THE ORDINARY VIRTUES

The Ordinary Virtues

Moral Order in a Divided World

MICHAEL IGNATIEFF

Harvard University Press

Cambridge, Massachusetts | London, England | 2017

First Printing

Book epigraph: "Meditation," from *New and Collected Poems: 1931–2001,* by
Czeslaw Milosz. Copyright © 1988, 1991, 1995, 2001 by Czeslaw Milosz
Royalties, Inc. Reprinted by permission of HarperCollins Publishers.

Library of Congress Cataloging-in-Publication Data
Names: Ignatieff, Michael, author.
Title: The ordinary virtues : moral order in a divided world / Michael Ignatieff.
Description: Cambridge, Massachusetts : Harvard University Press, 2017. |
    Includes bibliographical references and index.
Identifiers: LCCN 2017008712 | ISBN 9780674976276 (alk. paper)
Subjects: LCSH: Applied ethics–Cross-cultural studies. | Ethics–Social
    aspects–Cross-cultural studies. | Virtues–Social aspects–Cross-cultural
    studies. | Virtues–Political aspects–Cross-cultural studies. | Ethics,
    Comparative.
Classification: LCC BJ1521 .I36 2017 | DDC 170.9–dc23
LC record available at https://lccn.loc.gov/2017008712

Contents

Introduction

Moral Globalization and Its Discontents

ON FEBRUARY 10, 1914, THE RICHEST MAN IN THE WORLD— Andrew Carnegie—met in his mansion on 91st Street in Manhattan with a small group of clergymen and gave them a bequest of two million dollars to endow the Church Peace Union. Carnegie's idea was grandiose: to foster world peace by promoting dialogue among the world's faiths. Not all of the world's faiths were represented at the meeting—Jews, Protestants, and Catholics were there, but no Muslims, Hindus, Buddhists, or Shintoists. But there was a glimmering of an idea: that global conflict could be averted if men of faith—and they were all men—could learn how to transcend differences of theology and rise above a thousand years of inter-religious warfare.

The Church Peace Union was the capstone of an architecture of philanthropy that Carnegie had erected beginning in the 1890s, including the World Peace Palaces in The Hague and Geneva and the global network of libraries intended to educate the working men of each country and teach them as citizens to turn a deaf ear to the siren call of militarism and nationalism.[1]

Carnegie's faith in progress, in learning, and in dialogue among cultures was a product of Globalization 1.0, the period that catapulted Carnegie himself from a Scottish emigrant telegraph operator in Pennsylvania in the 1850s to the steel magnate he had become by the 1880s. If progress, especially moral progress, now strikes us a nineteenth-century idea, no one believed in it more fervently than Andrew Carnegie. His own life seemed to incarnate it.[2] It was axiomatic to him that the economic globalization that had made him his millions would also integrate the belief systems of the world and that moral globalization would bring peace, if not in his time, then in ours.

He told the assembled reverends in his study that February day: "Truly, gentlemen, you are making history, for this is the first union of the churches in advocacy of international peace, which I fondly hope, and strongly believe, is certain to hasten the coming of the day when men, disgracing humanity, shall cease to kill each other like wild beasts."

Carnegie's belief that ethical dialogue across contending faiths could prevent war strikes us now as innocent at best. Within months of his bequest, and as if out of a clear blue August sky, the First World War began and Carnegie's dreams of world peace through law and dialogue collapsed. The old man's astounding vitality ebbed away into brooding silence, and he died at the end of the war.

Yet his dream did not die with him. Carnegie may be an example of the strange staying power of moral naïveté. Without Carnegie, would there have been a League of Nations, and without the League, would there have been a United Nations? Without Carnegie, would there be a Gates, a Buffett, a Soros, and the gigantic philanthropic enterprises of our era? Even the Church Peace Union endured—thanks to the magic of compound interest—and over one hundred years metamorphosed into the Carnegie Council for Ethics in International Affairs, headquartered in a pair of brownstones on a leafy stretch of East 64th Street in New York. It is a quiet, thoughtful organization with a motto, Ethics Matter, that is a declaration of faith but also a question addressed to our age. It sponsors Global Fellows, research, and gatherings on the role that ethics plays in international relations.

In 2013, as the organization approached the centennial of Andrew Carnegie's gift, its president, Joel Rosenthal, and I were discussing how they should celebrate it. I remember saying "You need to get out of New York." To observe ethics in action, I suggested, the Council needed to take ethics out of the seminar room and study how it shapes people's judgments and actions close to the ground where conflicts start.

Rosenthal seized upon this spark of an idea and blew life into it. The Council had Global Ethics Fellows in academic institutions around the world, he said, and they could serve as our partners if we were to embark on a global study of ethics in action.

In this way the Carnegie Centennial Project—of which this book is the result—was born: to commemorate the illusions about moral progress that gave rise to Carnegie's bequest in 1914, as well as to investigate what moral globalization looks like in the twenty-first century.

In June 2013, a small team made up of program director Devin Stewart, a translator and a researcher, and me, together with local fixers and drivers, set out on a journey of moral discovery that was to take us, over the next three years, to four continents. Our subject was globalization, but there was no realistic way for our journey to be completely global. We went where we could count on Carnegie's network of Global Fellows, and we went where we ourselves already had some expertise or experience. Our trips to Bosnia and South Africa, for example, were for me return visits to societies whose travails and achievements had been recurring subjects of my writing for twenty-five years. In other countries, such as Myanmar and Japan, we drew on the expertise of my companion Devin Stewart. In each setting we convened dialogues with experts—academics, judges, journalists, and politicians. These interlocutors were themselves examples of globalization in action: most were English-speaking, familiar with the international literature on our topics, and well-traveled visitors to international conferences. At the same time, these local "cosmopolitans" were sometimes as distant from the realities of their own shantytowns, favelas, and poor neighborhoods as we were; when they accompanied us on site visits to these places, the journey was as much a voyage of discovery for them as it was for us. Our site visits took us to poor Hispanic neighborhoods in Los Angeles, immigrant communities in Queens, favelas in Rio, illegal settlements outside Pretoria, and poor villages near Mandalay. These visits proved crucial to our project, for they enabled us to ask whether global moral languages, commonly used by cosmopolitans, had any purchase on the lives and reasoning of people living in poorer communities.

We were commissioned by the Council to hold global ethical dialogues—focused discussions with experts, academics, jurists, and journalists—on a single question: Is globalization drawing us together morally? Beneath all our differences, what virtues, principles, and rules of conduct are we coming to share?

Instead of dialogues on values themselves, which risked becoming abstract and overly general, we decided to focus on practical problems we face in common. We wanted to find out whether we speak the same ethical language when we confront such issues as corruption and public trust, tolerance in multicultural cities, reconciliation after war and conflict, and resilience in times of uncertainty and danger. Through dialogues on these themes we hoped to evaluate the idea that, as economies, lifestyles, technologies, and attitudes globalize, ethical reasoning also globalizes. As we come to share the same goods, markets, lifestyles, and life chances, so we come to share similar patterns of moral reasoning. That had been Carnegie's hope: that economic progress would bring about moral convergence among the world's religions and value systems. A century later, that hope was still alive among globalization's champions, but fewer people than in Carnegie's time still believe that religion is a force for moral globalization or the world's religions remain the sole authoritative guide to moral conduct. We found that religion still matters—as consolation, inspiration, and guide—in the lives of millions, but new secular patterns of belief are making their claims on the allegiance of the world. One such belief—in human rights—figured in our collective mind as a possible candidate for a new global ethic, but we wondered: How far and how deeply had this ethic spread? Had it really displaced or challenged local moral codes? How did the battle between the local and the universal, the contextual and the global, play out in the moral lives of ordinary people? These were the questions we started with as we began to think about how to assess the thesis of "moral globalization" in our time.

We knew when we started that moral globalization is a very old story, coterminous with the long history of European imperial expansion. Our challenge was to define what was specific to the globalization of our time, just as Andrew Carnegie had tried to understand the globalization of his era. For as long as trade and travel have brought different races and tribes into contact with each other, human beings have asked what values we have in common.

The Greeks asked it of the "barbarians" they met on their travels. The Romans asked it as they pushed the frontiers of empire north to Hadrian's Wall. The Chinese asked it of the Jesuits, who disembarked on their shores in the sixteenth century, bringing the idea that Christ had also died for their sins.[3] As soon as Europeans began their conquest of Africa, Latin America, and Asia in the fifteenth century they puzzled over what they shared with the people they were subjugating. The puzzlement was mutual. When Michel de Montaigne met three feathered and painted "Indians" in Rouen, brought back to the French court by a buccaneer in 1562 who had taken them prisoner in the harbor of Rio de Janeiro, Montaigne asked them their first impressions of French society. Through a sailor who doubled as a translator, they replied—as Montaigne recounts in his wonderful essay "Of Cannibals"—that they were astonished at the inequality of Europeans, how some lived in castles while others starved at their doors.[4] Since the poor were so much more numerous than the rich, how was it, the "Indians" asked, that they did not set fire to the rich men's houses and steal all their goods? Why did these Europeans, with all their guns and sailing ships and wealth, not understand how much better it would be to live in the radical equality of the Brazilian forest? Montaigne took what they said seriously—he may be Europe's first cultural anthropologist—but he doubted that his fellow Europeans would do so. Such people, after all, were cannibals, and besides, how could you take them seriously when they didn't even wear breeches?

In Montaigne's essay, we catch our first glimpse of one of the enduring metaphors in which moral globalization has been understood ever since, through the vantage point of the noble savage, the so-called primitive, whose ascetic virtue and egalitarian ethic called into question the European equation of civilization and moral progress.

In 2014 a film crew flying over the Amazonian jungle, on the border between Peru and Brazil, spotted a tribe in a clearing whose members had never before seen an aircraft or had contact with other peoples. The photographers' footage signaled a moment of closure in the history of globalization that had opened with Montaigne's dialogue with the cannibals five centuries earlier. These newly discovered people may have been the last self-contained and unvisited human community on the planet. Globalization has now penetrated every human community and changed how we work, live, buy, sell, and above all, think about our relations to ourselves and our fellow beings. There is something astonishing, but also frightening about this. Who could watch the footage of these Amazonian peoples, with their bows and arrows pointed skyward, their warrior faces daubed in red, as they guarded their manioc fields and their grass houses, and not feel poignant apprehension at what would await them—disease, loss of language and culture–if globalization were to hack its way to their door? And who could deny that these people needed a new right to protect them: the right to remain uncontacted?[5] In their vulnerability to globalization's insatiable force we could feel our own.

In the long imperial era that ran from the 1490s to the 1970s, there were two basic narratives about moral globalization. In one, Christianity, commerce, the cash nexus, and imperial administration were inexorably uniting mankind in a shared story of technological and moral progress. This was the fable that sustained the confidence of imperial administrators for four centuries, the fable that Andrew Carnegie took as gospel and the myth that was so devastatingly exposed in Joseph Conrad's *Heart of Darkness*.[6] In the competing narrative, exemplified by Montaigne but then taken up by Rousseau and socialist critics from Proudhon to Marx, globalization was unifying the world around the logic of the cash nexus, but it was also crushing the local, the traditional, and the vernacular in favor of an alienating modernity organized around wage labor and imperial domination. This was the narrative that inspired critics of capitalist modernity from the French Revolution onward and that continues to animate antiglobalist and anticapitalist campaigns to this day. We have understood moral globalization according to these two narratives ever since.

But neither version helps us to specify what is new about the globalization of our era.

What is surely distinctive is that it is postimperial. The last western European land empire, the Portuguese, collapsed in 1974. The last empire of them all, the Soviet, collapsed in 1991. Yes, the United States is still the predominant global power, and its culture of images and consumption still delights millions while appalling others, but the dominance it enjoyed in 1945 is slowly giving way as new powers, especially China, rise to prominence. Its alliance system remains strong, and it continues to outspend its military rivals, but its share of global trade is declining, its global cultural hegemony is giving way, and its own citizens' faith in America's capacity to shape and dominate globalization in their own interests has declined sharply. In the 2016 election, millions of ordinary Americans made plain that they feel they are the victims of globalization, not its beneficiaries.

For all the loose talk about neoimperialism and neocolonialism in our day, for the first time since the 1490s no imperial power dominates the global economy. Trade no longer follows the flag: capitalist penetration of markets is no longer underwritten by the coercive power of imperial regimes. After eighty years of decolonization and the triumph of the ideology of national self-determination, there is no country on earth where white people rule over nonwhites as if by right.

For the first time, the world economy includes China and Russia, huge populations who, for much of the twentieth century, were closed off inside dire experiments in autarky, building socialism in one country.[7] These attempts to create a systematic alternative to capitalism failed utterly, and now the entire world is being drawn into the vortex of a common life organized around consumption, saving, capital investment, and wage labor. "To be rich is glorious," Deng Xiaoping is supposed to have said, in a succinct formulation of the ethic that now rules the once forbidden kingdom as well as the rest of the world.[8]

This does not mean, however, that we are all being drawn into one moral world. The more insistently cash nexus globalization presses upon national cultures and ways of life and on political sovereignty, the more insistently nation-states and the citizens within them push back. The antiglobal counter-revolution comes from political forces on the left who mobilize in opposition to the ecological destruction and distributive inequality of global capitalism, and it comes from the right from those who believe capitalism destroys traditions, national identities, and sovereignty.

This fear of global change, on both the left and the right, is apparent everywhere, but especially in the nations of the former communist world. For millions of people born in communist times, the arrival of the cash nexus has been morally devastating: they feel their former life vanishing and a strange and rapacious world, in which they have lost their place, taking shape.[9] The regimes in China and Russia have responded to this sense of moral disorientation by providing the authoritarian order of single-party rule while leaving the door ajar to allow their citizens to travel and experience the outside world. Instead of accepting that rights are indivisible, as Western human rights advocates believe, these regimes split rights in two, permitting the private economic rights necessary for capitalism while denying their people the rights that go with the exercise of political freedom. To use Albert O. Hirschman's memorable distinction, they allow exit—the right to travel, leave, deposit capital overseas—but they forbid voice.[10]

The world's economic system has converged around capitalism, but the world's rulers are creating systems of political authority, from the authoritarian capitalism of Russia and China to the illiberal majoritarian democracies of Hungary, Poland, and Turkey, that seek to protect their own power from the creative destruction of capitalism and the demands for freedom that capitalism generates.

Both the Chinese and Russian regimes dispute one crucial assumption widely believed after 1989, namely that democracy and capitalism would advance hand in hand.[11] Both regimes are betting their survival on the proposition that a controlled opening to the global economy is compatible with single-party rule. No one can tell whether they have made the right bet. It is not clear whether these regimes can control the aspirations that access to the global economy has unleashed, just as there is no guarantee that liberal capitalist democracy will succeed in taming globalization in the twenty-first century.

The period after the collapse of the last European land empire in 1989 now seems like an interlude of illusion, in which it was possible to believe that liberal democracy would spread inexorably as closed societies opened to capitalist freedoms. It was possible, but only then, to believe that our moral lives as individuals, inside liberal democracy, could be understood as belonging to a story of progress, a long, uneven, but unstoppable emancipation of human beings from tyranny and injustice. Reliance on such narratives now seems self-deluding. As the Russian exile Alexander Herzen said more than a century ago, history has no libretto.

By now, we should have freed ourselves from the illusion that there is, or ever could be, a single royal road into the future. In the twenty-first century, there will be many capitalisms and many possible political orders seeking to control and channel its destructive energies. At the same time, some changes in the accepted moral order of the world since 1945 seem irreversible. There may be competing roads into the future, but the great powers all accept, at least in theory, that the normative dispensation of this postimperial world is self-determination. In moral terms, self-determination brought two epochal ideas into the world: that all peoples have the right to determine their own destiny as political agents; and that all peoples are equal. Human rights added the third epochal idea: that all individuals are equal. The result is both a new international system and a new moral dispensation. In 1945, forty nations were independent members of the United Nations. Now the number is up to 193. To be sure, self-determination is often a cruel joke. Angola, for example, has replaced Portuguese rule with its own predatory elite, and the same dire story has been repeated across the continent, though the number of stable African democracies is slowly increasing. Yet the fact that self-determination has often been betrayed, or that great powers still push weaker countries around, does not lessen the force of the norm that peoples should have the right to determine their futures. From this premise, others follow: the old racial hierarchies that legitimized the rule of white Europeans have been delegitimized for good. New hierarchies and new exclusions, based on money, are replacing those based on race, but the key fact remains: we live in a postimperial world premised on the equality of peoples.

Two features distinguish the postimperial situation. New technologies are accelerating the interactions among peoples: air travel, cell phones, and the Internet bring the cultures of the poor and the lifestyles of the rich face to face, and the resulting envy, resentment, and ambition are powering streams of migration from poor countries and unleashing waves of discontent within rich societies about inequalities that used to be invisible. New ethical principles are also structuring the encounter between rich and poor nations, and between rich and poor individuals within nations. The new normative dispensation is the idea that every person, every faith, and every race and creed should enjoy the same right to be heard and the same right to shape national political outcomes. This is what the self-determination principle has done to the world. In addition, the democratic norm—each person counts for one and no one for more than one—now structures the expectations of the 60 percent of states that are democratic. But the democratic norm also governs moral conversations when individuals, faiths, cultures, and nations that are nondemocratic step into the same room to talk. This norm is anchored in the practice of the UN, which accords the same sovereign equality to states that are small and large, weak and powerful. The norm is anchored in international human rights and international humanitarian law; and much more important, it is rooted in the daily social practices and interactions of peoples around the world. Twenty-first century peoples live—or want to live—in a morally flat world, one based on equality of respect, meaning a world where everyone has a right to speak and to be heard. The new social media technologies have enormously empowered and enabled this aspiration for equality of voice.

As late as the mid-twentieth century, hierarchies of voice still privileged whites over blacks, northern peoples over southern ones, imperial holders of power over their colonial subjects. In the old dispensation, voices had standing not by virtue of what was said, but by virtue of who was saying it. The white race and the English language conferred automatic standing and a place at the top of a voice hierarchy. Everywhere today—this is one meaning of "populism"—traditionally accepted voice hierarchies are under attack.

Let us be careful, however, not to confuse aspirations and realities. The empires are gone, but asymmetries of power, influence, and resources persist—alongside and in contradiction to the emerging norm of equal voice. To this day, the voices that command a global audience and define academic and policy agendas still reside in London, New York, and Los Angeles. We say that all voices are entitled to be heard, but we know that some voices carry further, have more influence, indeed need only speak in a whisper for their orders to be carried out. Moreover, the memory of a time when your voice was not heard—because of your gender, race, sexual orientation, or subject status in an empire—continues to hold back those who want to speak in their own name.

Western intellectual and moral authorities that used to command global influence are now learning to listen and give standing to the rising authority of new voices and sources emerging in Beijing and Shanghai, Rio and Mumbai. As nations rise to power, so their intellectual voices gain a global hearing. Voice rights are being claimed and exercised by once silenced groups everywhere, especially women. New norms of consultation now structure development practices, for example, and require that the voices of those affected—whether by a new mine, dam, or irrigation project—be heard.

So, to summarize, the world we live in is split in two: between a normative commitment to equal voice and the reality that some voices are heard more than others. The result is an unstable but dynamic situation. The powerful no longer can refuse to give a hearing to the voices of the powerless; they realize that they can lose control if they fail to listen to the less powerful. Even in China, no modern leader could shut his ears to the cries of the people as Mao did. Even in Russia, no modern leader can ignore popular discontent as the czars did.

In postimperial globalization, the distances that once separated ruler and ruled have collapsed. The "subject races" once lived on the imperial periphery. Once dominant and once subordinate races live together, in hyper-diverse global cities, former colonists and the colonized cheek by jowl, in self-segregated communities to be sure, but thrown together in daily life in ways that would have been unthinkable in the vanished spatial geographies of the imperial world. Our moral problem—how people can create shared moral operating systems from hundreds of different origins, histories, faiths, and religions—is new; and out of this new situation a vocabulary has emerged in which the fact of diversity is transformed into a value. Our embrace of this value remains ambiguous. As we shall see, we embrace the ideal of "living together" even as we actually live apart.

Diversity itself is not new. Ancient Rome was a multicultural city. For millennia the great cities of the Mediterranean—from Marseille to Alexandria—were promiscuous and polyglot meeting places for diverse cultures and races. Every imperial dispensation has fostered its own system for managing and controlling diversity. The Ottoman *millet,* which mandated limited religious freedom for minorities in the Turkish empire, is but one example.[12] What is new is postimperial diversity conducted under the moral premise of equality.

The second observable feature of this postimperial world is that the agents of moral globalization are no longer the servants of empire. They are no longer European school teachers, the disillusioned administrators immortalized in Conrad's *Heart of Darkness* or Orwell's *Burmese Days,* and still less the rapacious buccaneers who captured Montaigne's Brazilians.

The first of the new entrepreneurs of moral globalization are the executives of the multinational corporations. They manage global supply chains that yoke together West African coffee growers and Western coffee drinkers, that link cell phone users to Congolese producers of the rare earth minerals that go into each phone, and that have cabled the world together into one virtual communications platform. A globalized "cash nexus," as Marx called it, has bound strangers together with the rates of exchange set by the powerful.[13] Cash nexus globalization coexists happily enough with a postimperial norm of equality.

The second entrepreneurs of globalization are the advocates, activists, and nongovernmental organizations (NGOs) seeking to moralize the cash nexus. "Civil society" has replaced the imperial agent, instructor, and administrator as the bearer of universal values. These mediators want consumers to understand the injustice of buying a soccer ball sewn by a poor Pakistani child or a T-shirt made by a low-paid Bangladeshi seamstress; how a cheap cup of morning coffee holds down family income in Colombia; or how U.S. government subsidies to rich American cotton producers impoverish West African cotton growers. Through their campaigns for the ethical sourcing of commodities, these moral entrepreneurs want to raise wages and living standards in an international economy driven by the logic of profit.

These entrepreneurs have made it fashionable for middle classes to "source" products ethically; they have increased pressure on large companies to sign on to the corporate social responsibility principles in the UN Global Compact.[14] They have promoted anticorruption as a new global norm. Global investment funds now apply human rights, anticorruption, and sustainability filters to the bets they place in the world's stock markets. Global moral pressures do influence corporate brands, but the deep logic of a capitalist system remains amoral, rooted in the unceasing search for profit and lower costs. All we can say is that in contrast to Andrew

Carnegie's Globalization 1.0, capitalist profit seeking in Globalization 2.0 faces unprecedented regulatory pressure from states, vigilant monitoring by UN bodies, and constant contestation by global civil society movements and the consumer.

Moral globalization, when seen through a geostrategic lens, is a competition to fill the space left behind by the departure of empire. The competition is intense because there are at least four regional powers—the United States, Europe, China, and Russia—each articulating the values of their own political traditions, competing for cultural, moral, and geostrategic influence in their immediate neighborhoods and, where they have the capacity, across the globe.

Moral globalization is best understood not as a tide of convergence in which we are swept together into a single modernity, but instead as a site of struggle over whether, and to what extent, the cash nexus can be made to serve moral imperatives of equity and justice and which civilizational model—Chinese, American, or some other rival's—will define the political and moral order of the twenty-first century.

What also defines the globalization of our era is the extent to which market relations between the "global north" and the "global south" have become a topic of moral reflection and mobilization. Since the Pearson Report to the UN in 1970, attempts have been made to quantify the moral obligation of rich nations to contribute a certain percentage of their wealth (the 0.7 percent target) to assist poor countries.[15] Few countries achieve these targets, yet in all the debate about whether development aid actually helps the poor or merely enriches local elites, no one questions the premise that rich nations have some obligation to poor ones. Likewise, the relations between citizens in secure democracies and migrants and refugees fleeing famine, persecution, and war are now framed, not just in the age-old language of compassion, but in a new vernacular of obligation enacted in the 1951 Refugee Convention and other international agreements on migration.

The language that since 1945 has come to frame these global debates is human rights. For the first time, the rights of individuals have been recognized by the international state system. No other language of the human good has proved so influential, in large part because the language addresses every single human being alive as a sovereign individual.[16]

Certainly rights talk begins its history in Europe, but its diffusion after 1945 was not an example of European and American cultural hegemony in action, but the reverse. Human rights went global because the language was picked up by colonial peoples as the vocabulary which legitimized their struggle to secure national independence against the European empires. The first human right, after all, the one that emerging nations put at the top of the human rights covenants, was self-determination. The diffusion of human rights into African and Asian states after independence should be seen as a process in which the global went local, in which universal rights talk adopted local vernaculars for purposes of legitimation.[17] Once independence was gained, the human right to self-determination sometimes went on to destabilize the newly independent states themselves. Inside these new states, every minority group struggling for freedom against a dominant majority cast their cause in the language of human rights, with the result that many newly independent states were soon struggling with civil wars and secessionist conflicts.

If this history of decolonization is taken into consideration, it is impossible to understand the globalization of human rights as a story of Western cultural imposition. Human rights both legitimized the struggles for national independence and then sometimes weakened the state structures that emerged. Within these newly independent states in Asia and Africa, women subjected to discrimination and exclusion embraced the language of rights, not because they wished to become Western consumers but because the language of rights spoke to them as individuals; minorities used to being treated as less than human could suddenly articulate a claim to inclusion. These beneficiaries of rights talk did not seek to become Western. They simply wanted to be free from local forms of oppression. The global would never have gone local, would never have been "vernacularized," if it had meant Westernization. National struggles, on the contrary, fused Western norms, local customs, and religious traditions in forms distinctly their own. The spread of human rights has been like the spread of English: through a process of adaptation the original universal acquires the accents and pronunciation of the local vernacular.[18]

The second universal language–international humanitarian law–also followed this vernacularizing pattern. In Muslim countries the International Committee of the Red Cross, for example, has sought to enlist local traditions of warrior restraint to find common ground between international law and Koranic injunctions against the infliction of indiscriminate harm on civilians.[19] The Red Cross had some success with this strategy of cultural fusion but as a Western organization it has learned the limits of its cultural and legal authority. Its efforts to teach the laws of armed conflict in the Middle East have been set at naught by the belligerent brutality of the Syrian regime on the one hand and the ferocity of Islamic jihadis on the other. More broadly, within the Islamic world as a whole, Western norms have only limited purchase on the battle of ideas that has ensued across the Islamic world as to whether the faith is a language of love or a language of war. These examples illustrate the extent to which moral conflict rather than steady convergence of norms marks contemporary globalization.

In addition to the vernacularization of human rights and international humanitarian law, a third language–environmentalism–

has been put into play to rally local struggles around the common battle to save our planet. In the moral imagination that sustains this perspective, a single image has had a galvanizing effect: a photograph of the planet earth taken from an orbiting U.S. spacecraft. This photograph, which appeared as a poster on the first Earth Day in 1970, symbolized the claim that we all have common responsibilities of care for our fragile home.[20] From this intuition has arisen a vast, loosely coordinated, internally conflicted but enduring movement to save the planet from greed, waste, and political foolishness. Environmentalism is an example of moral globalization in action, but it also lays bare globalization's limits. The campaign has been paralyzed by a conflict between rich countries that are able to cut emissions and poorer ones reluctant or unable to cut theirs. A moral vision of a common home has emerged, but even those states that accept the vision refuse the particular sacrifices that effective action will require. Here too, global convergence of values, at least in the abstract, has sharpened rather than reduced political conflict over environmental responsibility.

To these secular languages—human rights, humanitarian law, and environmentalism—should be added a fourth: the religious languages of global solidarity.

When the early Christian fathers, especially Paul, sought to expand an embattled Jewish heresy into the Greco-Roman world, they crafted a language of universal moral appeal that has moved men and women for two thousand years. In St. Paul's Epistle to the Galatians (3.28), we read: "There is neither Jew nor Greek, there is neither bond nor free, there is neither male nor female: for ye are all one in Christ Jesus."

Christian universalism is certainly not the only religious language of human brotherhood. Religious languages of human universality in general are the oldest, and they may prove to be the most enduring vernacular in which human beings recognize their common identity. In institutional terms, Catholic Christianity is the most powerful heir of the Christian language of moral globalization, replacing declining congregations in Europe and North America with new adherents in Africa, Asia, and Latin America. The pope draws crowds to masses that are complex amalgams of the traditional Christian liturgy and the rock concert, and the faithful listen to the pontiff's unswerving ethical challenge to the destructive and socially alienating regime of global capitalism.[21] The remobilization of the Catholic Church has given it new energy as a critic of globalization, but it has also sharpened the conflict with the secular moralities that defend the rights of women, gays, and transgender people. Here again, religious institutions and secular movements are battling each other for the attention and respect of the world, and when the stakes are this high, moral compromise, on either side, can seem like betrayal.

The other great global faith, Islam, is an avatar of globalization too, but its authority to speak with one voice has fractured. Leadership in the competition to promote an Islamic road into the twenty-first century has passed into the hands of radical jihadis. They have been empowered by social media and galvanized by the propaganda of the deed. It may be unwelcome to think of jihadis as avatars of globalization, but that is what they aspire to be, to shake the confidence of the infidel and mobilize all those in the Islamic *umma* who are seeking a radical alternative to secularism, the cash nexus, and capitalist consumption. The future they are willing to kill for is a holy caliphate in which the strain of living with unbelievers, amidst all the temptations of modernity, is done away with and they can await paradise without distraction. The attacks they wage are local—from San Bernardino to Nice and Paris—but the impact they seek is global. Their sworn enemies are the moral entrepreneurs of human rights, tolerance, and liberal democracy.

These then are the agents, old and new—secular, religious, academic, and activist—who are fighting it out to define which language of moral globalization will shape the characteristic virtues of our age.

In response to these trends and to lend support to the secularists, university-based theorists have sought to systematize a global ethic in the language of university-based moral theory. This global ethic, in the singular, has had a powerful impact beyond the academy. It has come to shape transnational activism around the world. Theorists have tried to imagine what moral duties should look like if we recognize that all human beings are entitled to equal moral concern and we share a single global habitat. This vantage point could be called the "view from nowhere" or "the view from nowhere in particular."[22]

The view from nowhere has had a powerful influence precisely because it works against the grain of ordinary moral intuition. Moral life is about drawing boundaries, defining who we are in contrast to who *they* are. A one-world ethical perspective asks us to justify the natural partiality we have for our own. It is the view we are trying to reach if we say, for example, that we are reasoning from behind a "veil of ignorance," forced to imagine what justice should look like if we cannot figure out in advance what our position in society would be. One-world ethics also draws on the ancient "natural rights" tradition, which asked what all human beings, in any situation, should be able to count on as a natural right of existence.[23]

Global ethicists have asked why states should have the right to impose visa and immigration quotas on some but not all human beings, why states have the right to expel noncitizens, and why they favor their own citizens over people living in other countries in the distribution of global resources.[24] Moral philosophers have argued that allocating global resources to individuals on the basis of the country they happen to have been born in carries moral luck too far.[25] Other philosophers have used global ethics to figure out a morally rational way to apportion responsibility for action on climate change.[26]

This one-world perspective has provided a common moral vocabulary for civil society NGOs everywhere. It is a sustained critique of cash nexus globalization and the way power is exercised by states, corporations, and national communities against the common interests of humankind.

As a politics, however, the one-world perspective is not making much headway. States are no closer to a morally rational way of allocating responsibility for action on climate change. Countries still impose immigration quotas, and few countries have met their global justice obligations to the poorest on earth.

Global ethicists attribute the failure of a global ethic to selfish national interest. Yet the problem runs deeper. Globalization has sharpened, not weakened, the conflict between universal principles and democratic self-rule. Citizens in most democracies believe that their own interests, democratically chosen, *ought* to prevail over the interests of peoples in other countries. This view is a symptom of a conflict, at least in states with popular suffrage, between democracy and justice, between the value we attach to the self-determination of peoples and the value we attach to abstract justice for all individuals.

Isaiah Berlin observed long ago that all good things cannot be had at once.[27] Justice and democracy, justice and mercy, liberty and equality are a few of the conflicts intrinsic to the values we hold dear. Given these conflicts, it is not obvious that a single global ethic is even a coherent idea. Certainly it can never amount to a noncontradictory ordering of moral goods. Instead, it is better understood as a site of argument in which the justice of a particular society is called to the bar of justification before universal claims. The view from nowhere has put the self-justifications of the powerful to the test, and if the powerful sleep less well at night so much the better.

In the world we have lost, the world where human beings could only travel as far as their feet or their horses could carry them, moral insulation was conceivable. In a globalized world, we do not have the luxury of moral closure. We are constantly asked to explain ourselves. Adversarial justification is unavoidable. Anyone who travels even some distance from home, anywhere in the world, is bound to break through the membrane of the moral world they take for granted and enter the moral membrane of another tribe, faith, or ethnic group. Ethical systems, whether local or global, are also competitive, constantly bidding for adherents, seeking to hold on to doubters and to ward off attacks. Moral universes are never separate: each is in justificatory dialogue with the other.

What is important to understand is what ordinary people from different cultures and belief systems actually do when they confront each other on specific issues of moral principle. How do these momentous clashes, between religious and secular principle, environment and profit, local tradition and universal rights, play out in the day-to-day lives of ordinary people? What is the nature of their moral transaction? How do they understand each other? What happens when they disagree, when conflict starts?

In other words, how, in an age of globalization, do we negotiate our differences if all we have to go on is a procedural universal: that all human beings are entitled to respect and a fair hearing, that no one's view must prevail by virtue of their race, gender, religion, creed, income, or nationality? This was the starting question in our global ethical dialogues.

The question we started with was not whether moral globalization was occurring, but whose moral practices it was shaping.

Research by other scholars has confirmed that human rights remains an "elite discourse," the lingua franca of an influential but thinly spread stratum of educated, middle- and upper-middle-class intellectuals, university teachers, students, activists, journalists, and bureaucrats.[28] These are, in fact, the students I have taught in my human rights classes at Harvard. Through them I've seen firsthand how deeply human rights and global ethics shape their ambitions, their moral solidarity, and their allegiances, no longer to their countries of origin alone but to the great causes of global civil society: war, migration, global inequality, poverty, and climate change.

Much as I have learned from them, I wanted to ask questions that these impressive young cosmopolitans could not answer. My question was whether moral globalization has spread to social groups excluded from their privileged social strata, how it was shaping the moral practices of ordinary people around the world. By ordinary people I did not have a special class or social location in mind, and I certainly do not want to accord "plain folks" any kind of moral privilege, of the kind that populist politicians commonly do, when they speak of the ordinary people ignored by liberal elites. I simply mean anyone, and that could include the prosperous as well as the poor, who is not paid to think abstractly or campaign for a living, whose business does not involve the regular use of human rights or moral philosophy as a modus operandi. That's why we made a special effort to get out of the seminar room and the faculty lounge and into the street. Our Carnegie ethical dialogues took us to community centers, favelas, police headquarters, monasteries, religious sites, and poor neighborhoods on four continents.

I wanted to find out what it felt like for ordinary people, defined in this way, to sort out the competing claims of the global and the local in their daily lives. Our research became an exercise in the intimate sociology and anthropology of ethics. Our focus was not, in other words, on what people *ought* to have in common, but on what they actually *do* share when they face ethical pressure in their lives.

The first of these pressures, it turned out, was the momentum of contemporary history itself. Explosive, disorienting, and destabilizing change is the defining feature of our era of postimperial globalization. Change has always frightened and exhilarated human beings in equal measure but it has only been in the era of the modern state that human beings have believed they could control the historical forces that determine their lives. In the imperial phase of European expansion it was sometimes possible, at least in imperial capitals, to believe that the empire—its rulers, its agents, its servants—was in charge. In the postimperial version that has taken hold since 1989, what is new is the anxiety that no one is in charge. The postimperial era has coincided with a deep change in how the state is understood. By 1945, Roosevelt's America, Atlee's Britain, and in another vein entirely, Stalin's Russia, had all vindicated, thanks to the experience of war mobilization, a new idea of the state as an omnipresent provider of security and public goods, as well as the key driver of social and economic change. The French phrase *"l'État providence"*—the providential state—encapsulated the comprehensive ambitions of the governments that emerged from World War II.[29] In 2016, it is hard to find anyone who still thinks of the state in this way. It is no longer the master engine of change, and it no longer gives itself the mandate to protect citizens from globalization. From the 1970s onward, these ambitions have been whittled back, partly because the state simply was unable to fulfill them, partly because the state itself was stripped of its capacities by the conservative counter-revolution we associate with Margaret Thatcher and Ronald Reagan. One ironic result of this conservative paring back of the state is that some of the voters who most embraced the ideology of "getting government off our backs" are now clamoring for protection from the unwelcome forces of global competition. But the state no longer has either the capacity or the ambition to serve as a secular providence. Like every other social actor, the state seeks to surf the tidal wave of technical, scientific, and social change safely to the shore, preserving its own powers, revenue, and capacities. The confidence in the state, in the foresight of the imperial capital, in the orders received from far away—all this has ebbed away, even in wealthy societies with robust welfare states. We all face change now, freed from the illusion or fantasy that someone, somewhere is in charge. We are all on our own, living by our wits, and perhaps only the very privileged retain the confidence that globalization can be their servant rather than their master.

In all of our dialogues, the starting condition was how to make sense of change: explosive economic growth and corruption in Brazil; hyper-diverse migration in Los Angeles and New York; the aftermath of the tsunami and the nuclear accident in Fukushima, Japan; a protracted transition from military rule to democracy in Myanmar; the fragmentation of Nelson Mandela's "rainbow nation" in South Africa; a downward spiral back to ethnic conflict in Bosnia.

The individuals we talked to never separated their own private dilemmas from the wider social context of conflict in which they lived. Generalities about human obligation and moral reasoning meant little to them: context was all. In each place, we listened for common ethical languages as our partners in dialogue struggled with the questions that they wrestle with in their daily lives.

The resulting book focuses on the ordinary virtues because these virtues—trust, tolerance, forgiveness, reconciliation, and resilience—emerged as the common thread through all our dialogues. By ordinary I mean commonplace and everyday as opposed to heroic and exceptional. By ordinary I also mean unreflexive and unthinking as opposed to purposive and rationally justified. When I speak of virtue I mean a life skill, a practice acquired through experience, rather than an exercise of moral judgment or an act of deliberative thought.

What is common to human beings, we found, is virtue, defined as acquired practical skills in moral conduct and discernment, not shared values as such. Wherever we went, whatever language barrier we were working across, we were able to recognize generosity when we saw it. It did not require translation. We felt trust, even when we couldn't explain why it had been accorded to us. Words were not required when we felt that we were included. We simply felt welcome.[30]

While there are some moral universals—do not kill, do not steal, do not bear false witness, do not have sex with members of your immediate family—these only define the outer limit of moral permissibility, not the detailed inner core which decides the mundane choices that most people have to make. It was this inner core of detailed choice that we wanted to penetrate.

How, we wanted to ask, do global norms like human rights work into everyday moral assumptions? For most of the people we talked to on our long global journey, human rights entered their moral perspective chiefly as an inchoate belief that all human beings, as individuals, are equal. By this our interlocutors, often very poor people, meant equality of voice. They did not confuse the equal right to speak with the equal right to be heard, and they were not so naïve as to believe that equality of voice conferred equality of opportunity, still less equality of result. But they did feel, both as peoples and as individuals, that their voices should count. By this they meant something primal: I matter. I am not a piece of garbage. I am a human being. From these assumptions, large consequences followed: Rich people cannot treat me like dirt. Police officers should not beat me when I seek their help. When rich foreigners come to my door—these people from the Carnegie Council, for example—it is right that they should seek my opinion. This normative assumption of equality is unprecedented in the long history of globalization.

We are in a new moral era in which the struggle for equality has produced a clamor, sometimes violent, for recognition and acknowledgment. The affirmation of equal moral worth was evident everywhere in our travels, but it was not always the dominant note in the quotidian struggle to do the right thing here and now. Here virtue showed its local face. Instead of using available universals, the people we encountered simply sought to practice the ordinary virtues, as best they could, in daily life. No matter how differently people thought about specific issues, they all took for granted that life was an ongoing effort to justify and explain themselves in moral terms. These exercises in moral justification were not abstract and theoretical, but intensely practical, contextual, and local. The audiences they sought to justify themselves to were not general ones but local: family, friends, neighbors, significant others. Ordinary virtue—local, contextual, nonideological, antitheoretical—turned out to be the moral operating system of hyper-diverse cities as well as smaller communities from Bosnia to Burma.

In using the term "moral operating system," I'm not making a neurological claim to the effect that moral reasoning is hardwired like a computer circuit or software program. I am using it in a metaphorical sense to capture the tacit, implicit character of the ordinary virtues, plus the sense that the moral order they create becomes a shared public good, like open source code, used by all but neither authored nor possessed by a single person.

Ordinary virtue does not generalize. It does not forget or ignore difference; does not pay much attention to the human beneath all our diversity; is not much interested in ethical consistency; works to live and let live as an organizing assumption in dealings with others, but retreats to loyalty toward one's own when threatened; is anti-ideological and antipolitical; favors family and friends over strangers and other citizens; is hopeful about life without much of a metaphysics about the future and is often surprised by its own resilience in the face of adversity; believes, finally, that ethics is not an abstraction but just what you do and how you live, and that displaying the virtues, as best you can, is the point and purpose of a human life.

Ordinary virtue, as Michel de Montaigne said five hundred years ago, is a struggle with the ordinary vices: greed, lust, envy, and hatred.[31] Ordinary virtue can also prove helpless in the face of extraordinary vice. In the face of terrorism, for example, ordinary virtues may be silenced and numb. But when the crisis of violence and brutality passes, it is the ordinary virtues that do the rebuilding, that reform the networks of trust and resilience, without which ordinary life cannot continue.

If ordinary virtue is what human beings truly share—and recognize in each other, despite all our differences—a couple of key questions are: What do these virtues need in order to flourish? What institutional conditions foster these virtues and in what political circumstances do they decay? These questions are as old as Cicero's reflections on corruption in the Roman Republic and as current as the "institutional turn" in modern development economics.[32] If the test of a decent society is that it allows people to display these virtues easily, what policies and institutions do we need to create so that virtue can remain ordinary? On this journey we witnessed downward spirals in the relation between virtue and institutions, evidence that good institutions cannot save a republic when its elites turn vicious and predatory. Rules, someone once said, are for people with no character. Woe betide a republic ruled by rules, in other words by persons without character.

On our journey we also found that the converse is true: good institutions, when supported by citizens of virtue, can stop the elites' downward spiral into predatory self-dealing. Good institutions can give courage to virtue and inspire an upward spiral toward repair and renewal.

This book seeks to deepen our understanding of this relation between virtue and institutions by looking at societies—South Africa, Bosnia, Brazil, Myanmar—that are struggling to make good institutions work in difficult circumstances. The book is thus an analysis of virtues at work in an unjust, dangerous, and uncertain world, a study of how people reproduce virtue—and moral order—in arduous circumstances. Its purpose is to help us all understand what it means to live in a postimperial global society and to realize how the ordinary virtues give us common cause with the human beings with whom we share this fragile planet.

1

Jackson Heights, New York

Diversity Plaza

THE JOURNEY FROM THE CARNEGIE COUNCIL'S BROWNSTONE
on East 64th Street in midtown Manhattan to Jackson Heights in
Queens takes about forty-five minutes by subway. It is a journey
from one reality of contemporary globalization to another. In midtown Manhattan, the privileged of the world compete for the best
jobs, educations, apartments, tables at restaurants, and seats at
concerts and the theater.[1] In these circles, postracial and postimperial cosmopolitanism is an easy lingua franca. The competition for
scarce positional goods is fierce, but it is understood as a battle
among equals. It's a contest between skilled individuals who share
the same global operating system–the competitive individualism of
elite cosmopolitans. I've taught many of these young men and
women in graduate school; they come from every country on earth,
and they've all been led to believe that there should be no barriers–
of race, creed, gender, or origin–that should stand in the way of their

own determination, brain power, and skill. For many of the foreign students I've taught, New York is the destination of their dreams because its universities, businesses, hospitals, and schools live by this cosmopolitan code more fully than any other place on earth.[2]

There is little doubt that this moral code of inclusive equality and competitive individualism is responsible for much of the innovation and growth incubated in a global city like New York. Yet the cosmopolitan code has another moral effect: so long as competitors believe the competition is fair, so long as no one has conclusive evidence that they were barred from succeeding by their origins or characteristics, then the competitors are inclined to believe, as well, that the resulting distribution of privileges must be fair too. In this unintended way, equality of opportunity ends up justifying severe inequalities of result. Yet the moral order of competitive cosmopolitanism, the moral order of Manhattan, does not always convince even its beneficiaries. As I have discovered with my own students, globalization lifted them from humble beginnings in faraway places to positions of prestige and prominence, yet they remain among globalization's fiercest critics, especially of the new forms of inequality and exclusion that it leaves in its wake. These students of mine defend the multicultural opportunity that globalization has made possible for them, in a place like Manhattan, but they remain keenly aware that numberless others have been left out.

Jackson Heights, Queens, presents another face of globalization, the precarious world of migrant cosmopolitanism, where the struggle is to arrive, to make it, to get a foot on the bottom rung and climb.[3] Those starting at the bottom may be less enamored of the moral virtues of the global city than those at the top, but for them too, the city has to keep some moral promises, above all the chance to climb and to rise.

Our journey from Manhattan to Jackson Heights ends in a bleak square that some right-thinking municipal official decided to name

Diversity Plaza. It is bounded on one side by the green girders of the El stop, first opened in 1917 and not much changed since, and on the other side by a former Bollywood cinema now converted into an all-night food mart and a row of single-story storefronts with signs that advertise Sunflower Driving School, Nepal House, Travel House Nepal, IME Money Transfer, Ra Ra Group, Fundacion Mazabel, New Menka Salon, Brown's Army and Navy, Farmacia Latina, and Al Muqsir's barber shop. In the middle of the plaza, there were a few umbrellas covering a couple of white plastic chairs. At nine o'clock on a weekday morning, in a light drizzle, Diversity Plaza is empty.

Around the corner, the owners of a Bangladeshi café, running a continuous loop of joyous Bollywood musical numbers on the TV behind the counter, serves me sweet milky tea and samosas. The teenage daughter behind the cash register does the talking in English; her father does the talking to the cab drivers in their native Urdu. Across the street, the Money Marts are already cashing checks and sending remittance money home to countries in every corner of the world. The little businesses fronting Diversity Plaza advertise, in English, Spanish, Urdu, and a dozen other scripts and languages, haircuts, massages, cheap apartment rentals, real estate, and notary publics; and little restaurants offer food from Nepal, Colombia, Honduras, India, China, Korea, and the Dominican Republic.

As you walk the streets of Jackson Heights, the ethnic character is marked chiefly by women's dress and this character changes block by block. On one corner the women wear hijab, on the next jeans, on the third the wigs and full-length dresses of Orthodox Jews. The food functions as another marker of ethnic territory. In one food store there is Jamaican plantain, while in the next the greens are all Chinese. Everybody seems to know which block belongs to the Dominicans, which is Honduran, and which is Nepalese. A hypersensitivity to turf, to defensible space, seems to possess everyone. The people seem to carry around in their heads a real estate map with rough pricing for every block, since this is the fundamental economics that determines who gets what piece of urban turf. The air is filled with conversations in dozens of different tongues, but by and large, like speaks to like, just as like lives with like, in separate neighborhoods. At the same time, turf changes hands constantly as better-off residents move up and out and poorer and newer arrivals replace them.

There are more different racial, ethnic, and religious groups living together in this part of Queens than in any other county in the United States.[4] Forty-seven percent of Queens residents were born in another country, and in 56 percent of homes the mother tongue is other than English. Whites—from a range of ethnic and religious backgrounds—compose a bare majority, with Hispanics, blacks, and Asians making up the rest.[5] In the neighborhood, there are half a dozen Hindu temples, two Sikh *gurdwaras,* several mosques, Japanese, Chinese, and Korean Buddhist temples, a Taoist temple, Korean Christian churches, Latin American evangelical churches, Falun Gong practitioners, Jehovah's Witness temples, and Mormon tabernacles, as well as several of the oldest Episcopal churches and Orthodox synagogues in New York City.[6]

In the course of several days I talked to community organizers, local politicians, police officers, urban theorists, and local passersby. I was always asking the same question: how does a place as diverse as this hold together? What common ground can there be? For most people the question seemed odd: it just *did* hold together, though no one could quite explain how.

Jackson Heights is to twenty-first-century globalization what New York's Lower East Side was to the globalization of Andrew Carnegie's era. Then as now, new technologies and declining transport costs, plus the galvanizing appeal of a new start, drew millions to America's shores. Then as now, the distance between the Carnegie mansion on 91st Street and the tenements of Orchard Street was just as great as the distance between East 64th Street and Diversity Plaza.[7] In Carnegie's day, immigrants were actually a larger percentage of the American population—almost 15 percent—than they have been at any time since, though the current figure, 13 percent, is close.[8] Whereas the languages of the Lower East Side were Yiddish, Polish, German, and Italian, today the languages of Jackson Heights span the globe, with Spanish and Chinese becoming more prevalent. Then as now, the question is how the urban order of commonplace interaction and exchange gets created from such staggering diversity.

This is a moral question as much as a sociological one. For diversity to work, there must be a code of tacit mutual acceptance, and for a place like Jackson Heights, which takes in an unceasing tide of migrants, there must be a tacit code of welcome. The first thing to notice about the moral code of Jackson Heights—and it distinguishes contemporary New York from Carnegie's—is that official, legislated discrimination against immigrants is a thing of the past. In Carnegie's day, Jews from Eastern Europe had to fight their way into American life against explicit anti-Semitism, Italians had to battle anti-Catholic prejudice, and blacks faced racial covenants that barred them from rental housing.[9] Between 1920 and 1965, America used country quotas to ban nonwhite immigration of all kinds. In 1965, the Hart-Celler Immigration and Nationality Act struck them down. President Lyndon Johnson went to the Statue of Liberty in New York and declared that a national origins system was "a cruel and enduring wrong."[10] It's fair to say that no one imagined the consequences of abolishing these quotas, but they have been far-reaching. In the words of one scholar, "At no one's request and by no one's design,"

America in just the past fifty years has embraced globalization as demographic diversity.[11]

The diversity of Jackson Heights is also the creation of the post-civil rights dispensation of equality for all. Few appreciated at the time that Martin Luther King's victory in securing the Voting Rights Act and the coincident abolition of racial quotas on immigration would create a new moral economy of diversity for the American city, but it did. This was no mean achievement, but it raised the moral bar: as a result, both immigrants and host communities experience diversity differently, with a sensitivity to slights, exclusion, and discrimination that in Carnegie's time were reluctantly accepted as the price of admission.

The site where the moral economy of a diverse city is most contested is in police-community relations. We were in Jackson Heights during a period of relative calm, but this was shattered soon after, in July 2014, when Eric Garner was arrested in Staten Island for selling individual cigarettes. For this trivial illegality, the consequences were dire. The arresting officers held him down in a choke hold and did not relent even when he whispered, at least nine times, according to shocked onlookers, "I can't breathe, I can't breathe." He died in the hospital an hour later. The eruption that came to be called Black Lives Matter dates, at least in part, to Eric Garner's death.

Fairness in policing is the absolute sine qua non of the moral economy of a global city. Poverty and economic inequality can be endured, as long as migrants or their children believe that there is a way up and out. But police abuse is an affront to basic moral expectations: it makes a mockery of the creed promoted in every citizenship class, school civics lesson, and Fourth of July speech. No society has more enduring difficulty reconciling its high ideals with its social realities than the United States and in no society is the debate about what these ideals mean, in practical terms, more contentious.

If fairness is the norm for police-community relations, what the police and the communities in question may think is fair are two different things. One small example of this disjunction surfaced when I talked to a policeman of Yemeni origin who works within the NYPD community relations unit. For the police, infiltrating New York mosques is crucial for early detection and deterrence of terrorist attacks. But for the congregations, it is an intrusive and insulting demonstration that they are citizens under suspicion. These Muslims are tired of having to prove that they are as repelled by terrorism as the rest of their fellow citizens. The Yemeni cop himself seemed caught between two worlds, having to explain why his own department deploys informers to his own community gatherings.

Fairness, it turns out, is a continual site of contestation between the police and community groups. Basic consent for policing is negotiated, minute by minute, in the housing projects and streets of the borough, and even a small incident can explode into something serious.

Jackson Heights's community groups—organized by religion, ethnicity, language, interest, and neighborhood—are the key mediating institutions that keep the peace, solve disputes with the police and knit diverse communities together.[12] The groups and organizations we talked to represent those who do not have citizenship or language skills and might otherwise be voiceless: they fight unlawful deportations, report fraudulent landlords, and negotiate parades and public gatherings with the police. They also sponsor classes in the languages of the city, and these go beyond basic English to include computer skills, financial literacy, and rights education. Acculturation to the big city means knowing your rights, learning not to be ripped off by scam artists, money lenders, notary publics, city officials, or employers.

I visited an agency that runs a hiring hall for undocumented Hispanic laborers. They only accept employers who will pay minimum wage and respect basic rights. In the Spanish-English phrase book they hand out, the sentences they teach young Hispanic workers offer a clear picture of what rights are at stake:

> I would like to discuss my salary with you.
> I only received...
> I should receive...
> I have the right to receive at least the minimum wage...
> I'm going to consult with my lawyer...
> Don't yell at me...

At dawn most mornings, undocumented workers from Latin America gather in a plaza adjoining a ramp leading onto the BQE expressway; employers show up in their trucks and hire them for cleanup, demolition, gardening, painting, repairs, and unloading. The police keep an eye on this early- morning job market, but they don't intervene. They don't enforce deportation orders on the undocumented—New York's Democratic Administration prides itself on being a "sanctuary city"—so the morning labor market operates in a no-man's land between legality and illegality.[13]

If fair policing is the key institutional precondition for order in a hyper-diverse city, the second precondition—manifestly not met—is a fair immigration system, one that allows a path to rights for undocumented workers. Being undocumented deprives workers of redress and rights and forces them underground.

The New York mayor's office can't fix immigration—that's a federal responsibility—but it can do something to help integrate an estimated half a million mostly Hispanic undocumented workers. While Congress remains deadlocked on immigration reform, the sanctuary cities whose economies depend on immigrant integration can't wait. New York is following Los Angeles, Portland, and other American cities in developing a municipal ID that will enable the undocumented to open bank accounts, arrange loans, and enter into mortgage agreements.

Any time spent in Jackson Heights brings home one central lesson about the diversity that globalization has brought to the modern city. The success of diversity depends, ultimately, on whether the city delivers, every day, a certain rough justice: jobs that don't discriminate, employers who pay what they owe, landlords who keep their places up, police who don't pick on the undocumented, courts who rule fairly.

Besides rough justice, there must be opportunity, some way of moving from precariousness to security. While many of the undocumented and unskilled will fall through the cracks, slip into the deportation system, and be sent home, some will learn good English, secure a steady job, get their papers, bring their families to this country, and move from illegal basement apartments into accommodation above ground. As they do so, as they become citizens, they get a stake in the city and in the country. All of this is dynamic, never secure, constantly at risk of unraveling.

The family is the survival unit of the immigrant experience: if it holds together, all can rise together; if it comes apart, everyone goes down. For all the talk about "community"—everyone I talked to said they were from some community or other—the one that matters most is the family.

If you start from Queens, making your way in America is not easy. You have to have papers and documents. You have to know how to open a bank account, get a Social Security number, learn how to deposit your check or insist that your employer pay you the full amount in cash. There are lots of people from your community who will offer to help—for a consideration. Trust flows naturally to those who speak the same language and have been through the same experiences. Immigrant integration can be visualized as a long human chain from the home country through to the final destination, linking the new arrivals to an ascending rank order of the more successful and integrated.

Precisely because ethnic chains of influence *seem* to an innocent newcomer to be the safest way to navigate the strangeness of a diverse city, these are the relationships most open to abuse. When I talked to the policewoman who works with the Asian elderly, the credit counselor at the Hispanic service agency, and the New York City financial literacy team, they told me about the Hispanic lawyers who promise to solve immigration problems and then disappear with the money, the Asian real estate agents who bilk new arrivals from China, and merchants who promise a special deal for "one of their own" only to charge them double. One of the key functions of urban institutions—the police, the courts, city agencies—is to protect newcomers from their protectors in their own community. Global migration upends the frameworks in which trustworthiness is determined. In the global city, they learn to trust strangers in institutions and crucially, strangers from other races.

What this means, in turn, is that no community in Queens can afford to be entirely self-contained, closed in upon itself. While the ties of common food, language, memory, and loyalty may tie immigrants to their communities of origin, the job and housing markets pull them out into interactions with strangers. The mass media—television, radio, Internet, newspapers, magazines—are engines of acculturation, pouring images of American life together with the goods, hairstyles, slang, deportment, and news values of the majority community into every basement bedroom and curtained front room in Queens.

Immigrants are exposed, like everyone else, to the tidal influences of the multichannel universe, but they also have native-language sources of information all their own. In what is called the "ethnic media" pride of place goes to immigrant success stories—the bright Bangladeshi girl who gets a scholarship to NYU, the Korean adolescent who makes sergeant in the Marines.

The Internet and satellite TV that beams native language programs from home make it possible for migrants to live in two worlds at once. Having transnational identities that span the globe is not new, but the ability to maintain simultaneous loyalties has been empowered by the TV satellite, the cell phone, and the Internet.[14] Queens's inhabitants keep up with the soap operas, Bollywood musicals, and news and commentary of their native lands. These allegiances used to be shed after the first generation, but now subsequent generations, born in the United States, maintain contact with their parents' countries of origin. Dual citizenship is more common, and both the new land and the immigrants' countries of origin are required to share the loyalties, values, and attachments of these global citizens.

Politics in the multicultural city is simultaneously the politics of the new land and the politics of the countries of origin. Immigrant diasporas commonly import the hatreds and exclusions of their home countries' politics, while at least nominally the politics of their new homes preaches tolerance and openness. In practice, of course, political leaders in the multicultural city recruit new party members along ethnic lines, using local power brokers, religious leaders, and community businesspeople to bring in money and party workers. Once Sikhs, Nepalis, Tibetans, Chinese, and Turks, to take but five examples from Queens, have been recruited into the democratic politics of their new homes, they reasonably name their price: support for the ethnic or religious demands of their

brothers and sisters back home. In this way, diasporas in the multicultural city pull politicians in their new homes into the fray of domestic politics in their home countries. Globalization has the effect
of making all politics, but especially the politics of ethnic and religious minorities, a global affair.[15]

Migration globalizes political struggles for recognition, and it
also transforms religion. Back in their homelands the spiritual is
always local. In Jackson Heights the spiritual is global. At Friday
prayers at a mosque in a converted warehouse, the key fact to notice is the diversity *within* diversity, the range of ethnic and racial
groups who pray together as Muslims. The heterogeneity of the
Muslim *umma*–the believers–was on full display: Africans, Asians,
Arabs, white and black Americans also. The imam who led the
hundreds of men in prayer–with the women in a separate room–was
a European Muslim from Bosnia. His sermon was eloquent, with
metaphors of struggle, *jihad* he called it, though the struggle he
meant was the battle of the immigrant experience itself, the
struggle with temptation, discouragement, loneliness and sorrow.
The men listened silently, some prostrating themselves, others
kneeling and bowing their foreheads to the carpet, side by side
with men who shared the same faith but did not speak the same
language.

I also visited a South Indian Hindu temple, ornamented in
splendid gray marble, located among small single-family dwellings
on a suburban street. Indian families from distant boroughs brought
generations together for a blessing or a wedding or the commemoration of a departed relative. They sat cross-legged on the marble
floors, clustered around shrines, beautifully embellished with
flowers, the matriarchs in saris, the younger generation in jeans,
shorts, and baseball hats on backward. One especially devout man
in Bermuda shorts and a T-shirt, made a continuous circle of one

shrine, praying and bowing, and every time he passed, he took care to say "Excuse me." Downstairs in the basement, spicy vegetarian food was served, and families lined up with containers to take the food away in cartons back to their homes. All of this interweaving of ancient Hindu ritual and modern American life seemed effortless and unstrained.

To live in the global city is to live the ancient time of religious ritual and to obey the contemporaneous clock of suburban life. It is to conjugate a meaning for life from different layers and to hold to this meaning in the face of secular temptations unthinkable in the village communities from which the ancient faiths originally sprang.

What is remarkable about the hyper-diversity of Queens is that so many groups touch, interact, share public space—Rockaway Beach, for example, and the public parks and subways—but largely live separate lives. Students of ethnic integration in other global cities, such as London, have described a "commonplace diversity" in which groups share public space but maintain their homes as private space. They welcome groups that mix with others, disapproving of orthodox religious communities that "keep to themselves." At the same time, in London at least, groups do not, by and large, eat in each other's houses or attend each other's weddings or funerals.[16]

The same pattern was evident in Jackson Heights. The public ethic, the one people used when they spoke to me, strongly endorsed "living with" people of other races, religions, and ethnicities. At the same time, they said clearly that, when it comes to choosing where to live or whom to associate with, they prefer to "live apart," with their own group.[17]

"Living apart" is most pronounced between native-born American blacks and the white population. Black communities in Queens remain effectively segregated from other groups. White flight from minority neighborhoods continues. A 2007 study of the United States as a whole found that neighborhoods in larger U.S. cities have a critical minority threshold—typically from 5 to 15 percent—beyond which white families leave for residential areas that are predominantly white.[18]

Though there are "global neighborhoods" where diverse populations live side by side, there is extensive voluntary segregation by race and ethnicity and income in Queens.[19] Everyone seems to navigate with an internal map of neighborhoods that are safe, dangerous, in transition, or up and coming. Residential segregation builds upon and compounds segregation in education. Many middle-class whites have seceded from the New York public school system and have gone to private or charter schools. In 2009, most black and Latino students were enrolled in public schools with less than 10 percent white enrollment. Blacks are educated with blacks, Hispanics with Hispanics. Only Asians and whites seem to share educational opportunity together. A study in 2014 showed that New York has the most segregated school system in the United States.[20]

In hyper-diverse cities, in other words, a strong commitment to equality, diversity, and tolerance—that is, living together—goes hand in hand with the actual practice of living apart. By and large Americans do not share neighborhoods with people of other races; do not school their children in the same public schools; and most of all, rarely marry outside their own racial or ethnic group. In the United States as a whole, intermarriage has increased over the past several generations—after legal barriers were struck down in 1967—but still only 8.4 percent of all marriages cross racial lines.[21] Indeed, as immigration has soared, the effect has been to increase the pool of same-race partners and thus reinforce patterns of racial endogamy, at least among first-generation immigrants. Some of their U.S.-born sons and daughters are "marrying out," but the numbers are small. While Americans interact on a daily basis and endorse the normative commitment to equality, when it comes to making intimate choices, they stick with their own.

Living side by side, as opposed to living together, does not require much meeting of minds or even shared culture. It requires passably fair public institutions, decent policing above all and a subliminal operating system—basic trust, basic reciprocity—constantly tested, constantly renegotiated, but usually reaffirmed in the ebb and flow of daily life. It is so often reaffirmed as to become second nature.

The most interesting thing about the tolerance on display in Jackson Heights was precisely how unremarkable and ordinary it was, rooted in everyday transactions at the grocery store, in nods exchanged between neighbors, in greetings in the streets, in occasional embraces at meetings. People I talked to were quietly proud of the moral order that this tolerance had produced, but they were not ideological about it. For example, they did not construe tolerance as an obligation, as a proposition they were obliged to respect with all people. It was determined by the person in question, the situation, the history they had managed to create with each other. Tolerance was not a universal value, just a workaday social practice. It was an ordinary virtue, fragile, contingent, easily damaged by violence, police brutality, or crime, dependent for its survival on nothing more than its humble reproduction in daily life.

As I headed back on the El from Diversity Plaza to midtown Manhattan, after three days walking the streets of Jackson Heights and talking to everybody I could, I realized that the expectations that modern globalization has instilled in us are hard taskmasters. As I sat there, rattling my way back to Manhattan, looking at my fellow passengers, some of them nodding off after a hard day's work, some heading to the evening shift, it was clear to me that opportunity is a promise that simply must be kept. If this dream is denied, then the whole order of diversity and tolerance in Queens will crumble. The virtues of resilience and endurance endure when promises are kept: when justice is done, when jobs are open to all, when the rungs at the bottom of the ladder are within reach.

Harder questions pressed upon me too, as I returned to Manhattan. If super-diversity works—in the limited sense that the soup does not boil over and overt conflict is avoided—what actually is so good about it if we live side by side, but not together, if tolerance goes hand in hand with self-segregation and avoidance, if, moreover, people don't actually choose this pattern of life? The tidal wave of migration can't be seen as a conscious result of democratic deliberation. It was an unforeseen consequence of changes to an immigration act in 1965. For at least some native-born Americans the new diversity is the key feature of the forces of globalization over which their democracy seems to have no control. So why do most politicians celebrate diversity? Why have we translated the fact of diversity into a value? Why has it become one of the moral signatures of twenty-first-century globalization's good conscience?

When Americans put a value on diversity, they are patting themselves on the back for avoiding the ethnic and religious violence that rages elsewhere. But they may just be lucky. They may also be engaging in a complicated act of self-deception. They pretend to live *together,* but in reality they only live side by side. It would be easy to dismiss this as moral hypocrisy, as the evasion Americans use to mask the distance between moral ideals and messy reality. But there is another more interesting possibility. It may be the case that the only realistic way for diverse populations to live together *is* to live side by side.[22] This paradox may be diversity's condition for success.

The other conclusion is that what we make of diversity in moral terms depends critically on our own origins and national story. When we—and here I mean non-American outsiders like myself—praise the diversity of Queens and New York more generally, we are making a declaration of allegiance to a postcolonial moral universe in which, if we are white, we claim to have jettisoned racial and cultural stereotypes. We are acknowledging that struggles for freedom and justice changed us, the privileged ones, for the better. If, on the other hand, we come from one of the racial, religious, or ethnic minorities, our embrace of diversity is still an unfulfilled promise, a demand addressed to the privileged and the institutions we continue to control. All of this is to say that we who praise diversity do not mean the same things by it or have the same interests in its preservation.

Diversity Plaza leaves me thinking that diversity as a value and diversity as a fact do not closely correspond. It is fundamental to the reality of Queens that its neighborhoods are places people are prepared to come from, not places most of them want to end up. They are starting points, not final destinations. Outsiders like me invest Jackson Heights with a meaning—that is, a validation of postimperial diversity—that most of its inhabitants might be happy to escape, if, for example, they could only get together the money to get a place in one of the new bedroom communities in Long Island or the stable neighborhoods elsewhere in Queens itself.[23]

Queens, moreover, is not the United States. Super-diversity remains the exception rather than the rule in American urban settings, and not just in the United States. Around the world, billions of human beings still live in villages where cultural diversity has no recognized value, where strangers are viewed with suspicion, and where moral codes are still defined by local religious, tribal, and family leaders, mostly male. Diversity as a value would not mean much, if anything, in Shanghai and Beijing, Mexico City, Delhi, or Mumbai, because these cities are not diverse in the sense that Jackson Heights is diverse. They are undergoing rural-urban migration by groups sharing the same ethnic and religious composition, not postimperial emigration of the kind flooding into Europe and North America.

It may be an illusion particular to the empowered and educated middle class of Manhattan to believe that where "we" tolerant cosmopolitans lead, the rest of the world will follow. In fact, there are more competing paths into the future than the rhetoric of globalization allows us to see. We are not all becoming the same. We are not all on the same path. For that we should actually be thankful.

Moral life in the global city should be seen as one of the most consequential experiments in mankind's history, one that tests whether we can reconcile egalitarian commitments to human equality with ongoing loyalty to tribe and faith, whether democracy can build civic commitment across diverse populations or whether the tidal wave of human movement across borders will produce a populist backlash against democracy itself. The moral order in Queens is fragile, its fate uncertain, but it also represents an especially modern kind of hope: that we can master globalization itself by showing that peoples from every corner of the earth, without coercion or force, can evolve a moral order that coheres, endures, and protects the ordinary virtues. There are no guarantees here, no certainty that the diversity we praise today will survive the pressures of populism and politicization or the adverse forces of global economic downturn. In every ethical judgment we make about the facts, we are also making a bet on how we hope the future will turn out.

2

Los Angeles

The Moral Operating Systems of Global Cities

LOS ANGELES, LONDON, TORONTO, NEW YORK, AND SYDNEY: in 1960, none of these global cities were "super diverse."[1] By 2000, all of them were. The United Nations anticipates that the world's cities—especially the twenty-three megacities with populations larger than 10 million—will absorb all of the 2.3 billion population increase expected between now and 2050.[2] Nearly 70 percent of the world's population will live in cities by then, and we can expect that many of these will be multilingual, multiracial, and multicultural.

If you had asked anyone in 1960 whether, in a city like Toronto or London, people from a hundred different cultures and faiths could share the same space, you would have been met with disbelief. Some predicted disaster.

In the 1960s a British politician, Enoch Powell, contemplating the prospect of London's becoming a global magnet for migration, gloomily quoted the nightmare vision in Virgil's *Aeneid* of the Roman river Tiber foaming with blood.[3] Today the river Thames flows through a London that is the more or less peaceful home to populations from the entire world.

In Jackson Heights, Queens, several of the conditions for the moral success of globalization became apparent: fair policing, non-discrimination, effective institutions of integration, and above all, a moral culture of living "together" if not "side by side."

If these are the rough-and-ready conditions of success, we also came away thinking that there are no guarantees. The work that courts, police, elected officials, and civil society organizations have to do in order to keep the show on the road is unending. In unequal societies, the burden of legitimacy is squarely on the shoulders of those who uphold the rule of law. What happens when the rough justice of the rule of law breaks down? What happens when the global city fails? How does it repair itself when its operating systems fail?

The place to ask that question is Los Angeles, for its recent history is a story of how moral operating systems collapse into violence and how they are slowly rebuilt from the ruins.

Los Angeles is the capital of the world's entertainment industry, a port shipping huge volumes of goods to and from Asia and a vast metropolitan area that has opened its doors to mass migration.[4] Latinos now make up 48.5 percent of the City of Los Angeles, and they come from every nation and community in the Americas; Asians, again from every country, faith, and region, now make up 11.4 percent of the city's population. Whites and African Americans are now a declining percentage of the population. Their antagonism defined the life of the city from the Watts riots of 1965 to the Rodney King insurrection of 1992.[5]

The Watts riots that devastated south central Los Angeles over six days in August 1965 were triggered by a bungled arrest of a black man for drunk driving. In the ensuing uprising, thirty four people were killed and whole city blocks were destroyed before police and the California National Guard restored order. Public order collapsed again in April 1992 after charges levied against the police responsible for the beating of Rodney King were dismissed in court. The disturbances of 1992 claimed fifty-five lives and were not brought to a close until the Marines and the National Guard were deployed to the city. The uprising was not an episode of "mindless" violence and looting, but a moral phenomenon at its heart, triggered by the insufferable spectacle—caught on videotape and broadcast around the world—of police officers relentlessly beating a black man, Rodney King, who was not offering resistance and whose later plea for calm, when rioting engulfed the city—"Why can't we all get along?"—was a poignant appeal for moral order. In the wake of the chaos and fury that this episode triggered, leaders across the city understood that they had to repair the ripped fabric of civic life together.

Since 1992 the city has become a laboratory of intercommunal coalition building. Let us look at Los Angeles through an ethical lens, searching for "the moral economy" the tacit but shared assumptions that enable neighborhoods and communities to overcome their own differences and then reach out and forge links with other racial, ethnic, or national communities in the metropolis.[6]

The central ethical problem of the global city is how to generate collaboration among strangers who do not share a common origin, religion, or ethnicity. To ensure coordination among strangers, the city needs an operating system. Like computer code, such a system is a set of shared procedures or routines that enable millions of people, from different races, origins, and social backgrounds, to live together.[7] There has to be some tacit moral equilibrium, some rough-and-ready, live-and-let-live attitude that allows strangers to share public space. Transactional indifference, though there is plenty of this in any city, is not enough. People want their gaze returned. They want to hope for the kindness of strangers, no matter how rare it may be. Shared interests make for business deals, but not for the electric excitement of city life or its promise of human connection. All of this presumes that city dwellers are willing to gamble on trust, to reach out to strangers in the hope that their gesture will be reciprocated. Even the "cash nexus" can only function effectively on the basis of limited trust; and when interests collide, conflict can only be avoided if parties share some basic willingness to adjudicate their differences and find a compromise.

There's nothing new about the idea that economies cannot function without moral order or that moral order is a self-generating organism or system. Adam Smith's *The Theory of Moral Sentiments* (1759) was perhaps the first to emphasize that moral order could be generated through human "sympathy," through each uncoordinated individual's capacity to imagine and follow through on the conduct necessary for effective social cooperation. Moral life, on this account, is not rightly understood as obedience to top-down commands but rather as a largely automatic display of ordinary virtues.[8]

The ordinary virtues—trust, honesty, politeness, forbearance, respect—are the operating system of any community. Los Angeles's operating system has to work for people from 115 foreign countries speaking 224 different languages. It has to work, moreover, in a city with a history of bitter conflict, with people whose memories are still not reconciled to a violent past.

Ethics can be modeled as an operating system because, like software, it guarantees the predictability necessary for stable human interactions. The most important condition for predictability is security: interactions that are free from violence. Without security, trust between strangers is impossible.

In a global city, people want more than just to be safe. They want a space to experiment, to emancipate themselves from the roles they left behind in small communities where face-to-face interactions were the norm. The often lamented anonymity of city life has provided the safe space for individuals to become individuals, to find and express identities that might have been suppressed in rural or village settings.

Besides safety and privacy, cities have to provide opportunities for seeking, earning, and giving respect. In any anonymous urban environment, according respect to strangers is a risky business. If you are rejected, you recoil. In a city with a healthy moral economy, moral risks are rewarded, trust is returned, and basic reciprocity is strengthened.

In the multicultural city, people arrive with the moral operating systems they inherited from their cultures and countries of origin. Some women arriving from traditional societies, for example, will hesitate to step out beyond their front doors, because the public sphere was denied them in their home countries. It takes time, sometimes a generation, before these women feel comfortable sharing public space with strangers. What weakens these traditional operating systems is what drew the immigrants to the city in the first place: the dream of equality and opportunity. Over time, traditional operating systems lose their purchase with city dwellers because the traditional codes cannot keep up with the highly individualized choices of urban life. The immigrant experience is an experience of individuation: women become breadwinners, children leave the authority of the family for the disciplines of the school, patriarchs lose some of their authority when they leave for work in a factory. The younger generation learns the new language of the city first, and the older generation struggles to catch up, sometimes transferring their own dreams onto the shoulders of their children.

In this battle between the traditional operating systems that immigrants bring with them and the new operating systems of the global city, the city's advantage is always the promise of equality. It creates the moral expectation on which civil peace depends; opportunity is the ladder that all wish to climb. Beyond this, as many city dwellers as possible must share a few basic rules: prohibitions against violence, false witness, and lying, and a few positive injunctions that stress reciprocity: do unto others as you would be done by. Provided that these moral injunctions enjoy majority support, those who do not share them can be contained and controlled.[9]

These expectations may be codified in law, but law alone cannot ensure that everyone complies. If law and law enforcement were the only powers maintaining the moral order of a city, it would soon be a jungle, ruled by the gun and the night stick. Coercion alone cannot hold together the order of any large city. Most of the work of moral order is done by the tacit live-and-let-live approach that city dwellers internalize from their city's moral operating system. Ethics can be seen as an operating system because, when we start up our lives every morning, our moral systems start up with us, without enforcement or top-down supervision, and guide us in the common interactions of daily life.

Cognitive psychologists and neurologists have tried to show that many of the shared moral reflexes in any urban operating system—empathy, sympathy, fear, and repulsion—are hardwired in our brains.[10] Yet we do not understand how an individual's neurological processes, especially as they relate to ethical behavior, interact with those of other individuals to produce the iterative social patterns of trust, accommodation, and friendship or conversely, aversion, suspicion, and hostility that I am calling the moral operating system.

Whatever cooperative or aversive moral impulses we may have in our neurological makeup, they become imprinted features of behavior only if they are reinforced by experience. A moral operating system comes into being when certain impulses—limited trust, conditional accommodation, mutual assistance under certain conditions—are recurrently reinforced by the rhythms and demands of urban life itself. The reinforcement occurs when interactions with strangers come to have a predictable and reliable form. The reinforcement occurs in public institutions, in our interactions with police officers, judges, and public officials, and when our children interact with teachers in a classroom. A moral operating system is a collective social invention made possible by the reinforcing interaction between public institutions and the moral expectations of ordinary citizens. We learn the cooperative behaviors required for an effective urban operating system as children if we are lucky enough to have stable families, if our public school systems do their jobs, if our places of worship tell us how to live right with ourselves and with others. Even if some virtues are hardwired, public institutions have to reinforce a shared set of expectations for civil cooperation to become our second nature.

A city's moral operating system is a tacit set of framing assumptions—the default settings, if you will—about other people's likely behavior that enables us to make choices: in second-by-second interactions, whether we trust or avoid, engage or avert. To speak of an operating system is to use a metaphor, and metaphors can mislead. The system frames choice; it doesn't make the choices for us. We have to take ownership of the ethical operating systems inside our own conscience. As with our computers, we personalize our operating systems so that they allow us to share with others and serve our personal identities and needs. It is up to us to forge what we have learned and what we have inherited into the principles we live by.

Our operating systems have to contend with a lot of noise coming from conflicting perspectives. One source of noise is the media and entertainment industry. Los Angeles itself, as the global capital of this industry, has probably done more to structure our moral imagination of the city than anywhere else in the world. From *Chinatown* to *Blade Runner* to *Reservoir Dogs* and *Pulp Fiction,* the movies fill our imaginations with dystopian and utopian visions of city life, so that in all our interactions with strangers we are working our way toward them, across stereotypes that often create paranoia and distrust.

Operating systems filter out most of the noise and provide us with stable expectations and guidelines. When the noise is filtered out, we don't have to make constant choices about trust in the city. The operating system we take for granted allows our moral behavior to feel reflexive, unconscious, and, as long as things go well, unproblematic. Ethical life then feels like merging with traffic on the freeway: most of the time we can count on the other drivers to do what we expect, and they can count on us to do the same.

The default settings of an operating system are not propositional, general, or theoretical. If we behave decently it is not because we believe we have some general obligation to mankind that we must fulfill.[11] Human rights doesn't come into it. When we live side by side with people from other races or religions, our question is not, What do I owe persons who are different from me as a general proposition? but simply, Do I trust this particular person? Can I do business with this one? Should I stay away from him or her? The gradual, life-long training in these moral reflexes that we receive in the course of life in a super-diverse city imperceptibly makes these judgments so much a matter of habit that we are hardly aware we are making judgments at all.

In these interactions, justification and self-justification occur only when there is conflict or some rupture of expectation. It is then that the moral evaluations that divide begin: just / unjust; fair / unfair, us / them. Otherwise, the global city is a scene of "everyday togetherness," banal, unexamined, and yet efficient precisely because it tacitly frames our moral expectations of each other.[12] Central to these aspirations is the search for community, for groups or neighborhoods where we feel at home. Community is the key word in any moral operating system for it defines the boundaries of trust.

There is no shortage of communities in Los Angeles. Some are the spatial territories we call neighborhoods, while others are faith communities. Still others are virtual communities, where, to use an L.A. example, young Muslim believers use social media to share opinions and identities in more casual ways than those allowed in a traditional mosque. These virtual communities, needless to say, start in one global city and then rapidly deterritorialize and draw in adherents from other cities around the globe. Very occasionally they become organizing sites for the countermorality of jihad.

In a global city, community aspires to be elective, a matter of choice rather than of fate. In Los Angeles, the elective communities that provide hope, refuge, and belonging for the poor are the churches, temples, gurdwaras, and mosques. Along Slauson Avenue the storefront churches, black and Latino, some of them Pentecostal, welcome the new immigrant arrivals, one proclaiming "Holiness or Hell" on a sheet hung over a doorway. At the Mount Moriah Missionary Baptist Church, if you show up when the University of Southern California gospel choir visits and preacher and congregation join in, you soon experience what community *feels* like: bodies swaying together in the pews, voices intertwining in exuberant harmony, the sound filling the hall and expressing kinship, belonging, relief from daily cares, and oneness with others. Even at Mount Moriah, however, the community is not stable. The preacher has to hold his congregation together—many are leaving for the suburbs—and young people do not automatically elect to show up for worship on Sunday.

The question for Los Angeles is whether there is a community of communities, transcending and uniting the diverse peoples who make up the population of the 400-square-mile area of the city. To be sure, no one can experience the city as a whole. Each city dweller may know only her own daily commute, the streets of his immediate neighborhood or a nearby shopping plaza; yet it is important to believe that in principle at least there are no no-go areas, no places where civic trust has entirely collapsed. It is important for a city to present itself as a moral whole, for it to believe that it shares some basic identity as a community.

Everybody in L.A. is searching for community, affirming it, defining it, or defending it from attack. Community has civic meanings denoting the shared values that unite people across their differences, and it has ethnic, religious, or racial meanings denoting the particularisms of language, culture, cuisine, and neighborhood that give people a sense of belonging that separates them from others.

The salience of community in any global city is so obvious—the neighborhoods where all the shop signs are in one language, where all the places of worship are one denomination—that it would be reasonable to suppose that primal belonging to race, religion, and ethnicity must be stronger than any general civic attachment to the larger community of the city as a whole. Yet if we had no shared operating system, if our values were exclusively directed by primal affiliations and loyalties, it is doubtful that a multicultural city as complex as Los Angeles could function without recurrent conflict and violence.

Some thin (rather than thick) moral consensus, mandating limited trust, nonviolence, and a default setting in favor of cooperation, appears necessary to keep a multicultural city functioning.[13] The consensus has to be thin because it has to be pluralist; that is, it has to accommodate the fact that inhabitants live in many moral universes at once—ethnic, religious, familial, and traditional, the ones they were born in, the ones they work in, the ones they wish they lived in.

The moral operating system of the global city cannot deliver a sense of common ground by suppressing or supplanting these competing allegiances or values. When races, religions, and ethnicities share space in the city and interact every day, they do not suppress their primary loyalties. In a diverse city everyone balances primary and secondary affiliations as a matter of course. They may live their most meaningful hours "inside" their own communities of language, race, or origin, but they also live "outside" because work leaves them no choice or because they like spending time with people different from themselves. The negotiation between inside and outside is complex, but no one would venture beyond the stockades of their inside identity unless the city's pattern of daily life succeeded in creating an expectation of fluid, peaceful, and sometimes rewarding interactions with strangers.

The complex meanings of community came into focus when the Carnegie Council team met with teenagers in a police station in Boyle Heights, a low-income community that is 95 percent Latino. The high school students meet every Saturday to work on the *Boyle Heights Beat*, a bilingual student newspaper that serves the entire community, produced with assistance from faculty at the Annenberg School at the University of Southern California.[14]

The students come from immigrant homes where most of their parents speak only Spanish, but the young people work in both languages and the newspaper they edit is bilingual. They are constructing identities between two linguistic worlds, keenly aware that when they leave for college—which most will do—they may take a significant step away from the Spanish-speaking world of their parents. This fact has complex meaning for them. One young woman said she wanted to go to college so that she could return to help her community, but when I asked her when that might be, the return she had in mind was too distant to come into any kind of focus. You could feel her struggling to reconcile the ambitions she had for her own life with her own desire to return and serve her community.

When the young Latino students used the word community, they gave it contrasting meanings: "a place where you are at home," "a place where you are safe," "a place where the people know you or they know your parents or grandparents." Boyle Heights had not always been a community, they said. It had been too dangerous, but now it was safe. The women said you could go home late at night; the men said the police didn't hassle them. One sixteen-year-old girl whose parents are undocumented workers, laboring at a bakery on the night shift, portrayed community as a prospective project people could share into the future. She said, "A community is a place where people are trying to make things better."

So, following her lead, we could say that a community is more than a safe place; it is also a political space where you can work with strangers to improve the lives you share. These high school students have been as good as their word. They put out—and deliver to people's homes—a newspaper that creates the common currency of reliable information. A community has moral properties, but as Manuel Pastor argues in *Just Growth,* it has epistemic ones too: without shared knowledge, a community is prey to rumor, panic, disinformation, or manipulation.[15] With shared knowledge, a community can defend its interests and do politics together.

Within communities, however, the battle over who defines the operating system will be competitive, sometimes violent. L.A. has seen decades of gang warfare–Crips versus Bloods is the best-known example–with desperate citizens caught in the crossfire. Gangs reject the very idea of a moral operating system that makes a city work. Pluralism meets the limits of its tolerance here: a global city is not safe if there are zones where strangers cannot venture without the permission of predatory enforcers or where two warring codes are fighting each other for control of the streets. This is still the reality in many city blocks of south Los Angeles.

In south central L.A. at the Stentorian Community Center, we met former gang members who had set themselves up as an intervention team, mediating between gangs, preventing retaliation shootings, reaching out to young people and turning them away from gang life. These battle-scarred, heavily tattooed men–black and Latino–have done time in prison; they have watched brothers and sisters being killed in the battles over turf and pride. They know that if they don't stop now they will end their lives in prison or die in the streets. A Better L.A., a private nonprofit established by sports figures and business leaders, bankrolls their attempt to turn the next generation around.[16]

When the former gang members talked about their "license to operate," I asked them who hands out the licenses. One of their leaders explained the license as a form of community consent that they secure by being known, by being disciplined, by working with the police and not against them. To have a license in a community is to have legitimacy. Theirs is earned, it seemed to me, through redemption. Their work is ethical–repairing themselves so they can repair others–but it is also political: trying to retake the operating system of their neighborhood from the gangs.[17] As long as these neighborhoods are as poor as they are, however, the streets of their neighborhoods will remain a battleground between competing moral systems with the outcome in doubt.

Like the software engineers who write code for our computers, these gang veterans and the young high school students from Boyle Heights are writing code for themselves, but also for their city; their actions, however small, are helping to change expectations and repairing the system breakdowns that keep communities apart.

We are all moral code writers. What we say and do, in our everyday interactions, creates expectations and frames of reference for others, which in turn change how they behave. The operating system of a city is not proprietary—no one owns it or writes it alone. It is an open system, constantly adjusting to people's lived experience of daily life. Through billions of daily interactions, as we experience the pleasure and pain of city life, we recalibrate our expectations of strangers and our own behavior.

Unlike the operating systems in computers that are designed to function identically all the time, ethical operating systems are homeostatic: they adapt to experience and they can be damaged by trauma. When policing breaks down, when one group feels that it is systematically exposed to police violence, or when others—Koreans in Los Angeles, for example—feel they get no police protection at all, trust collapses, communities cease to reach out to them, and they hunker down to defend themselves.[18] Koreans tried this in the Rodney King riots by defending their shops with guns, but their actions only deepened the hatred and resentment on both sides. The chaos and violence of 1992 taught communities that no operating system could function across racial lines unless a police force, more or less trusted by all, was there to keep relations peaceful.

The Los Angeles police department was shaken to its foundation by the Rodney King uprising and the corruption scandal in the department's Rampart Division in 1998. The LAPD was placed under federal judicial supervision, and it has taken many years to slowly rebuild relationships with Los Angeles's communities.[19] When the

Carnegie team visited with them, their officers told us that they have abandoned a "them versus us" fortress mentality; they have come to understand that, in the words of one officer, "we can't arrest our way out of any problem." Legitimate policing depends on finding the religious leaders, teachers, parents, and local politicians who are defending the operating system of a community and then working with them to strengthen it.

Their policing methods are politics in action: identifying community leadership, making deals, forming iterative and provisional relationships of trust. For instance, they may broker an agreement with other municipal agencies to improve garbage collection or recreation space in a disadvantaged community. In that way they earn the community's trust. In this process of policing as political exchange, maintenance of a shared moral operating system turns out to be crucial. As one LAPD officer put it, "Never write the community a check they can't cash, or you will lose trust."

It would be foolish to ascribe too much to the change at the LAPD. One bad night on the street, one death of a civilian or a person in uniform, can undo twenty years of progress. Yet it is a fact that police-community relations are better than they were in 1992. It is also true that Los Angeles's crime rates have declined for the past fifteen years.[20] The riots that have erupted in other cities, such as Ferguson, Mo., and Baltimore, Md., have not occurred in Los Angeles. Many communities are no longer under siege from the police, and because they have control over their own operating system they can reach out and make common cause with others.

In the moral repair work that occurred after the 1992 riots, religious communities played a crucial role. In the days after the uprising, Cecil Murray and Mark Whitlock of the First African Methodist Episcopal Church had to perform contradictory feats of moral leadership: articulating the rage of their congregation as victims of police brutality, while calming them down, reaching out to adversaries, and repairing the fissures that had opened up with the Korean community, while also drawing together business people and politicians to fund the rebuilding of burned out neighborhoods.[21]

Mark Whitlock was a senior executive at Wells Fargo Bank when the police responsible for beating Rodney King were acquitted. He resigned from the bank that day, determined, as he told us, "to stop making rich people richer." Within a month he was negotiating with street gangs in his neighborhood, eventually mounting bail for a gang member arrested by the police. In the global city, such unlikely partnerships between gangs and religious leaders illustrate how a concern for the overall moral fabric of a city can overcome deep differences of experience and perspective. The partnerships are political: power brokers working together to ensure that the competition over whose operating system will prevail stays peaceful.

To repair the damage after 1992, faiths had to work together. This cooperation also involves a complex navigation over doctrine. If an evangelical Christian joins hands with Muslims or Jews to pray before a meeting and he evokes the blood of Jesus Christ and the agony of his crucifixion, it can be hard for his brothers to accept. Yet, as one of the reverend leaders joked, you can't build interfaith dialogue by praying "to whom it may concern." When repairing an operating system, after the trauma of riot and violence, therefore, what is common can only be strengthened if differences are acknowledged and affirmed. What the faith-based groups learned is that common ground can be found so long as no one is asked to trade away what makes them distinctive. So for the sake of community peace, religious leaders manage to put aside these differences and join hands to pray together.

This is leadership displayed as forbearance and it is critical in repairing broken systems of trust. Besides mutual forbearance, there is the leadership of empathy, reaching across the competing narratives of what happened in 1992 to find common ground. The leaders in L.A. have learned that the work of forbearance and empathy is never done. These leaders know, deep down, that the very metaphors they use—the religious and therapeutic language of healing—is misleading because these words imply that wounds, caused by violence, rage and hatred, can be forgotten with time. Memories of 1992 may be fading but a new generation is growing up in the city that is still aware that basic fairness and basic justice for all remain a work in progress. Wounds endure and the work of healing is unending. Many of the leaders in L.A. are veterans of decades of community work since the riots of 1992, and they are tired, openly wondering who will take their place. Getting new leaders ready is a constant challenge, and if a new generation fails to step up, networks of trust can dissolve and communities can go backward.

Ethical systems are both operative and normative, maintaining the equilibrium of daily interactions but also pointing out what is disturbing the equilibrium and must be rectified.[22] Ethical operating systems point communities toward the injustices that must be overcome together.

Now that Los Angeles is a majority Latino city, there is a new expectation at the heart of its operating system: a path to citizenship for the undocumented. In Boyle Heights the Latino high school students want to go to college, but they fear that their parents' undocumented status will deny them access to financial aid. Pursuit of the American dream encourages them to reach for the stars, while their immigration status keeps them grounded.[23]

As long as the issue of documentation is seen as a Hispanic issue alone, it will not be solved. The question is whether other communities also make it their concern. Middle-class families in Los Angeles depend on nannies, housekeepers, and drivers to look after their homes and possessions and take care of their children and aging parents. When these employees are arrested for being undocumented, their problems become their employers' problems. In this way immigration status issues cease being a Hispanic issue alone. They enter the political agenda of the white middle class.

Despite the emergence of political causes that unite different communities, the central question remains: Does the word community describe what is shared or what divides? Is Los Angeles an example of "segregated diversity" or "multicultural diversity"?[24] Does the city live diversity together, or do its communities live it apart?

Los Angeles residents, like the people we met in Jackson Heights, have an acute consciousness of the racial and ethnic geography of their city—which neighborhoods are white, black, Latino, Asian, or a mix; which ones are safe, which ones dangerous; which ones are middle class, which ones up and coming; which ones are sliding down the real estate scale. People's residential choices are a practical plebiscite on whether they are willing to live among people different from themselves.

Many communities in Los Angeles are mixed: more than one-third of L.A. zip codes do not have a clear ethnic majority, but in two-thirds, like does cluster with like, language with language, community of origin with community of origin.[25] Some of this segregation is morally innocent, reflecting patterns of group self-selection; some of it, however, is morally problematic, reflecting fear and dislike of other groups.

At the same time, the segregation and self-segregation are extraordinarily fluid. The neighborhoods of L.A. seem to change rapidly. Groups move in, groups move out, neighborhoods prosper and decay. As a result, while there are some desperately poor parts of the city—17.6 percent of the city's population lives below the poverty line—nowhere in L.A. has the ladder of opportunity broken down. Someone is always moving up and moving out.[26] Most remarkably, a city that is constantly absorbing new immigrants still manages to maintain opportunity for newcomers. Forty-four percent of Mexicans who live in Los Angeles but were born in Mexico own their home in L.A. Once they own a place, they have the collateral to move on and to move up.

"Segregated diversity" is also offset, to some degree, by intercommunal alliance building at the political level. No one ethnic or racial group has a hammerlock on power. Every candidate for mayor has to put together inter-racial coalitions that reach across the city in order to win.[27] Political coalition building is crucial to the maintenance of a shared operating system, and it is one reason why Los Angeles has avoided a recurrence of the riots of 1992.

When cities are as ethnically diverse as Los Angeles, they cannot be governed from the top down in command-and-control style. Instead, they need horizontal governance, with power dispersed through networks of community and business leaders committed to the maintenance of its shared operating system.[28]

These networks must ensure that no single group secures exclusive control over contracts and patronage. Favoritism can set off sparks that, when fanned, burst into flames of conflict. Cross-ethnic political mobilization can prevent "segregated diversity" from exploding into conflict only if coalitions arrange for the fair distribution of patronage.

A moral economy, however, will break down unless the real economy is robust. As the travails of other cities, like Detroit, seem to suggest, cities cannot hold together unless the local economy generates jobs and tax revenue. Los Angeles does have a broad-based manufacturing and service sector based in small and medium-sized enterprises that provides jobs and a tax base.[29] A recent report indicates, however, that L.A.'s unemployment rate has stayed above the national average for the past quarter-century, and it is no longer creating the jobs it needs or the tax base to fund its pension liabilities.[30] So the real economy is fragile, and if it is fragile its moral economy will be too.

Global cities are vulnerable, too, because their economies are linked into global supply chains over which they have little control. L.A.'s garment trade has to compete with Bangladesh. Hollywood competes with Bollywood. In the cash nexus that ties the global economy together, not even as powerful a city as Los Angeles gets to control the terms under which it competes in a global order.[31]

The cash nexus, however, is not lawless. City and federal regulations limit hours and conditions of work. The Los Angeles garment sector may be a tough place to work, but if a building is not up to code, it can be shut down. Enforcing labor and building standards may be a constant struggle between unions and management, with understaffed municipal authorities in between, but in this battle over labor standards, workers are not powerless.

There are pessimists, many of progressive or left-wing credentials, who claim that the defense of labor standards in Los Angeles is a lost cause. Since wages are lower in Shanghai or Manila, the cash nexus in an open international economy imposes upon Los Angeles a race to the bottom.[32]

Optimists deny that Los Angeles is fated to lose the race. L.A.'s constant influx of immigration and its small-scale and flexible manufacturing base enable it to maintain a competitive advantage. Moreover, many of the jobs that sustained L.A. in 2013 did not exist in 1960. Even low-wage immigrants have agency: they will move north only if they perceive it to be to their advantage. Immigrants still believe they gain by coming here. The promise of opportunity provides the moral legitimation of low-wage economies. Without that legitimacy, cities fail as moral communities.

To sum up, our visit to Jackson Heights and Los Angeles illuminated the dynamic relationship between institutions and the ordinary virtues. The virtues of interethnic trust, tolerance, and accommodation depend on institutions doing their jobs: police and the courts grinding out a rough-and-ready equality before the law, politicians maintaining a reasonably fair distribution of patronage to all groups, real estate and job ladders remaining open to all irrespective of religion or ethnicity. In the virtuous upward spiral that Los Angeles has tried to maintain since the riots of 1992, more or less acceptable institutional performance has strengthened the ordinary virtues and rebuilt the social trust on which a peaceful city depends. But an upward spiral of institutions and virtues is easily reversed. L.A. carries the memory of what a downward spiral looks like, and this memory, as much as any other single factor, keeps the dynamic between virtues and institutions moving in the right direction.

One prevalent image of the modern hyper-diverse global city, purveyed in movies and TV shows, is that it is a moral jungle. The actual L.A., as opposed to the L.A. in the movies, gives the lie to these dystopian images. Human beings do not want to live in a jungle. Los Angeles shows how deeply they strive for community, for places they can share, for people they can trust. This is not a sentimental fiction. As a matter of hard economic fact, cities simply cannot function without some key elements of a shared moral operating system: leadership networks that have the same aspirations, share the same knowledge, maintain solidarity between classes and races and common practices of justice and fair policing on the streets. None of this can ever be taken for granted. Just keeping the show on the road is an unending struggle, requiring everyone to recommit daily to the task of seeing each other anew, cutting through the stereotypes, taking people as they find them, one by one, finding and building connections with strangers and rewriting the code that keeps a common operating system in place.

This is no mean achievement. Nineteenth-century thinkers—John Stuart Mill, for example—doubted that it was possible to sustain moral community among people of different religious and ethnic origins. He questioned whether representative democracy was conceivable without ethnic and racial homogeneity in the citizenry.[33] We are trying to prove him wrong, to demonstrate, as the motto of the United States proclaims, *e pluribus unum,* that out of the many who come to her shores America can forge a community of civic equals.

Americans are conducting this experiment under conditions even more arduous than Mill imagined, for the forces of economic globalization that he witnessed in his era were still controlled by the power of empire. Today's globalization obeys no sovereign master, not even the United States. Yes, states and international bodies have greater power than they did in the nineteenth century to regulate markets and corporations. Thanks to the welfare state systems developed since 1945, modern nation states have more capacity to protect their citizens from globalization's dislocating effects. States now impose increasingly stringent border controls to protect their citizens from the adverse impact of global migration. But do modern sovereign states control globalization, as the British imperial system believed it did in John Stuart Mill's time? Certainly not.

Securing control over globalization so that it creates jobs rather than killing them, sustains communities instead of wiping them out, protects the environment instead of wrecking it, is the core problem of modern politics, in powerful and weak states alike. Many of the people we met in Jackson Heights and south Los Angeles can be forgiven for believing that such control is out of reach, both for them directly and for the politicians they elect.[34] This feeling of being in the grip of forces beyond political control is sharpest among globalization's losers, the bottom 10 percent, but it even expresses itself in the cosmopolitan 1 percent who count themselves as winners. There are few people left with Andrew Carnegie's confidence that the historical forces shaping their era could be mastered, understood, and controlled.

So what do we all do in the face of the acceleration of history and the feeling that our jobs and our lives are held in the grip of forces our democracies do not control?

This is where the view from the bottom up, the ordinary-virtues perspective, becomes useful. It suggests that for most people the larger questions posed by globalization, together with the larger threats and opportunities, are simply beyond their reach or grasp. This is not a reaction of ignorance. Everyone we talked to knew perfectly well that Los Angeles competes with Manilla, Ho Chi Minh City, and Shanghai and that this competition may well have very large impacts upon their lives. The real issue is whether an ordinary person can do anything much about these large determinants of their lives. Politicians and theorists may talk about "taking back control," but most people's experience of global change makes them skeptical of such rhetoric. Ordinary virtue is thus a strategy for making do, for getting on with life, for bracketing larger questions that do not admit of answers. From the ordinary-virtues perspective it is enough to do your job, to give your neighbor a lift when her car breaks down, to loan the renter across the hall your hair dryer or take in her package, to mix in the streets with people from a hundred different lands, to join in your neighbors' festivals, to make sure your own kids do their homework and do your best to maintain a marriage or relationship through good times and bad.

This is not the politics of resignation, but of resilience. It focuses on what can actually be achieved, and those who live by the ordinary virtues seek, to the best of their ability, to reproduce the moral order around them, without which their lives would no longer make sense. When citizens in a global city achieve the fragile common good called community in the neighborhoods of Jackson Heights or south L.A., they achieve an important victory in relationship to globalization itself. In the local domain, they cease to feel that they are the prisoners of impersonal forces. Through successful interactions of trust with others, they cease to feel like pawns in someone else's game. To have a moral community in a city is to recover some semblance of sovereignty over life as it is lived. It is to have the sense that you can work together with others to shape common life to humane ends. In a city like Los Angeles, ordinary human beings, in billions of interactions, struggle to turn what might have degenerated into a moral jungle into a community that every day delivers meaning, security, and prosperity to millions. This is a precarious achievement, an unending experiment that violence could destroy at any moment, but one that gives hope that we can make order out of the forces that globalization has unleashed upon the world.

3

Rio de Janeiro

Order, Corruption, and Public Trust

SANTA MARTA IS A VIBRANT, CHAOTIC, AND VERTIGINOUSLY
poised sliver of shanties, shacks, and breeze-block dwellings built
into the steep and verdant ravines of Rio de Janeiro. For at least
eighty years it has been home to a floating population of five thousand poor people of various races. This is not the hyper-diversity of
Jackson Heights or Los Angeles. Instead it is the locked-in poverty
of the shantytowns that abut the prosperity of the new global middle
class. This middle class, now numbering more than 1.8 billion worldwide, has brought prosperity and growth to Istanbul, Mexico City,
Mumbai, and Rio, but the gap between their lives and those of the
very poor in the shantytowns has grown markedly.[1] Santa Marta
raises different questions than Jackson Heights or Los Angeles. We
went to Rio to understand what rapid globalization looks like from
the bottom up, to examine what rapid economic growth has done to
the moral and political relations between enriched and empowered

middle classes and the teeming populations of poor people left behind. As we had done in Jackson Heights and in Los Angeles, we approached these larger questions by looking specifically at relations between the police and the people they are supposed to protect. Without rule of law in this key domain, we had found, moral order in social and class relations more generally will be fragile and vulnerable to the violent eruptions that had recurred in Los Angeles. These were the assumptions that sent our team clambering up the steep and winding walkways of Santa Marta. We were going to meet the person everyone in the favela knows as Major Pricilla.

Pricilla de Oliveira Azevedo grew up far from the favela in a middle-class family. Instead of pursuing a career as a lawyer or a judge, she enrolled in the federal police. She now commands the Unidade de Polícia Pacificadora (UPP), the police pacification unit, whose job is to wrest control of Santa Marta from the criminals and drug gangs.[2] She is thirty-five years old.

All of the global campaigns against police violence and corruption have heard of her. Transparency International, Revenue Watch, the World Bank, and the International Monetary Fund all sponsor campaigns against corruption. No global norm has spread faster or received more authoritative international endorsement than the anticorruption norm, and no form of corruption is more dangerous or more difficult to root out than police corruption. These anticorruption campaigns need heroines, people whose stories can mobilize strangers far away. Major Pricilla is one of these heroines, caught betwixt and between, mediating between global norms and local realities. She is there to tell visiting journalists and academics like our group what we want to believe, but she also knows what is actually happening on the ground, in the violent reality of favela life.

In 2007, when Pricilla was twenty-nine, a gang of seven criminals hijacked her car, threw her in the back of the trunk, and drove her to a favela where they held her for hours while they phoned around seeking a ransom. She was off duty at the time and believes that if they had seen her uniform in the trunk they would have killed her. Somehow they never realized they'd taken a policewoman hostage. While the criminals were on the phone, she escaped and took herself to a hospital where she received treatment for cuts and bruises. She returned to work the next day and decided to track down her own kidnappers. Weeks later she returned to the scene of the crime with other officers, burst in on her attackers, and arrested them at gunpoint. Every single one of them went to jail. For this exploit a Brazilian magazine called her "the defender of the city" and put her on the cover. The U.S. State Department invited her to Washington to accept an award as an International Woman of Courage. There is a photograph of Major Pricilla in her uniform, smiling shyly, holding her award, flanked by Hillary Clinton and Michelle Obama. In 2008 the federal police appointed her to lead the UPP, the federal police unit in charge of Santa Marta. UPP is one of the most closely watched experiments in global policing.

Rio is a very violent city, and Brazil is a violent and deeply unequal country.[3] A poor person in a favela learns to fear the municipal police as much as the drug gangs. One-fifth of all homicides in the city are committed by people in uniform. In some cases the police simply execute their victims with a bullet in the back of the head. In very few cases are the police prosecuted.[4]

Favelas grew up in the late nineteenth century as illegal settlements of ex-slaves and poor workers who settled on the hillsides of Rio because they couldn't afford anywhere else to live. These were places without police, sanitation, streets, or urban services. They were beyond the state and beyond the law, ruled by gangs who provided jobs, justice, and security. In the 1970s, Rio mayors tried to bulldoze the favelas only to realize that doing so pushed the poor into middle-class neighborhoods. So the municipality began to provide the favelas with electricity, streets, and sewers instead. That's when the once muddy and slick hillside paths of Santa Marta were paved over and the sewage that used to flow down the hillsides was piped underground. Incorporating the favelas into the municipal infrastructure did not succeed in every way: the drug cartels still ruled.[5] The authorities then embarked on a brutal process of pacification, shooting it out with the drug gangs. Favela dwellers were caught in the cross fire.[6] The violence became so extreme that middle-class neighbors nearby had to fit bulletproof glass on their windows.

In 2008, the state sent in paramilitary units in armed personnel carriers to surround Santa Marta and apply overwhelming force. Once the drug gangs were driven out, police units—the UPP—specially trained in human rights and community policing were deployed to "pacify" the favela. Pacification, Major Pricilla knows, has two objectives: to wrest control from the gangs but also to protect the poor from the police.

Her exploits have indeed pacified Santa Marta and set the paradigm for UPP operations elsewhere in Rio. She is the soft-spoken, energetic, outgoing, and engaging poster child of police anticorruption in Brazil and now spends as much time taking international delegations around as she does actual policing. We were one such delegation, treated to a short pep talk and then a video, in the UPP headquarters at the summit of the steep ravine down the sides of which the shanties of Santa Marta descend. Children gathered around Pricilla as she led the way down the steep labyrinth of streets between shacks, shanties, brick and breeze-block structures slapped together and hanging over the hillsides at crazy angles.

Judging from the hours we spent exploring the labyrinth of Santa Marta, it seems that the UPP is working. Consent-based community policing does empower the ordinary virtues of residents. We watched, for example, as a stretcher, carried by two teenagers from Santa Marta and two policemen, gingerly navigated the steep and winding steps of the favela, transporting an old man with a heart condition to an ambulance waiting in the main thoroughfare below. Passersby put down their shopping, from their long trudge up from the supermarket, to help the stretcher pass. Others asked after the man's health, and he nodded weakly in reply.

There were signs that good policing had brought other institutions back to life. Religious faith never left Santa Marta, but now it can be celebrated in peace. There were tiny evangelical and Pentecostal churches with their names and denominations stenciled on the doors and inside neat rows of benches facing an altar and a crucifix.

The order in Santa Marta was reminiscent of, though different from, the super-diverse order in poor neighborhoods in Jackson Heights or south L.A. Santa Marta was home to poor blacks and poor whites, and although there was a clear social hierarchy—some of the houses were plastered and had windows and heating, while others were fragile tin shacks open to the winds—there was a palpable sense of living in a community with shared pride. It was the order of hardworking women, who swept the steps in front of their front doors, who prepared their children's dinner on the stoves inside the tiny houses, who looked in on their mothers snoozing on a sofa. We met few suspicious glances or stares. Everyone seemed at ease with strangers passing by. The neatness of the streets, the scrupulous cleanliness of the interiors, the total absence of garbage or evil odors all added up to a moral statement: that, collectively, house by house, neighbor by neighbor, a fragile kind of control over surroundings was being maintained. The open doors and windows, the people leaning out and talking, all suggested a micro-order of trust between neighbors. A child doing her homework by an open window looked up as we passed and then resumed her sums; mothers prepared dinner or instructed their daughters in how to stir the soup; men smoked by their windowsills and open doorways. Drying laundry hung over the narrow streets. Overhead from every junction box a forest of wires ran to TVs and refrigerators that hummed in the heat. Tiny shops, with their wares festooned on the doors, sold toilet paper and razors and soft drinks. There were beauty parlors with women getting their nails done and bars where men watched football and drank beer; there was a community room where kids could get on-line with computers. Everyone knew Major Pricilla. A poor black woman, her hair neatly braided, came out and swept the steep steps outside her doorway. Yes, she said, she had lived there forty years. It was a good place, safer now than before, when the drug kings ruled and their enforcers patrolled the streets with AK 47s. As Major Pricilla passed by, the old woman paused in her sweeping and gave her a nod of recognition.

In one small square we came upon a surprise: a life-size statue of Michael Jackson, arms outraised toward Rio bay. Apparently he came here in 1995 with Spike Lee to shoot a music video for his single "They Don't Care about Us." The Rio authorities allowed Jackson and his team to film in the favela, but they worried that the singer would only draw unwelcome attention to the city's problems. The inhabitants of Santa Marta thought differently. Maybe the singer's presence would draw attention to *their* problems. He came and went. Only his statue remains.

Santa Marta has become a destination, the favela that draws celebrities in search of a location for a music video or tourists who come for the astounding view, for a brief look through the doorways into the lives of poor people and come away, or so the local leadership and the municipality hope, believing that crime and poverty in Rio are actually under control.

Moral globalization, at least from the perspective of Santa Marta, is a complex two-way process of symbolic interaction in which industries like tourism and causes like anticorruption go in search of new venues and new good causes and the locals scramble for whatever benefits the global presence can bring. The people try to get something out of the interaction, even if they don't always get what they bargained for. Santa Marta, for example, welcomes delegations like ours. They even have a sign at the lower entrance to the favela announcing themselves proudly as a tourist destination. Their only quarrel, a Norwegian research team found, was that tourists didn't buy much in the local bodegas and the tour guides weren't local: they came from outside.[7]

Caught in the middle of the encounter between the local and the global is Major Pricilla, trying to make Santa Marta a safe place, yet also aware that she is serving agendas over which she has little control. When we were there, Rio was bidding for two global spectacles—the World Cup in 2014 and the Olympic Games in 2016. The spectacles promised to be a bonanza for local elites, announcing Brazil's arrival as a global power. In order for these spectacles to go smoothly, the political elites in Rio needed to have crime under control. Pricilla feels the pressure to deliver even as she knows that driving the drug gangs out of Santa Marta simply drives them into other neighborhoods.[8]

Major Pricilla's police work provides moral cover for local politicians and entrepreneurs seeking to benefit from global recognition. It provides global visitors with lessons and examples they hope to apply elsewhere. But she is not fooled—and it is doubtful that the long-suffering inhabitants of Santa Marta are fooled either. They both know the moral order in Santa Marta is fragile. UPP policing has changed their lives for the better. What no one knows is whether the funding will last, the political commitment will remain, or whether, once the tents of the Olympics have been folded and put away and the caravan moves on, the bad old days will return. With the Brazilian economy in recession, a huge bill for the Olympics coming due, and a political crisis in Brasilia reducing the elites to paralysis, the chances are slim that the fragile order that good policing and ordinary virtue have brought to Santa Marta will survive.[9]

In the global cities of the twenty-first century—Mexico City, Mumbai, Istanbul, Johannesburg, and Rio—globalization has rained a cascade of corrupting money into local political systems, while mass migration from rural towns and villages has flooded shanty-towns and informal settlements with a tide of new people. These two trends converge in a place like Santa Marta. The state needs control of these ungoverned spaces, and the people in the shantytowns want order. The police battle it out with the drug gangs to determine whose order will prevail. Ordinary virtues cannot flourish unless the police win, and the police cannot win unless the culture of corruption infecting the political elite is cleaned out. The people in the favelas understand this. They are well schooled in the unchanging realities of injustice and corruption in their society. While there is nothing new about corruption or police brutality in Brazil, what does seem new—a sliver of hope, at least to us—are rising political expectations at both ends of the social spectrum: a fury among a new middle class electorate over the corruption of their political elites and a new found awareness in the favelas that their ordinary virtues don't stand a chance of sustaining moral order in Santa Marta unless the police turn honest.

When the Carnegie team arrived in Rio the Brazilian Supreme Court had just finished hearings on the appeals of senior members of President Luiz Inácio Lula da Silva's government against convictions for bribery in what had come to be known as the Mensalão scandal. A member of parliament had revealed that he had been paid a monthly retainer (*mensalão*) by officials in the governing Partido dos Trabalhadores (PT, or Workers' Party) to pass their bills in parliament.

Why, we wondered, had Lula stooped to bribery? The fragmentation of the party system was one reason. A Brazilian president, we learned, cannot expect to control more than 25 percent of the votes in his lower house. Lula's own party was a fractious coalition held together as much by presidential patronage as by conviction. To keep his own coalition together and to win over a gaggle of minority parties, President Lula's staff, or Lula himself, decided that they had to resort to bribery. After a year or so undetected, the affair exploded into public view. Forty members of parliament were punished and excluded from public office. Lula pleaded ignorance, but the scandal tarnished the reputation of a president who came to power claiming he was different from the others. When we arrived in Rio, the Supreme Court's televised public hearings on Mensalão had made the issue the chief topic on everyone's lips.[10]

On a sultry June day our team met with judges, politicians, journalists, and academics to discuss corruption. The setting was the cultural hall of the federal judiciary, a magnificent nineteenth-century building on one of Rio's wide tree-lined avenues. Presiding over our deliberations, I noticed, were plaster casts of Cicero and Justinian. Now this was a pair, I thought, who knew a thing or two about corruption. Cicero's *De Officiis* has taught civic virtue to European elites for a thousand years, and Justinian's Codex implanted Roman jurisprudence into the fabric of legal systems across Europe and the world. Modern global anticorruption norms and discourse all descend from these Roman origins.[11] Justinian and Cicero both understood that good institutions can reinforce virtue in an upward spiral and bad institutions can corrupt virtue in a downward direction. Both would have thought of a specific type of corruption—the power of money in politics—as the cardinal threat to republican freedom and self-rule.

Our "global ethical dialogue"with Brazilian experts plunged us into the complex local codes that make it so difficult to enforce global norms. What we really had to understand, the experts told us, is why ordinary Brazilian citizens keep reelecting politicians who are known to be corrupt.[12]

Some of our experts traced Brazil's problem back to the Portuguese language. It has no word for "accountability." Others argued that corruption had become endemic to Brazilian political culture during the Portuguese empire, while others located the problem in the period of Brazil's national independence, while still others maintained that the problem lay in modern Brazilian attitudes toward the law. There is a Brazilian way of bending the rules—*jeitinho*—and those who display jeitinho are admired not scorned. The rules themselves do not command support because the public knows that bureaucrats use them to "create difficulties in order to sell solutions." For some legal scholars the root cause of voters' lassitude lay buried deep in historical attitudes toward the Latin American state. Public institutions were regarded in patrimonial terms as the property of ruling elites, who were allowed to do what they wished with public goods provided some benefits trickled down to the poor. The only corruption that shocked a Brazilian voter, one expert argued, was corruption that did not give the poor a piece of the action. "He may steal but he delivers" (*rouba mas faz* in Portuguese) was a term of praise.[13]

A political scientist told us that corruption, bribery and patronage were the essential lubricants of a political system that both ratifies and reflects deep social cleavages while struggling to keep these cleavages from fracturing the society altogether. In Brazil, which has one of the highest levels of income inequality anywhere in the world, an expert told us, vote buying was the only way to forge coalitions of the rich and the poor.

One such coalition had brought Lula to power. Brazilian voters, we were told, gave Lula the benefit of the doubt, during the Mensalão scandal, because during his presidency an estimated 29 million Brazilians climbed their way into the middle class. Poor families especially benefited from the Bolsa Familia, a program that paid 11 million poor families a benefit if they sent their children to school.[14]

The transition from military to democratic rule in the 1980s had led to the creation of independent courts, NGOs, and a free press, and these institutions, by shining the light of democratic transparency on the culture of corruption, had actually made the problem more visible and more politically explosive. So good institutions—and Brazil had them—had a paradoxical impact on virtue: courts and a free press made it possible for whistle-blowers to go public, but the avalanche of disclosures seemed only to convince the general public that Brazil's political culture was incorrigible.

Other experts told us that we should not exaggerate the lassitude of the Brazilian public. Brazil did not lack for vigorous advocates of global anticorruption norms; there is Transparência Brasil, as well as a free press, and an independent judiciary who brought offenders to justice in the Mensalão case. These independent institutions commanded enduring public support. Yet the pressures on them all, and on judicial independence in particular, were constant. In our global dialogues one of the young judges told us that when she was starting out, on her first assignment to a tribunal in a small town, a local bigwig paid a visit to her office and his first question was: "Is your door open?" When she told him, no, it was not open, not for him or for anyone else, he decided to leave her alone. Her predecessor's door, it was only too apparent, had never been closed.

Our Brazilian experts concluded our day-long dialogue on a pessimistic note. They all agreed that the global norm against corruption was helpless in changing the political culture as long as politicians and the electorate colluded in the maintenance of a corrupt status quo. As they were drawing these conclusions, however, a strange commotion began outside the windows of the federal judiciary building. Glancing out, we noticed that demonstrators decked out in the national colors of green and yellow were eddying past the building in ever larger shoals, carrying placards and waving signs.

I suggested we should go down into the street and find out what was going on. So we deferred further meetings, and together with a couple of the federal judges we joined the demonstrators, now numbering in the thousands.

For the rest of that week in June 2013, we were in the streets, as Brazilian cities were paralyzed by huge demonstrations against corruption, including the capital Brasilia, where demonstrators clambered onto the roof of the parliament buildings and fought with police to gain entrance to the president's office.[15] The experts had told us that Brazilians were resigned to corruption. The demonstrations told us a different story.

The initial spark, it turned out, was a hike in bus and transit fares. Why, I wondered, had this burst into the flame of mass protest? One of our global dialogue partners, a journalist, offered part of the answer. When we asked her what sort of corruption might tempt her personally, she replied: tax avoidance. Because, she said, in a remark we were to hear everywhere, "we already pay twice." We pay for health, transport, and police, and what we get from our taxes is worthless. So we have to pay for them again with our own money:

private schools for our children, private security for our houses, private transport to get to work. All this, she went on, in a year in which the Lula government is spending billions on renovating football stadiums so that the country can hold the World Cup.

This explanation gave us our first inkling of why the streets were full of demonstrators, why a hike in bus and transit fares had caused such fury. Cutting public services while spending billions on elite sports facilities struck demonstrators as more than just a stupid choice. It was a contemptuous insult, a clear sign that politicians favored their own opportunities for enrichment over the interests of the people who put them in office. In the background, too, lingered the bitter aftertaste of the Supreme Court hearings on the Mensalão case.

The crowds we joined in the streets that June week in Rio were young, white, and middle class: office workers, bank tellers, legal secretaries, human resource clerks, and technicians from the offices in the downtown, together with university students from nearby campuses. We didn't see many executives in suits and ties or favela dwellers either.

The marchers were quick to tell us that they were not political. For many this was the first demonstration they had ever joined in their lives. Few of them seemed interested in avant-garde or radical political gesturing. This was ordinary virtue on the march: citizens deciding enough was enough. Many draped Brazilian flags across their backs to demonstrate patriotic rather than party affiliation. There were no indications that the demonstrations were organized beforehand. Planning of any kind was minimal. Mobilization on Facebook seems to have done the trick. We came across groups painting their own placards with their own slogans. One group of municipal librarians sitting on the grass of a city park were debating what to put on their sign. Finally, one of them took a felt-tip marker and scribbled: "There's so much wrong, we can't get it all on one poster!"

As we weaved our way among the thickening crowd, that first afternoon, I saw one young woman carrying a handwritten placard that read: "The People Are Awakening!" Another said, "A New Brazil Is Coming." Other signs denounced legislation before parliament that would curtail the rights of prosecutors to investigate cases of corruption. These demonstrators were campaigning against their politicians, not against their institutions. They still believed, apparently, that the prosecutors could bring the guilty to justice, if given a chance.

On that first afternoon, as their numbers continued to swell, the crowds were full of wonder, feeling their own power and realizing their kinship with protests elsewhere in the world. One demonstrator told me it was their Arab Spring, like Cairo's Tahrir Square, another that it was like the demonstrations in Gezi Park in Istanbul, just weeks before. For a radical minority, it was their moment to join the global anticapitalist movement. Some had donned the Joker masks first worn in the anti–Wall Street protests in New York a few years earlier.

By the time the demonstrators converged in front of a classical eighteenth-century colonial basilica, shadowed by tall office buildings, in the heart of Rio's business district, the crowd had filled the square, and the sound of the drummers playing on the back of a flatbed truck had become deafening.

Suddenly a group of middle-aged men and women in red T-shirts unfurled the banners of CUT (Central Única dos Trabalhadores, or Unified Workers' Party), a union affiliated with the ruling PT party. Young men in the crowd suddenly surged forward, pulled down the trade union banners, seized the leaflets the unionists were handing out, and hurled them into the air. A chant went up: "Out! Out! Out!" Within a minute the PT supporters had been hounded down a back alley and had disappeared, dragging their banners behind them.

Immediately the mood of the crowd darkened. Having driven away the political opportunists who had tried to co-opt them, the demonstrators now faced a question that the people in Tahrir Square in Cairo and in Gezi Square in Istanbul had also faced. How can antipolitical protests succeed unless they become political, unless they put a leadership structure in place, forge a coalition platform, impose discipline, repel infiltrators?

One of the demonstrators had told us, "If there are no leaders, then no one can be corrupted." The problem is, if you have no leaders, you have no direction. If you despise the politicians you've got, whom do you put in their place? With no answer to these questions, and the leaders on the platforms failing to rouse or capture the demonstrators' mood, they began drifting away.

As night fell, a more violent group took over, and soon rocks were smashing into windows in the business district and glass was spraying onto the sidewalks. Later, roving bands of masked men began taking baseball bats to the cash machines. The violence unleashed was astonishing, vandalism legitimizing itself in the tropes of global anticapitalism. The next morning, as shocked crowds gathered to gape at the destruction, the ebullient mood of the day before disappeared and a new anxiety crept in. I heard one person say, as she looked at the gutted, glass-littered cash machines, "God help us if the favelas join in." The new middle class had begun the demonstrations. Now they were frightened that those with nothing to lose would take them over.

When we left Rio at the end of that week in June 2013, the anticorruption demonstrations had faded away. Yet the fire that had been lit kept smoldering and burst into flame in the years that followed. After the Mensalão scandal, a still bigger one—involving Petrobras,

the gigantic Brazilian state oil company—burst onto the front pages
in 2015. Billions of dollars were transferred from Brazil's energy rev-
enues to operatives in the ruling PT party.[16] The Petrobras scandal
reignited the anger of 2013. Street demonstrations and a vigorous
judicial investigation eventually swept President Dilma Rousseff
from office despite her attempt to portray herself as the victim of a
"constitutional coup." Her attempt to tarnish the prosecutors and
judges failed because popular support for their operations remained
unshaken. Then in June 2015, a third scandal erupted, this time
involving the gigantic Brazilian construction company, Grupo
Odebrecht, whose chairman Marcelo Odebrecht was arrested on
charges of bribing politicians, including the ones who had brought
Dilma Rousseff down.[17] These politicians, including the new president, Michel Temer, then found themselves under investigation, and
as they were dragged under, an angry public wondered whether
there was anyone left who could clean the stables. A country that
had believed itself on the eve of greatness, a rising giant from the
global south, found itself, in 2016, paralyzed by a collapsing economy
and the most serious constitutional crisis since the end of military
rule. As for Major Pricilla, she had moved on, from Santa Marta to
Rocinha, a tougher favela where the battle with the drug gangs was
still in full swing. Major Pricilla had to fight on two fronts: against
the gangs and against her own police force. The previous commander in Rocinha had been dismissed and prosecuted for tor-
turing and then murdering an innocent favela dweller whom he
suspected of being an informer.[18]

As a story about moral globalization, Brazil offers several lessons.
It lays bare the resistance that elite cultures of collusion can mount
against global norms, in this case, the world-wide incantations about
the evils of corruption. Indeed, global norms themselves, and all
their international advocates in the NGO community, don't stand a

chance of changing the political culture of a country unless the global goes local, unless these norms find a fierce domestic constituency. In Brazil, the cause of anticorruption caught fire only when it enlisted popular support and when institutions like the federal prosecutor and the judiciary understood that they could increase their own power and strengthen their institutions by enlisting in a global cause.

If, finally, the question is why the norm caught fire, what really counted is that masses of people revolted against a local culture of excuses. The purveyors of the global norms—the international organizations like Transparency International and the World Bank—could only stand by and watch. In explaining the Brazilian revolt, what seemed crucial, in those dramatic June days, was moral revulsion, a sense among the demonstrators that their politicians were treating them with contempt. It was a feeling that came as a surprise. Young Brazilians had been resigned for so long. No longer. They discovered civic virtue, the feeling that a country belongs to you and depends for its moral health on your willingness to stand up for its true values.

The final implication of the Brazilian case is less hopeful. After three years of popular anger and judicial investigations, the political system in Brazil remains broken, and the culture of self-dealing remains intact. Brazil shows just how thoroughly a nominally liberal democratic constitution can be corrupted, as Cicero and Justinian warned a thousand years ago by a culture of entitlement and self-dealing. While corruption is the oldest temptation of republics, as Cicero and Justinian warned, what is distinctive about twenty-first century corruption is the malign interdependence between the political elites and state capitalist giants like Petrobras and private capitalist giants like Odebrecht. Without the money of the big companies, politicians can't run mass-scale democratic campaigns.

Without the licenses and regulatory concessions that only politicians can provide, capitalist giants can't secure oligopolistic domination of their markets. Good institutions—in this case, a free press and an independent judiciary—will usually catch on once the deals have been done, and through disclosures in the press and judicial prosecutions, they can punish the wrong-doers, but the systematic patterns of collusion seem bound to recur. Good institutions cannot save a republic if the virtue of the political elite fails and if the broad mass of an electorate colludes in their rapacity. Economic globalization, in particular the money that has flowed into Brazil since the 1990s, corrupted the political elite and overwhelmed the institutions that liberal democracy created to control corruption. Globalization also widened the gulf between rich and poor, weakening the norms that ought to have made decent policing for Santa Marta and for all the other favelas a shared value for rich and poor alike. International actors—the media, the anticorruption NGOs, the international banks and aid agencies—have denounced these trends, and these forms of global vigilance, reinforced by global spectacles like the Olympics, keep the pressure on. But in the end only Brazil itself, only its democracy, its free institutions, and above all the avenging fury of its people, can reverse the complicity and collusion that holds their country back.

4

Bosnia

War and Reconciliation

JUNE 28, 2014, BEGINS AT DAWN WITH THE GUTTURAL lament of the *muezzin* calling the faithful to prayer. There are two mosques close by, built in the 1540s by the engineers and masons of the Turkish Empire, a small one behind the Europa Hotel and the magnificent grand mosque itself, with a large flagstoned courtyard and a fountain and a marble and brass washing place near the entrance. It is Ramadan in Sarajevo. The mosques will be full today.

When I was eleven years old my family visited Sarajevo on a holiday. While my mother waited outside, my father, brother, and I washed our feet and entered the grand mosque, the Gazi Husrev Bey, and sat down in the great domed space, streaked with beams of light falling on the old carpets. For a small boy, used to Christian churches, it was a disorienting moment that has stayed with me for life. There was no image, no altar, no focus for the eye, only the vast, echoing, silent circular space and, in the distance, in the shadows, an old man sitting cross-legged on the ground reading a book.

When the Serbs in the hills above Sarajevo shelled the mosque during the war, between 1992 and 1995, it was an attack on a certain idea—or was it just an illusion?—about Europe as a continent where Islam had belonged for centuries and where Jews, Christians, and Muslims, not to mention Serbs, Croats, and Bosnians, had lived, at least sometimes, in peace.

Because I had lived in Yugoslavia for two years as a child and had no inkling about who was a Serb and who was a Bosnian or Croat, its break-up seemed especially tragic and inexplicable to me. When Serbia invaded Croatia in 1991, I spent weeks going between the lines of the village war in eastern Slavonia on the border between the two new countries. I was shot at in the ruins of Vukovar, and I spent a night at the Serbian front lines a couple of hundred meters from the Croatian enemy.[1]

A village war was an intimate affair, conducted between men who once worked in the same gas stations or took out the same girls and now fought each other in bunkers so close that they actually hooked up a phone connection so that they could exchange verbal abuse at night, between rounds of gunfire. I spent days with both sides trying to figure out how virtues of trust and living together could vanish, as if in an instant, replaced by such mystifying and intense hatred. They were puzzled themselves, how brothers could become enemies and former friends could be trading gunfire. It seemed that such virtues had been easy when both Serb and Croat could count on the protection of Prime Minister Josip Broz Tito's authoritarian state. When Tito died, when the communist system collapsed and free peoples could have elections, they chose nationalist politicians whose appeal was that they had an answer to the existential question posed by the collapse of the Yugoslav state: who will protect me now? Friends and neighbors who had once trusted a common state now fled to the protection of nationalist warlords and gunmen. The ordinary virtues vanished, replaced by hatred, fear, and loathing.

I wrote three books about the Yugoslav catastrophe, including *Blood and Belonging,* but from the safety of London, while journalist colleagues shared the dangers of Sarajevo itself, racing from the airport to the Holiday Inn, along sniper alley, past the devastated ruins of the *Oslobodenje* (Liberation) newspaper building, with the bullets from the Serbs in Pale pinging on the concrete beside them.[2]

When the war ended, the questions that outsiders asked about Bosnia changed. Now the issue became how to help enemies reconcile, how to recover those lost virtues of trust and tolerance. For the so-called international community, Bosnia became a vast demonstration project in the re-creation of lost virtues of tolerance and intercommunal living. NATO troops patrolled the streets, the International Criminal Tribunal in The Hague sought to enforce the justice that was supposed to bring reconciliation in its wake, the European Union sent in administrators to guide the warring peoples back toward democracy, and a small army of young people, trained in the best universities in North America and Europe, flooded in to teach conflict prevention, transitional justice, human rights, reconciliation, and economic development. Looking back now, Bosnia was the high point, the apogee, of an important exercise in moral globalization: outsiders, trained in the moral disciplines of universalism and the techniques of reconciliation and forgiveness, trying to persuade battered insiders to adopt their moral codes.[3]

Now, most of these outsiders are gone. The International Tribunal is winding up its work; the European administrators have gone home; the army of universalists has headed elsewhere, to Afghanistan, Central African Republic, Sudan and Myanmar. Bosnia is on its own. There are new causes, like corruption and police brutality in Brazil, the resource curse in Nigeria, climate change everywhere.

Nineteen years after war's end and exactly one hundred years after the start of World War I, our Carnegie Council team arrived in Sarajevo to observe the centenary of the bequest from Andrew Carnegie that created the Council and the centenary of the world war that destroyed so many of Carnegie's dreams. No man had higher hopes that the globalization of commerce and technology, and with it the globalization of moral ideas, would make war impossible, and no one had a crueler awakening to reality when the guns started firing in 1914.

We gather for the commemoration in the Gazi Husrev Bey Library, next door to the grand mosque. The building, like the mosque, was damaged by the siege. When it came to rebuilding the library after the war, the money came, not from the European Union, but from the Qataris. It is all part of an eastward drift in Sarajevo, now that the war is over. Mosques all over Bosnia, their minarets toppled by Croat and Serb gunfire, have been rebuilt with Gulf money. It is as if Europe has given up claiming this place as its own.

The Gazi Husrev Bey Library is five minutes' walk from the narrow street, where a hundred years ago the car bearing the Imperial Austro-Hungarian couple took a wrong turn, backed up, and gave Gavrilo Princip, a consumptive Bosnian Serb teenager, the nationalist jihadi of his era, time to pull a pistol out of his pocket and fire point blank at the archduke and his wife, Sophie, setting in train the cascade that, within six weeks, had six empires committed to a global war that would end with the eventual destruction of all of them.[4] Princip's gunshot blew apart the Austro-Hungarian empire in Bosnia, only to usher in a struggle to the death between the Balkan nations for supremacy, a struggle resumed once Tito's regime of "brotherhood and unity" collapsed with his death in 1983.[5] The long history that has ushered in our postimperial age began here, in the Balkans, with a struggle for self-determination that destroyed the Ottoman Empire, then the Austro-Hungarian Empire, and finally the European order itself.

Anywhere else, the commemoration of World War I brings old enemies together in common celebration. Today French and German leaders will stand side by side and remember shared follies that they have vowed never to repeat. Not in Sarajevo. Serbs are boycotting because they believe the Muslims will use the ceremony to blame them for both wars, for Princip's role in igniting 1914, and for the martyrdom of Sarajevo from 1992 to 1995.

As we gather in the auditorium of the Gazi Husrev Library—all-white Gulf-state marble, like an airport or a shopping mall—many seats in the auditorium are empty. Sarajevans themselves are staying away. They'd prefer to leave commemorating 1914 to the foreigners, for they know that outsiders want to preach reconciliation, forgiveness, accommodation, virtues of which they are mightily tired. Our host for the occasion, the grand mufti, the senior Muslim cleric in the city, in robe and turban, gets up and reads slowly from a text in Bosnian. Instead of lapidary platitudes, he says something that has everyone listening intently. Peoples do not reconcile with the past, he says, until they feel they have a common political future together: "We do not share a common vision of the future. It is the only way to open us to a common vision of the past."

More than twenty years after the 2005 Dayton Accords, Bosnia is without a political future. It is a frozen conflict, with a political system divided among its "constituent peoples": Serbs have their republic in the north and east; Croats are agitating for an entity of their own next door to Croatia in the west, and Bosnian Muslims fear the Croats and Serbs will carve up the rest of their country between them. While there are federation institutions that all three peoples are supposed to share, in practice every job, every position, is rotated or allocated to each one of the groups; in effect, the Dayton agreement has set in concrete the ethnic apartheid it sought to overcome.[6]

Joel Rosenthal, the president of the Council, an intense and wiry ethicist of gentle mien, follows the Grand Mutfti to the stage. He speaks of reconciliation as an opportunity to "recommit to the idea of using reason and experience to build life together." George Rupp, a Carnegie Council trustee, follows him and places reconciliation within the context of a global ethic of common values that is pluralist, respects differences of religious and political authority, but also works on the principle that sources of authority in our exchanges must be accessible to all.[7]

David Rodin, co-director of the Institute for Ethics, Law and Armed Conflict at the University of Oxford, speaks next and argues that people divided by war can now reconcile on the basis of common commitment to a global ethic that includes, as it did not in 1914, human rights and the laws of war.

Sir Adam Roberts, a professor of international relations at Oxford, is less sanguine about the relevance of global ethics in these parts. He points out that Princip's bullet destroyed the interethnic accommodation that had flourished under the Ottomans and the Austro-Hungarians. A century later, an interethnic order here remains out of reach. The twentieth century, he said, was a story of "learning through burning." We burn and we learn too late.

Margaret MacMillan the preeminent historian of the Versailles Treaty and of the origins of World War I, points out how deeply late-nineteenth-century Europeans believed that globalization had brought hearts and minds together and rendered war impossible. Yet at least one core element of their emerging ethic—democracy—actually propelled European elites toward catastrophe. Once the modern state drew to itself the loyalty of mass electorates, these electorates then became its most ferocious defenders. Before mass democracy, war had been "cabinet war," battles for prestige and honor decided by the cabinets of kings and fought for the purposes of elites. Cabinet wars were limited in their ambitions and in their violence. General Helmuth von Moltke, Bismarck's general, the old Prussian who had defeated the French at Sedan in 1870, warned when he retired that in an era of mass democracy, cabinet wars would be replaced by what he called "people's wars." "Woe to him," Moltke warned, "who lights the spark."[8] The century of democracy's greatest advance also turned out, not coincidentally, to be the century of total war.

A Croatian-American historian, Ivo Banac, returns the meeting back to the Bosnian context. He offers a gentle rebuke to all those outsiders who flooded into Bosnia after the war seeking to teach the locals new techniques of reconciliation and conflict prevention. Banac suggests that reconciliation is not a technique or a process; it's not something for outsiders to teach and insiders to learn. It is a process of slow sedimentation, as aging and death claims combatants on both sides and once ferocious enemies slowly accept to live as adversaries. Banac concludes the commemoration with the story of Cain and Abel, in the version retold by the blind Argentinian writer Jorge Luis Borges:

> Abel and Cain met each other after Abel's death. They walked through the desert and recognized each other from afar, because they were both very tall. The brothers sat on the earth, made a fire, and ate. They remained silent, in the manner of those who are tired at the end of the day. A star appeared in the sky, one whose name nobody can remember. By the light of the flame, Cain noticed the mark

of a stone indented in Abel's forehead and the bread he had raised to his lips fell before he could eat it and he asked whether his crime had been forgiven.

Abel answered:

"Did you kill me or did I kill you? I already cannot remember, and here we are, together like before."

"Now, you must have forgiven me," Cain said, "because to forget is to forgive. I will, too, try to forget."

Abel replied softly:

"That's right. While the remorse lasts, so does the guilt."[9]

The next day, Devin Stewart, our translator Leila Efendic, and I are driving on a winding two-lane road through undulating farming country to Srebrenica, two hours east of Sarajevo. Muhamed Durakovic is our guide in the front seat, a heavy-set, pale man in his mid-forties, working overseas for the ICMP, the International Commission on Missing Persons. He usually works in Libya, but the warlords have taken over and it is too dangerous, so he is back home.[10] As we get close to Srebrenica, his birthplace, he looks out at the scraggy grazing pastures with an occasional horse sheltering under the shadow of a tree, and he begins talking softly. His voice rises and falls just above the hum of the engine. As we listen, it is like "The Kreutzer Sonata," the Tolstoy novella about a man pouring out his life secrets to a fellow passenger in a darkened railway carriage. Muhammed is the stranger pouring out his life story, and we are the silent listeners.[11]

"There were 37,000 people in Srebrenica once. We had mines—silver and bauxite—as well as timber. My father worked as a forester in the state forest. It was 83 percent Bosnian in the old days, but my best friend in high school was a Serb guy called Dragan. Suddenly, in 1992, the Serbs started leaving the city, as if they had been warned what was coming. Then the paramilitaries came from Belgrade and they burned our house, leaving us only the garage. Our neighbors said we should move into the empty Serb houses, but we didn't. We stayed in our garage for three years. Refugees from other villages began flooding into Srebrenica. In '93, the French general Morillon came and spoke from the second story of our post office and he told us the UN would come and protect us. First there was a French battalion and then a Canadian one, young guys, pretty spaced out, but they were great. The internationals were here too—*Médecins sans Frontières,* International Red Cross, UNHCR. Then the Dutch came, 500 of them in '95, and they moved into the factory in Potocari. I spoke some English so I became a liaison between the local police and Dutchbatt. We turned our weapons into the UN, but the Serbs didn't. They were up in the hills and they could see us through their sniper scopes and they began picking us off in the streets. Then food began to go short. The UN sent convoys to feed us, but the Serbs stopped them and the UN did nothing. Then in July the Serbs moved in and the Dutch stood by and watched. Mladic paraded through the town, I remember him saying on Serbian TV, 'we have taken the town from the Turks and now it is time for revenge.'

"They loaded all the women—including my mother and two sisters—onto buses—and sent them to Tuzla while Dutchbatt watched—and they took the men away." He points at the woods through the car window. On either side of the road, deep in the lush forest, are places where the men of Srebrenica were shot and thrown into shallow graves.

"I was with the men who decided to go over the hills and escape to Tuzla. I was well prepared: I had a compass, backpack, water and food, and I left with my father. It was chaos, night-time, they were shelling us. We found a trail then we lost it again. There were wounded all around us, people in shock. I was separated from my father. I thought I had lost him. When the men I teamed up with reached a road—this one here, he points at it, as the mini-van rolls past—the moon was up and I said, brothers if we cross this road, they will kill us all. So we turned back. I found my father again. We had a terrible argument. He said he wanted to go back to a Serb village and ask them for shelter. I have done nothing wrong in my life, he said. They won't kill me. I told him he was crazy. We walked on and the next days we saw horrible things, decomposed bodies, bodies that were alive but booby-trapped by the Serbs. My father's eyes glazed over, he was in shock, and exhausted, he couldn't take in what he was seeing. Soon our group was down to six people. We passed deserted Bosnian villages, no one there, everyone gone, just animals wandering about. I remember how a little calf followed us. It was in shock too. By then we were making for Jepa. I remember one night, we snuck up on a house, where there was a Serbian soldier with a huge beard who has chopping wood in the yard. My father recognized him and wanted to talk to him. But I whispered no.

"We traveled by night. I remember once how three Serbian soldiers with a horse passed within inches of us. When we got to Jepa, we could not find my sisters, so we walked on to Kladanc, where the front lines of our soldiers were. It took us thirty-seven days, from the night we left Srebrenica, to reach our front lines. We made it together, my Dad and me. I was bearded, filthy, I had lost so much weight. I went to the barber shop for a shave, and I asked if the phone line to Sarajevo was still open. They said it was and I remembered my grandfather's number, so I dialed it. He answered. I said we were alive. We all cried.

"You know, he says, my father had a pistol, with enough rounds to kill himself and me. Once, when we were in the woods at night, he said that he was going to pull the trigger on me and then on himself, and he asked, in tears, would I forgive him for that? I said I would, but I told him not to.

"Basically, he was hard on me all my life, criticized me for everything. But I saved his life. Dad agrees, but now he says, 'is that all you did, save my life?'"

He looks at the passing trees, the once lethal forests, where he persuaded his father not to shoot himself, and then he looks away with that fixed expression that men adopt when swallowing back tears.

The factory in Potocari where Dutchbatt was billeted, where the women were loaded onto buses and driven away, where the men were lined up and marched off into the woods, is still there, shuttered and locked. Across the road, there is the mass grave where the recovered bodies of the murdered men of Srebrenica have been buried.[12]

We meet the mothers of Srebrenica, four women in kerchiefs and Bosnian trousers who have campaigned for twenty years to secure the proper burial of their menfolk.[13]

Their achievement lies before them in the rows of white marble graves stretching for two hundred meters, several thousand of them, each with a name, a date of birth, and the same death date, July 12 1995. Had it not been for the Srebrenica widows, it is doubtful that the international community—the International Tribunal, the International Organization of Missing Persons, NATO—would have devoted resources to finding the mass graves, sending out the forensic teams to match DNA samples to the remains that were found in the forests round about. The women kept faith with their fathers, husbands, and sons, and there is a ferocity in their remembering, but it is a bitter fate to have become professional mourners. It is a trap to remember so intensely, because they are old now and there is no other life left for them.

They also live, day by day, with the Serbs they hold responsible. Some of them are still in the municipal offices or in the police station. That is what it means to live, as a Bosnian Muslim, in Republika Srpska, an "entity" they believe protects people who committed genocide.

They do not believe "such a project"—as they call genocide—could have been invented by ordinary people. They had lived with ordinary people, side by side, as neighbors. Everyone kept their distance, but it was possible to have one as a godfather of your children, for example. They had a normal life with the Serbs—*normalne zhivot*—though now they ask themselves what normal could have meant if from one day to the next a Serb godson could cut his Bosnian godmother's throat.

No, they maintain that this "project" of extermination was not invented by ordinary people. It was the work of "scientific people," by people with ideas, from outside, from Belgrade.

The widows could have moved to Sarajevo, but they stay in Republika Srpska because this is their home. If they leave, the project will have won.

They get called Turks by little children who are taught this language in homes not two hundred yards from their own houses. They see the "spite churches," the Serbian Orthodox churches going up on the hills around. They listen to the church bells being rung on the anniversary of the massacre, and the sound of the bells is like mocking laughter.

Shahida Rakmanovic, a thoughtful, well-dressed woman with blond hair in her fifties, lives about a mile from the Potocari graveyard in a beautiful valley, lush with kitchen gardens, rippling streams, and orchards. She managed a store in Srebrenica. Her husband was a schoolteacher. On May 8, 1992, a paramilitary gang from Belgrade, led by Zeliko Raznatovic—a nationalist gangster known as Arkan—broke into her house and took her husband away. They killed him that day at the police station.

When the Serbs overran Srebrenica in July 1995, they ordered Shahida's sons to show up for deportation at Potocari. They refused and fled into the woods instead. What happened with Dutchbatt, she says, with icy understatement, was "below any standard of decency": the Dutch soldiers abandoned the Bosnians, and once they had been safely evacuated they filmed themselves dancing and drinking in a hotel in Zagreb. In any account of moral globalization since 1989, the failure of the UN and Dutchbatt at Srebrenica would figure as a moment of decisive fracture, when the twin fictions of the "international community" and human rights solidarity among strangers were shown to be cruel and empty delusions.

She herself was loaded onto a bus and went to Tuzla, where she lived for two years. Her children went to France and now live on the Swiss-French border.

I ask her whether she will stay in the valley or join her children in France. "I am confused," she says quietly. "My kids want me to be with them. But for now I'm staying. I don't want them to win. If I'm the last Bosnian woman in this village, then they will not have won."

"I sacrificed my life," Shahida says. "I am a guardian." Her face reddens, but she does not weep. She stares fixedly out at the lush kitchen garden through the window, at the light sparkling on her apple trees.

I say: "You won the battle of memory." Thanks to the women of Srebrenica, the town's fate is known to the whole world. She nods.

They won the battle over the past, but they are losing the battle for the present and future. Bosnians like Shahida were once the majority in eastern Bosnia. Thanks to ethnic cleansing, massacre, and migration, they are now down to 5 percent of the population.

As dusk begins to gather, Shahida and I make a visit to one of the "spite churches," as the Bosnians call them—built on a hill overlooking the Potocari cemetery, its Orthodox onion dome visible atop the trees from every viewpoint in the valley. The church, more like a small chapel, is at the end of a stony track, with farms on either side. There is scaffolding above the entrance and a nearly completed image of Christ above the door. A Republika Srpska flag leans against the doorway. As we approach, we are passed by a skinny, tanned young man in a paint-stained T-shirt and shorts, who nods as we pass and then stops when we turn and hail him. It turns out he is an icon painter, a Serb from Belgrade, commissioned by the local priest to paint the image of Christ above the chapel entrance. His English is fluent; he smiles when I say that the only icon painter I know about is Andrei Rublev, in the film by Tarkovsky. Of the great medieval Russian master he says, "He is the Rembrandt of our tradition." There are fifty images of Christ an icon painter can choose from, and for this church, above the graves of Potocari, he has chosen one depicting Christ the peacemaker.

Next to the country track, where we stand talking, is a barbed-wire fence, with solid concrete posts holding it up, fencing off a field full of waist-high grass. The fenced area is about fifty yards from the church door. I ask him why the field is fenced off like this. He says it must be because the field is someone's private property. He smiles absently. Shahida suddenly shakes her head and casts a furious glance in his direction. In an urgent whisper, she says the icon painter is lying. He must know. How can he pretend otherwise? The field is fenced because it is a secondary grave. When the original graves began to smell, the Serbs dug up the decomposing remains and trucked them to more remote places like this. This field was full of body parts, and it took years of DNA analysis before they could receive decent burials in Potocari. The icon painter listens to Shahida, but he does not meet her implacable gaze. His face is mild, expressionless, almost, you might say, like an icon. It is as if he is not there. Then with old-fashioned formality, he shakes my hand, hands me his business card, and resumes walking up the country road.

After Srebrenica, we travel, mostly in silence, to Prijedor on the river Sana, close to the border with Croatia. During the war, I remembered how foreign journalists took to calling Prijedor the "heart of darkness." That was when it was the center of a network of concentration camps for Bosnian Muslims. Nowadays it is a regional capital of Republika Srpska, and the population of Bosnians, once about 20 percent, has fallen below 5 percent. In the town offices, it turns out that the mayor who had agreed to see us, has pulled out of the meeting, but the Serbian deputy mayor will see us. She is a busy municipal official, in a wood-panelled office, with a desk piled high with files awaiting her attention. She is polite but uneasy. I ask her about memorials to the Bosnians who were imprisoned or who died in Omarska, Keraterm, and Trnopolje, the pig farms and industrial sites, which the Serbs converted in the summer of 1992 into the largest network of concentration camps in Europe since World War II.[14]

What has been done by the authorities, I asked her, to remember these "events"? She and the mayor had attended a mass funeral in 2005—or was it 2006? She couldn't remember—for "the war dead," as she called them, those who had been exhumed from graves and reburied. She sighed and looked out the window. "What happened, happened," she said finally, with a clouded and unhappy look on her face. "Let's hope it never happens again."

Outside the municipal offices, Sudbun Mujdzic, a thin, middle-aged man with bright red hair, wearing jeans and a cloth jacket, is waiting for us. He is one of a small number of Bosnian Muslims still living permanently in Prijedor, "the last of the Mohicans," as he puts it.

In July 1992, he and his mother were preparing lunch in their village house in Carakovo, and his father was scything the grass down at the riverbank when they saw uniformed men with rocket-propelled grenade launchers on their shoulders standing in the road, taking aim at their house. His mother rushed outside waving a white cloth, begging them not to fire. The paramilitaries grabbed Sudbun and his brother and demanded to know how old they were. Sudbun lied and said they were seventeen, too young to be fighters. Don't take them away, his mother begged. They were loading men onto buses at the end of the road. The paramilitaries pointed their weapons and told Sudbun and his brother to lead them to his father. When they reached the edge of the river and could go no farther and their father was nowhere to be seen, Sudbun looked down at the muddy water and thought, "Here I am going to die."

Just then, one of the drivers of the buses shouted for the men to stop. The driver, a Serb, had worked with Sudbun's father in the local bus depot, and he told the paramilitaries he would handle them himself. He loaded Sudbun and his brother into his bus and drove them to Trnopole, a pig farm the Serbs had turned into an internment camp. They were locked up in low pens reserved for pigs. It was there, from a neighbor, that Sudbun learned that when the Serbs found his father, down by the riverside scything hay, they shot him and threw his body down the village well.

Sudbun leads us up a rain-soaked and muddy road to a bleak excavated field where a forensic team had recently found a further thousand bodies, all killed that summer day in 1992. It was a secondary site, like the one at Potocari by the spite church, a place where human remains were dumped, months after the killings, when the smell in the primary site grew too offensive to the locals. It has taken a year of patient DNA work to identify the mangled hair, teeth, and bone tissue.

So as the rain fills the pitted holes of the gravesite, I think: this is what ordinary virtue does in the face of atrocity. Teams in lab coats comb the area, millimeter by millimeter, bent over, recovering dirty, abandoned, desecrated tissue. They take the remains to a lab, where DNA is extracted. The lab connects the DNA samples to swabs taken from surviving cousins, mothers and uncles, and after months of work they connect the samples to vanished lives, to existences ripped apart. Then people like Sudbun take the remains and give them a decent burial.

I cannot understand how Sudbun has done this work, with others, for so many years. I cannot grasp what quiet dispassion and disciplining of rage, despair, and futility is required to keep at the recovery and burial of remains day after day, year after year. How do you manage this work and live, every day, among people who did this to your people? I also recall our commemoration in Sarajevo two days before, and I think, Borges was wrong: no one ever forgets or forgives. No one ever mistakes Abel for Cain or Cain for Abel.

Why, I wonder, did outsiders ever try to preach reconciliation here, why did they ever think they had the moral standing to tell the insiders to forget, forgive, and move on? Who gave them this right? Why did they ever think it was their business at all?

If ripped and desecrated bodies are still being dug out of miserable pits like these, twenty years later, why are outsiders surprised, why do they express disappointment that reconciliation has been glacial to nonexistent, ethnic resentments still smolder, and Bosnian politics remains trapped in the politics of suppressed hatred?

I am angry at moralizing outsiders—I am angry at myself—as I walk back from the burial site. Why do we inflict our expectations upon people like this? But Sudbun himself is in a very different mood. He is cheerful. His story turns out to be too complicated to imprison him in simple, vengeful longings. At the pig farm in Trnopole, a Serb colonel bundled him and his brother into a bus and took them to another site, where they were able to escape and make their way to Germany and then to Chicago. His brother had been beaten so badly at Trnopole that he stayed in Chicago. Sudbun never felt at home in America, so he returned to the family house in Carakovo, where he lives to this day.

"They" murdered his father, but "they" also saved his family. "They" rule in the mayor's office; "they" are in the police cars that patrol his village, but "they" have not stopped the search for the remains and "they" have not prevented Sudbun from completing his work of memory—the due burial of the dead. "They" now acknowledge, "We know what you suffered," and then they add, "but we suffered too." He lives among them, the last of the Mohicans.

In Carakovo, the village houses are newly plastered in bright and cheerful colors, their sashes and blinds are from Germany, and in the driveway there are Volvos with Swedish and Danish plates. Almost all the Bosnians in the village, Sudbun explains, live in northern Europe, and they come back only in the summer, to give their children a taste of what they still call "home." Sudbun is funny about it all. The Bosnian absentees hire local Serbs as watchmen to keep their places safe. Some of the watchmen who patrol the village at night were once in the paramilitaries who did the killing. They now protect Bosnian properties for their absentee owners. Everyone understands what is going on.

At the top of the village is the graveyard. Three hundred and ninety-three Muslim men, women, and children, plus a dozen

Croats, were killed here on one day in July 1992, and they are all buried here in white marble graves. The Croats are recognized as "brothers." This marble graveyard, empty and sunlit in the July afternoon light, with the view over the valley and the newly refurbished houses below, is Sudbun's work. He led the village to get it done, on land owned by his father and mother. As he shows it to us, the last of the Mohicans seems at peace with his work of memory.

On one of the marble stones, Sudbun has inscribed a verse from the Koran: "Whoever does an atom's weight of good will see it, whoever does an atom's weight of evil will see it."

It takes us four hours, winding through the mountains and ravines of western Bosnia, to reach Mostar, in the baking-hot olive groves and vineyards of the southwest. The river Neretva, deep blue, fast moving, runs through a gorge that divides the city of 120,000 people in two. For four centuries there was a famous bridge, a soaring, light, single-vaulted structure of stone, that linked the mosques and teahouses of the Muslim side and the Catholic churches and Viennese-style pastry shops on the Croatian side.

The war that broke out in 1993 in Mostar was a frenzied, neighbors' conflict of small arms fire across the river, at terrifyingly close range, Muslims on one side, Croats on the other, so that even in 2014, more than twenty years later, the houses on the front lines by the river are still pockmarked with bullet holes, their roofs smashed in, trees and scrub growing up in the vacant ruins.

In November 1993, after days of shelling, a Croatian artillery team finally succeeded in bringing the Mostar bridge down, with one blast that sent the soaring arch tumbling into the river like a rearing horse felled in mid-flight. Afterwards there was a general sense of shame, even among the Croats, about what happened. The bridge had given the town its very name, so its destruction—everyone knew which commander had done it—was widely regarded as a complex act of self-mutilation.[15]

Now the bridge has been rebuilt, but it is not the same. The old one had soared over the water, no wider than a donkey cart, a wonder of sixteenth-century Ottoman engineering, held together by gravity, without mortar, by iron pinions. The new one is a pretty good copy, but no one takes it for the original, and while Muslims use it, Croats don't because they don't feel safe on the other side. On the Muslim side someone has stenciled a message in black paint: "1993: Don't Forget."

Of the legions of outsiders who came to Mostar to practice the latest techniques of post-conflict resolution and reconciliation, only a handful remain. The Nansen Center, a Norwegian aid charity, runs programs that send Muslim and Croat kids to Norway for a summer holiday together. It works wonders when they're there, the aid workers say, but when they return they never see each other again.

Instead of practicing the politics of reconciliation, the local Croatian elite use control of the municipality to plunder everything. The thieving is shameless, and while there has been a protest against corruption—it began in February 2014 and spread across Bosnian towns, leading to marches and attacks on particularly corrupt municipal offices—the political system, whether run by Serbs, Croats, or Muslims, seems impervious to the anger of its own citizens.

The "international community" once believed that the road to reconciliation lay through joint schooling for children from both sides, and so the European Union rebuilt the Mostar Gymnasium (high school) to give Muslims and Croat students a common education. By the time the local teachers and officials had taken it over, however, there were two schools inside the Gymnasium, one for

Croats, one for Muslims, with separate curricula, separate entrances, separate hallways, even separate toilets.

An American anthropologist from Syracuse who spent a year as a supply teacher in the Mostar gymnasium discovered something very interesting was going on in the bathrooms of the school. Muslim and Croat boys and girls had found a way to sneak off together into the cubicles, to smoke, joke, and flirt. None of the teachers knew about it, and it was the sole contact between the two groups of teenagers. If there was a single sliver of hope in Mostar, it was to be found in those toilets.[16]

The Carnegie team spend our last evening together on the roof terrace of a fish restaurant in the Muslim quarter overlooking the old town, in sight of the bridge, lit from below by searchlights. Leila, our translator, broke her Ramadan fast and joined us for the meal.

I had noticed on some of the war memorials we passed that each group used different words to denote their dead. In my notebook, Leila Efendic wrote me out a lexicon:

> Croatian: Victim: *zrtve domovinskog rata*
> Serbian: Victim: *zertve otodzbinskog rata*
> Bosniak: Victim: *sehid odrombenog rata*

The word *rata*—war—is the same in all three languages, but the words for its victims are different. *Sehid,* the Muslim word, means holy martyr, and that is not what *zertve* and *zrtve* mean.

I had noticed that when people in Srebrenica, Prijedor, and Mostar talked about how it was to live nowadays with the other side, they all said: we live "side by side," but we do not "live together." I asked Leila to write those phrases down:

> Side by side: *jedni pored drugih*
> Together: *zejedno jedni sdrugima*

I had noticed too how people bristled whenever we used the word "reconciliation" and how they looked dismissive or surprised whenever Leila translated the word. The people we had talked to said, one after another, "We are not reconciled. We merely coexist." What were the words they used? I ask Leila again.

Reconciliation: *pomirenje*
Coexistence: *suzivot*

Whenever I asked about tolerance, Leila noticed, the word they used instead meant "put up with."

To put up with: *podnositi*
To tolerate: *uvazavati*

When the meal was over, and we were looking down at the bridge and the blue-black Neretva running through it below, I asked Leila what she made of Sudbun's story of looking down at the river and thinking his life was over; of Muhammed and his father, with the pistol, lost in the Srebrenica woods; or Shahida confronting the icon painter. Instead of a direct answer, she told us her own story.

Besides Srebrenica and Jepa, there was another "UN safe zone" in eastern Bosnia—the town of Gorazde. She grew up there and went through three years of Serb siege in that city, with her brother, mother, and father, while the Serbs, camped on the hillsides, cut off the water and electricity and shelled the town day after day, and the UN, which was supposed to protect them, did nothing to stop it.[17] Leila was sixteen. Her mother's family died in Visegrad, a town nearby on the Drina, her people thrown from the Ottoman bridge in the center of town. Her grandfather, she says, was killed by her own mother's Serb brother-in-law. The family dug trenches so that they could get to and from the shops; otherwise the Serbs on the hillsides would gun them down. She remembers what it was like to cross the bridge over the Drina, bent double as you ran, dodging fire from the snipers. "We knew exactly who they were. They were locals. You could see them clearly on the hillside."

From the age of sixteen to nineteen she lived under bombardment. She remembers the sound of a rocket when it is still in the air, when you don't know where it is going to land. "It still makes me shiver. It is like the sound of a sheet of paper slipping off the table and falling to the ground. And then the explosion."

"They robbed us of our childhood," she says.

I ask her what she thinks about it all now, nearly twenty years later, now that she has a job, a motorbike, a life in Sarajevo as a translator.

She thinks for a while. "There were Serbs trapped with us in the siege too. We helped each other. I guess I learned not to generalize." Now, she says, things are good in Gorazde. The local factory turns local leather into car seats for BMW and Mercedes. Serbs and Muslims flock into the city for the work. She shrugs, smiles. We walk back to the hotel, across the old bridge in silence.

"I learned not to generalize." Yes, it must be true, if you are to live here, you cannot blame whole peoples for stealing your childhood and murdering your kin. You have to keep responsibility individual. You try not to believe in collective guilt. It is not a useful thought, since even individual justice, for individual crimes, is hard to come by. The international tribunals have come and gone, the preachers of reconciliation have departed, and you are left in a society where perpetrators and victims confront each other every day in the streets.

But really, I ask myself, how can you avoid generalizing? What else is moral life but extrapolation from the particular to the general, from this experience and this person to the general and even to the universal? Isn't moral life one long exercise in synecdoche, taking the part for the whole?

So long as people did not generalize, she might be telling me, so long as words like "nation" or "faith," words like "us" and "them" did not enter their heads, as long as it was only "me" and "'you," people could live together, side by side, difference abutting difference, each in its terrain of ritual and certainty, not making claims on the other, living together *and* side by side, all at once. They came to your christenings, you went to their funerals. Respect was shown. Nobody tried to impose anything on anyone else. This is the deep logic of ordinary virtue, the tolerance that comes from taking people as they come and taking life one day at a time.

The nationalist ideologies that brought death to this region from Princip's bullet to the war of the 1990s were generalizations: claims that the land belonged to "us," not to "them," the claim that "we," by virtue of our faith, language, or superior power were fit to rule here while "they" were only fit to leave or die.

If that's the case, then, if generalities sowed poison, there is no "general" reconciliation available here, certainly none that outsiders can do much to promote. Of course public gestures can help, and political leadership always matters. Think of German chancellor Willy Brandt kneeling at the Warsaw ghetto memorial in 1970—but such nobility is too much to expect from leadership in these parts. No, the reconciliation that matters will be very slow, like a process of deglaciation, one heart, one mind at a time, over generations, as the pain of memory slowly gives way to history. The bodies, every one, will have to be given a decent burial. There are no shortcuts, no easy remedies. It will be ages yet before the history books in high schools teach the same history to children. Everything that matters will take place slowly, in individual hearts, as Sudbun completes the graves at Carakavo, as the Serb deputy mayor goes home and asks herself when the curse of the past will ever be laid to rest, as Shahida decides whether she should stay in the valley or leave for France, as Leila, one day, decides what she wants to tell her children about her own childhood under bombardment in Gorazde.

In Bosnia you learn that nothing, not even hatred and bitterness, endures forever and that barriers of pain cannot last forever because humans, whatever their memories, have to live with each other in the present, here and now, day by day.

It is happening, this glacial reconciliation, not with the enemy, not with "the other," not with "them," but simply with the fact that the past is past, over and done with. It happens so slowly that no one can see it, but it is happening. The only visible sign of it is that no one has died in Bosnia, for the sake of murderous generalizations, at least since September 1995, and so long as the rest of Europe keeps watch, no one is likely to do so in the future. The war, the one that began in June 1914 and raged, only with intermissions, from then until 1995, is over. For this, we should thank those brave souls today who have learned through suffering that it is not good to generalize.

5

Myanmar

The Politics of Moral Narrative

MASOEYEIN MONASTERY IS A CAMPUS OF DORMITORIES, classrooms, and gold pagodas glowing in the late afternoon sun of Mandalay. As we drive through the gates, the monks' belongings are visible through the windows of the dormitories, hanging in plastic bags on hooks at the end of their bunk beds. The trunks they carried from their villages are piled in racks by the dormitory doors. Robes are hanging outside on lines to dry. Monks, their shaven heads gleaming in the sun, pass by, but when they see foreigners getting out of the van, they cover their exposed brown chests, tossing their robes back over their shoulders.

Earlier we had seen them strolling through the leafy streets of Mandalay, in languid ochre processions, going from house to house to receive food, which they take back to the monastery in neatly stacked steel pots. The families who donate the food earn merit and can count on the monks' protection.

Burmese monasteries have an authority that rivals the military, the Tatmadaw—that black box of brute force, political power, and rent-seeking—that rules Myanmar and since 2010 has been edging the country, in a crab-like motion, toward a democratic transition.

A closed society, under military dictatorship for seventy years, is opening to the world. A global human rights heroine is poised to take power. For the first time, Burmese society is having to ask itself what a democratic country means and who it belongs to—the Buddhist majority or the hundreds of minorities, especially Muslim, who make it their home. Global discourses—human rights, Buddhism, and Islam—are battling over who gets to shape the Burmese transition.

Myanmar is to global civil society movements in the early twenty-first century what Bosnia was in the 1990s: a cause, a laboratory, a fund-raising opportunity, a training ground, above all a place to demonstrate that universalizing outsiders can help guide a divided society toward reconciliation and peace. As in Bosnia, outsiders are learning hard lessons about the limits of moral globalization, as universalist and secular ideologies encounter the authority of religious ideologies of resistance.

We've come to the Masoeyein Monastery to talk with one monk in particular, who, more than any other, has stepped into the political arena and staked his claim to defining the future of the Burmese nation.

We are led into a library that houses the holy books of Theravada Buddism, all encased in clear plastic covers. Through the windows we can hear chanting coming from a building behind us. In the still afternoon heat, novices are chanting religious texts, over and over, a buzzing roar of sound I've heard only once before, in a *madrassa* in Pakistan.

Burma—now renamed Myanmar—is a frontier country of 51 million people, squeezed between the civilizations of India and China, home to a medley of peoples determined to keep their own identities distinct. A British colonial official called Burma "a plural society," where ethnicities and religions live, as they did in Ottoman Bosnia, side by side but not together.[1]

Burma occupies a central place in the creation of our postimperial imagination. Next to the works of Joseph Conrad, there are few more pitiless depictions of imperial disillusion and outright racism than George Orwell's *Burmese Days*. Burma also offers hard truths about the liberation movements that overthrew the European empires.[2] The independence movement led by Aung San Suu Kyi's father never sank the unifying roots that enabled Nehru's Congress Party to hold India together after 1947. In Burma, nationalists like Aung San never commanded a broad-based popular uprising. Instead they maneuvered their way to freedom through a series of elite negotiations with a British Labour government, already divesting itself of British India and Palestine and only too willing to let Burma go.[3] The father of the nation, Aung San, was killed by political rivals before he had time to complete the work of nation-building.

Independence began an unraveling that no central government has been able to fully stop. Groups on the frontier and in mountainous regions rose in revolts that are still going and have made Burma the site of the longest civil conflict anywhere in the world. Burma's post independence rulers failed to stem the unraveling. The army seized power in 1962, claiming they were the only institution capable of keeping the Burmese frontier periphery under control.[4]

In a plural society, each ethnic and religious group has its temples, mosques, schools, and churches, its feast days, marriage customs, and funerals. To this day, all citizens of Myanmar carry an identity card listing their ethnic origin. There are 135 recognized ethnicities. We live as neighbors, a Burmese intellectual will tell me, but "we do not know each other deeply at all. We coexist, we do not live together."[5] It is one thing to coexist, as in Los Angeles or Queens, when the constitutional identity of the state has been settled, once and for all. It is another to do so in a state where the basic rules of the constitutional game have yet to be defined. To the Burmese Buddhist majority, diversity produces a state of continual political irritation, because the existential question that all politics anywhere has to solve remains unanswered: Whose country is this? Is it mine or is it yours?

Besides the frontier peoples, the minority whose claims most threaten the Buddhist majority are the Muslims, despite the fact that they number only between 6 and 10 percent of the population.[6] Rohingyas—the Muslim minority in Rakhine state, the poor rice-growing coastal belt around the Bay of Bengal—are the most despised and feared because they are Muslim, because they are poor, and because the steady growth in their numbers, through immigration from Bangladesh and their own robust birth rate, makes them competitors for land and jobs in one of the poorest states in the country. Most of all, it seems, Muslims are feared, not just because of their growing numbers inside Myanmar, but because of Islam's global march.[7]

In the monastery library a young man in jeans is setting up a camera to film us. A young monk, with the harried demeanor of political assistants everywhere, comes in carrying no fewer than three cell phones and asks us what the subject of our interview will be. We say we want to talk about ethnic and religious relations. He vanishes. There is a long pause. Minutes pass. Then suddenly, as if he had been watching us from behind the bookshelves, Ashin Wirathu appears.

He is a small man on a round frame, in his early forties, with smooth, light-colored skin and watchful, imperious eyes. He wears the orange robes of a monk. He removes gold-rimmed glasses, lays his cell phone on the table, and asks who we are and what we want.

We explain the Carnegie Council. He interrupts. Andrew Carnegie? He pronounces the name in English, and when we nod, he inclines his head significantly, but he remains suspicious. Americans, he says, returning to Burmese, have been the worst.

Time magazine put him on the cover in 2013.[8] His face appears above the headline "The Face of Buddhist Terror." Inside is a story, "When Buddhists Go Bad," in which he is quoted as saying that Barack Obama is "tainted by black Muslim blood" and that the Muslims in Burma are "radical bad." The military regime imprisoned him in 2003 as a troublemaker, but since it loosened its grip in 2009, Wirathu has built a national organization called 969 to fund his political tours.[9] His meetings are attended by thousands, who come to hear him denounce the Muslim takeover of his country and then follow him on Facebook and take home his CDs and pamphlets, full of graphic stories about the danger that Muslim men pose to Burmese womanhood.

This is a very global monk indeed. The battle he believes he is fighting is for embattled Buddhist civilization as a whole. He is not the only Burmese we meet who mentions the dynamiting of the incomparable Buddhist statues in Bamyan, western Afghanistan, in March 2001 by Taliban jihadis or the steadily weakening role of Buddhism in Muslim Indonesia. These are portents, Buddhist fundamentalists believe, of what may happen to Burmese Buddhism unless the Bangladeshi and Pakistani preachers are banned from Burmese mosques, if the tide of Islamic migration into Rakhine state isn't stopped, if the demographic surge of the Muslim birth rate in Burma isn't reversed.

In this vision of Buddhism under threat, Wirathu has extremist allies in other countries, especially Sri Lanka.[10] The more he succeeds at making himself an international defender of global Buddhism, with followers around the world, the more followers he will have at home.

I ask him what makes Burmese Buddhism special. He leans back and taps the books on the shelf behind him. There are three holy books, he says, and some Buddhists do not follow all of them. The Japanese for example, allow monks to marry and wear a gray rather than an ochre robe. "They think there is latitude for interpretation. We do not. Whatever the scripture tells us to do, we do. We are the original faith."

This is fundamentalism, Buddhist style, the belief in doctrinal purity fighting for its life in a global sea of relativism and decline. If there is a fundamentalist Islam on the march, Wirathu is saying, Buddhism must also rise up and reclaim lost glories. The Bodu Bala Sena movement of extremist monks in Sri Lanka, with whom he has an alliance, says much the same. Their name translates as "Buddhist Power Force," and like Wirathu's 969, they are widely accused of inciting the Buddhist majority in Sri Lanka to acts of violence.

It can't be an accident that religious extremism is on the rise in two countries, Sri Lanka and Burma, where the ultimate question—Whose country is this?—remains unsettled after decades of civil war. Fundamentalists have followers because they offer an uncompromising answer to the existential question of national identity.

The sound of novices chanting reaches us from the next building, a steady, monotonous drone like bees. Wirathu pats the books behind him. "We want to protect our religion," he continues. "If Buddhism were to disappear, the whole world would collapse."

In 2013, when Buddhist mobs were rampaging through the town of Meikhtila and more than thirty people died in a riot sparked by allegations that Muslims had raped a Buddhist girl, Wirathu had said: "Now is not the time for calm. Now is the time to rise up, to make your blood boil."[11]

Muslims are attacking Buddhists, he says, so we have campaigned in parliament for the race protection acts. These are four laws that forbid polygamy and forbid Buddhist women from converting to Islam after marriage. These laws are not really about polygamy or even about protecting women from forcible conversions. They are essentially political vehicles for the monks' claim that Burma is Buddhist, and that the monks are the guardians of what is most sacred to Burma, the honor of women.

Why, I ask him, do Buddhist women need your protection?

"Our females are taken from us and forced to convert. If she doesn't convert, she will be rejected, thrown out, lose her inheritance. Our women are beaten if they meditate or practice our religion in the house of a Muslim husband. They are beaten and lose their children. Thanks to Muslim polygamy, they are breeding faster than we are. Soon they will be a majority in Rakhine and our people there will be threatened."

In a voice that never rises above a low hum, interweaving with the chanting next door, he recalls the jihadist pogroms against Rakhine Buddhists in 1942, in which 30,000 Rakhines were killed. Today in Sittwe, the capital of Rakhine state, the Buddhists are outnumbered in their own home province. Buddhist counter massacres of their Muslim neighbors in Meikhtila are never mentioned.

We may be struck by his moral selectivity, but he jabs away at ours. The internationals, from Barack Obama to Human Rights Watch, have taken up the Rohingya cause, but fail to consider the poor, helpless Buddhists.

I ask him what the situation for Buddhists will be like after the election in November 2015. "If the government copies American and British democracy," he says, "there is a danger the country will come apart. Equality, human rights, democracy, these are dangerous things, especially for women. They are simple creatures, timid and easily deceived." Judy, our Burmese translator, relays all of this to us with sphinx-like imperturbality. Much later, when we are on our own, she laughs. "What can these monks possibly know about women?"

"If the election result hands Aung San Suu Kyi's National League for Democracy a victory," Wirathu continues, "the Muslims will gain the right to build mosques, the right to own land, there will be even more arms in the mosques than there are now."

The message he offers is a closed loop that is impervious to contradiction.

"The strong Muslims always win," he says. "The weak Burmese always lose."

Wirathu's sexual paranoia and his atrocity stories remind me of similar tales I heard in the former Yugoslavia in the 1990s. Serb commanders used to say much the same, and the Croats too; even a Muslim occasionally had his own variant. There always was a weirdly airless character to these diatribes: time slowed down so much you lost track of whether the atrocity they were talking about happened in 1392 or 1992; since they all made the same accusations you lost track of who was the perpetrator, who the victim. In this airless medium, facts ceased to exist; all discourse was self-confirming and self-reinforcing.[12]

These diatribes always have an enabling context. When the existential security provided by state order collapses anywhere, and with it the social trust that institutions provide, the ordinary virtues wither away. People quickly become Leninists: the only issue that matters to them is Who/whom? In a situation of radical existential threat, moral life is reduced to the search for protection: so you listen only to your own. As we saw in Bosnia, this suffocating moral climate can linger, even twenty years into a shaky peace.

Myanmar is not Bosnia, not now and hopefully not ever: the state has not dissolved, the national army and police can snuff out a pogrom or a riot, and they do not always stand by when Muslims are massacred.

But Myanmar does face a transition that is existentially threatening and open-ended. It was not safely concluded with elections in 2015. Indeed it will take decades, long after the international community has rolled up its tents and moved on to the next affecting moral drama. A democratic transition does not answer the question of who Myanmar belongs to: it merely creates the institutions within which the battle for the answer to that question will be conducted. The majority do not know how much they will have to concede to keep the country together; the minorities are uncertain what they can possibly gain from peace and a federal union. It is in these conditions of existential uncertainty that extremist monks gain a hearing.

Wirathu's discourse exculpates real perpetrators and targets imaginary threats. He vests paranoia and incitement in the language of a religion of peace, yet he may not be speaking in bad faith. On the contrary, he wouldn't be effective if he didn't appear utterly sincere.

His discourse conceives of his nation as the guileless female and Burma's enemy as the potent, duplicitous Muslim. It is a discourse of menace, but also of hope. It points to a happy future in which Myanmar is exclusively Buddhist, the nation's morals are protected by the monks, and the Muslims have been given their just deserts. Wirathu's discourse of sexual paranoia has a deeply appealing answer to the Burmese national question. The nation is ours alone. No wonder his audiences flock to hear him.

A year before in the streets of Mandalay, his Facebook posts let loose a deadly rumor to the effect that two Muslim owners of a tea-shop had raped one of their Burmese female employees. Crowds quickly gathered, one thing led to another, and before it was over a

Buddhist and a Muslim had been murdered.[13] The police had to declare martial law and suspend Facebook to tamp down the rumors. A year later, when we were there, Mandalay was still walking on tiptoe, uneasily awaiting the next spark.

After Wirathu had escorted us to our minibus and we posed, unsmiling, for a picture together, we traveled to see a group calling itself the Mandalay Peace Committee. It is made up of Buddhists, Muslims, Christians, Hindus, political activists, and journalists who, when the riot broke out, quelled rumors, quieted the enraged, and helped the police to clear the streets. The peace committee was a collection of elderly men and one woman, gathering in the upstairs meeting room of a Mandalay church. In the void where you'd expect a state to keep the peace, Burmese civil society had stepped in. The peace committee, fanning itself in an upstairs room, is the cautious, modest face of ordinary virtue in Mandalay.

When I said I had been visiting with Wirathu, one of the monks on the peace committee took me aside and whispered, "Such a person could not say what he was saying unless the military gave him permission." "We monks cannot stop him," he added sadly. "This is politics, not religion." Then he said he had to slip away, back to his monastery. Meeting with other faiths had become a little difficult these days, he said, as he bowed, smiled gently, and hurried off to his car.

The interfaith group was fragile, as the monk's departure showed, but it had held together because moderate Buddhists as well as Methodists, Hindus, and Muslims felt equally threatened by the Buddhist extremists. The Methodists, for example, were keeping their seminarians locked up inside their theological college after 9:00 p.m., even a year after the disturbances. The imams and merchants in the Muslim community were equally concerned. They had deputized a dapper young man in T-shirt and shorts, named Harry, who told the group that radical Islamists—with sermons, CDs, visits from Pakistani radical preachers—were inflaming their own Muslim community. The long-standing tolerance of Mandalay was now under siege, Harry told the group, by a radical Islam coming from outside.

It was so tense in this room of peacemakers that no shared narrative of the riots emerged, except a belief, greeted with nods of agreement, that the troublemakers—Islamic on one side, Buddhist on the other—came from outside and that a "hidden hand," presumably military intelligence, was fomenting the trouble in order to frustrate the slow advance toward democracy. This analysis seemed plausible in itself, but it was also the peace committee's way, I thought, of pushing the blame away, of struggling with the puzzle of hatred and how groups can live together in a plural society, and then one day, out of the blue, find themselves divided into stick-wielding, rock-throwing mobs.

Significant by their absence from the peace committee were any official representatives from Aung San Suu Kyi's National League for Democracy. When we went to visit them in their headquarters, plastered with reverential oil portraits of the Lady, party members told us they assist the committee "in a private capacity," but the party didn't want to get drawn into the politics of religious violence, especially not with an election looming.[14]

No one in the peace committee challenged the narrative of the riot itself—that it was triggered when two Muslim brothers raped a Buddhist employee. Then we crossed town and paid a visit to another monk, Galon Ni Sayedawa, in his office in Mandalay.

On the night of the riots, when the Buddhist crowds surrounded the mosques, one of the imams reached Galon Ni Sayedawa on his cell phone and said he had better come quickly. Wirathu's posts on Facebook were swelling the crowd. He and his fellow monks were on the streets into the early hours, trying to get enraged Buddhists to go back to their homes, reassuring frightened Muslims that they were not about to be attacked. Eventually, the religious leaders calmed the city down. When I ask Galon Ni Sayedawa whether peace has actually been restored, he looks doubtful. Yes, he confirms, there are Islamic extremists circulating among the mosques—from the Pakistani Taliban—and so he works with the local imams to keep whatever peace they can. Their joint message is: "Don't listen to rumors, live peacefully, and don't let instigators start anything."

As we are getting ready to leave, he adds casually that the story we've heard about how the Mandalay riot started is quite wrong: The girl who said she was raped wasn't Buddhist. She was a Muslim, and she wasn't raped at all. The police circulated the story, after it appeared on Wirathu's Facebook posts, but it wasn't true. It was all a business dispute between two Muslims in the city, and one of them paid the girl to accuse the other of rape. Galon Ni Sayedawa looks at us coolly through his gold-rimmed glasses and says nothing further, a smile playing on his lips, as if to say, nothing here is what it seems.

It is a June evening in Yangon, heavy with the heat, the monsoon thundering on tin roofs, the gutters running brown with garbage and detritus; the traffic is immobilized in the downpour and everyone is in a cheerful mood, especially the boys and girls in school uniforms crammed into the jitney next to our minibus, sheltering from the downpour by bunching together, giggling as they duck the sheets of rain sloshing down the open sides of the old vehicle taking them home. The traffic jam is a happy scene of disorder, drivers swearing and waving their arms, ladies fanning themselves in front seats, ragged street children darting to and fro between the cars selling drinks and sticks of meat. Through the sheets of rain, we can see the brightly lit car showrooms lining the jammed highway, that display the cars only the elites can buy: BMW, Audi, and Mercedes. Billboards by the roadside announce twenty-four acres of "exclusive" condominiums coming soon. The land used to be a barracks and a parade ground, our translator tells us, until the military sold it off to their cronies.

Since the junta began allowing people to import vehicles in 2009, Yangon's cracked road system has been jammed.[15] Chinese, Indian, and Singaporean businessmen are snapping up land, resources, and marketing concessions. The international hotels are doing a rich business, and all this new wealth gushes, like monsoon rain, into a city where the gutters run with sewage, weeds still poke out from the ruins of old British imperial buildings, poor folk squat by roadside stalls selling charred skewers of meat, and everyone scrambles in the perilous jumble of transition, some people accelerating into wealth and luxury, others standing still as the caravan passes them by, others thrown back to the side of the road.

The military regime let Yangon decay, and its hold on the city was never secure. In 2002, they began building a sterile new capital, Naypyidaw, in the middle of nowhere, so that they could feel safe. Yangon feels too pleasure-seeking, too chaotic, too much of a jumble to submit to military rule again or to succumb easily to the purgative hatreds of an Ashin Wirathu.

Yet the question for which Wirathu provides an extremist answer—Who does this country belong to?—is still not answered.

There was a time when a watching world thought one person had the right answer. She was the beautiful daughter of the nation's founder, who had sacrificed a quiet life as an Oxford scholar to return to assume the leadership of a movement of monks, students, and veterans of her father's independence struggle. Together they sought to free the country from the Tatmadaw's grip.

Her answer to the national question was resolute: Myanmar belonged to everyone who was prepared to live together under democracy and the rule of law. Her answer had the authority of her own courage, her willingness to pay a very nearly ultimate price for her beliefs, a price that included losing her husband, losing contact with her children, and fifteen years of house arrest.

Her story became a demonstration of the power of moral example in international politics. Without her, the human rights abuse of the regime might never have become a global issue for international campaigners everywhere. Without her, the regime might never have felt compelled to open the country up and gamble that it could cede authority without losing power.

Without her, Western governments might not have invested so heavily in the Myanmar transition. Certainly the West had strategic and economic interests at stake in Myanmar—oil and gas concessions, as well as countering the power of China—but its primary interest has been moral. Her example provided Western democracy with a narrative it needed: vivid personal proof that the yearning for freedom, democracy, and rights was universal. Campaigning for her release became a cause célèbre. As the campaigns for sanctions on South Africa had galvanized campuses in the 1980s, as intervention to save Bosnia became the cause for liberal intellectuals in the 1990s, so Burmese freedom became the rallying cry for a global alliance of young activists in the early twenty-first century. To enlist was to proclaim who you were. Looking back on the Burma campaigns, one old hand told me, we fought for a Burma that existed mostly in our imagination. Now, he added ruefully, we're waking up to Burma as it really is.

The waking up began in 2010. "The Lady" was released, ran for parliament, won, and took her seat in an assembly where the constitution guaranteed the military a controlling share of the seats. She ceased to be a symbol and lost her halo. She became a politician.

Almost immediately she began to disappoint. When asked to chair a committee to investigate police and army brutality against civilian activists and monks at a Chinese-operated copper mine in the interior of the country, she authored a report that failed, at least in many outside activists' eyes, to condemn the military with sufficient force. For outsiders, the military were culprits. For the Lady, the military were a national institution. Outsiders realized she was not just a Western-educated human rights activist, but also the daughter of the man who founded the Burmese army.

Then along came the Rohingya issue. As Rakhine Buddhists attacked their Rohingya neighbors in the poor villages on the shores of the Bay of Bengal, as Rohingyas took to their boats to escape, drifting miserably in search of refuge in Malaysia or Indonesia, as the Myanmar government confined displaced Rohingyas in camps and forbade them to exit, international outcry grew, but the Lady's message remained equivocal.[16] We had to understand, she kept saying, that the Rakhine Buddhists were just as poor, just as miserable as the Muslims. She told an audience in Australia that she would not condemn the persecution of the Rohingya as "ethnic cleansing." The Human Rights Watch Asia director, John Sifton, hit back, lamenting her failure to wield her "moral authority." She insisted she could not take sides between the Rakhine and the Rohingyas. "I want to work towards reconciliation between these two communities. I'm not going to be able to do that if I'm going to take sides."[17]

Kenneth Roth, head of Human Rights Watch, scathingly observed, "The world was apparently mistaken to assume that as a revered victim of rights abuse she would also be a principled defender of rights."[18] Chris Lewa of the Arakan Project, a Rohingya advocacy group, went further, arguing that her silence amounted to complicity with the abusers.[19]

The Lady was undeterred. Politicians, she was saying, can't afford to dismiss their own people's fears. She would leave moral condemnation to the human rights absolutists. Her job was to get her party into power and to ensure that the democratic transition itself was not swept away in a wave of interethnic warfare.

She was already barred from the office of president because she had children who were not Burmese. Her standing in her own country was constantly questioned. If she condemned monks like Wirathu and Buddhist troublemakers in Rakhine, she satisfied the international human rights community but put her domestic authority in jeopardy. She had to choose which audience mattered most, and she chose, as one would expect the daughter of Aung San to do, her own people.

At her party's central committee in a small office in a back street in Yangon, senior figures, many of them veterans of long bouts of imprisonment, insisted, with weary but unyielding intransigence, that outsiders had no business bringing up the Rohingya issue with them. Any use of the word, they said, was a humiliating neo-colonial interference in an issue of identity that the Burmese must decide for themselves. Yes, they admitted, the NDA has lost support among their "international friends" on this issue, but that's how it is.

The only Burmese I met who had a good word to say for the Rohingyas, who seemed to know them as actual people rather than as ideological abstractions, were political prisoners who had been imprisoned with them in Sittwe, the Rakhine capital. From these ex-prisoners there was a genuine sense of having been through something terrible together: long years behind bars, with awful food, rats, humiliation, and oppression, along with a recognition that the Rohingya were being imprisoned for ridiculous reasons—for example, for performing their own marriage ceremonies without police permission.[20]

Activists who had been imprisoned with the Rakhines were the exception. Others, who had also done time in prison for their politics, showed no sympathy. Ko Ko Gyi, a wiry and athletic fifty-year-old whom some diplomats pick as a future president, was scathing about President Obama's last visit to Myanmar in 2014. The president should never have used the word Rohingya in his remarks. Every time he did so he added fuel to the sectarian fire in our country. Outsiders need to mind their own business, Ko Ko says. "It is like the situation in Eastern Europe," he explains. "When democracy arrives, nationalism comes with it." He says, "Democracy is majority rule first. It will take time and space before it also includes human rights. You need to give us time."

It's not the job of the international human rights movement—Amnesty, Human Rights Watch, and the rest—to give anyone time. Universalism means a willed indifference to political trade-offs, especially moral compromises for the sake of transition. The internationals have built the juggernaut of their membership and influence because they stick to their guns, no matter how inconvenient their truths may be for those struggling to pilot a country toward democracy.

Some other internationals, however, feel the absolutism of the human rights community is, at the very least, unhelpful. At the U.S. embassy there is deep frustration at the inability of visiting politicians, columnists, and international NGOs to grasp how complex the politics of transition truly is.[21] Yes, quiet pressure on behalf of the

Rohingyas is a good idea, but public calls for Aung San Suu Kyi to give them equal citizenship only play into the hands of Ashin Wirathu and the extremists.

The election on November 8, 2015, gave Aung San Suu Kyi a decisive victory. She is barred from the presidency but she holds the power. For the moment, the military goes along, biding its time. The election was only one of many steps in a process of transition whose final shape remains unclear. Ashin Wirathu's influence may fade away, as many extremists do when people tire of apocalyptic rhetoric. In the two-steps-forward, one-step-back transition that never seems to reach a destination, the internationals may well decamp to more exciting venues. Other societies, other heroes, will become the beneficiary of their moral enthusiasms.

The full weight of the international community—the U.S. secretary of state, UN human rights rapporteurs, NGOs, the high commissioner for human rights—has not budged the Lady from her refusal to enfranchise the Rohingya. She needs political "space," she says, to move the peoples of Rakhine state toward dialogue and reconciliation, and in the meantime, outsiders should avoid "controversial" terms. No human rights hero or heroine of recent memory has so disillusioned the internationalist universalists who made her plight their cause.[22]

The Burmese story shows the decisive role of moral narrative in everyone's politics. The debates that matter most in any society are always about who belongs. Everyone—in Los Angeles, in Queens, in Bosnia—turns this from a question of fact to a question of value—in other words, into a question of who *deserves* to be counted as one of "us."

In Bosnia we saw where these battles of belonging can lead—to a war to the death to carve out ethnically defined political space—and afterward to a political stasis that frustrates outsiders who have discovered they cannot persuade the leaders of these ethnic enclaves to hammer out the terms of a common citizenship.

In successful multiethnic societies, at least in ones where there is more wealth to fight over, the question of who belongs is ordered, at least in theory, by functioning rule of law, by institutions that guarantee procedural equality and by the rhetoric of full inclusion. Thanks to the moral operating systems of these societies, diversity is transmuted from a quotidian reality that always falls short into an aspiration that can never be abandoned. This aspiration is multicultural society's saving grace, its safety valve, its shame when these values are traduced—but also its inspiration on the long, slow walk to freedom.

In a plural society like Myanmar, a society at war with itself since 1947, no such language has taken root. The nationalist struggle created a state, but not a nation. The question of who belongs is still unresolved, and it remains the question of questions that the political system—the Lady, the military, the monks, civil society—is still battling to resolve.

What all our journeys have upended is the idea, an axiom of American political lore, that all politics is local.[23] In fact, there is no politics, American, Bosnian, or Burmese, that is local anymore. In the American city, the politics of race and policing is forever framed by a history of slavery that was global in scope. No demonstrator in Ferguson is ever just demonstrating against the police in a small town in Missouri, but against the global heritage of white privilege as well. In Myanmar for Buddhists, the fate of the country is tied to the fate of Buddhism as a global religion, locked in battle with an Islam on the march.

The globalization of these struggles is a fact of life, but their worldwide amplitude makes them hard for local authorities, spiritual or temporal, to keep under control. Every local battle between faiths, creeds, or races can be fanned into an international fire once someone claims that what is at stake are ultimate questions of global, not simply local, identity. The solutions that might have been possible if local elites could just get down and do politics together—as the Mandalay Peace Committee tries to do—escape local resolution once everyone in the battle reaches for the global clichés of ultimate confrontation.

In all the groups who have had any success tamping down fanaticism and violence, from the civic groups in Mandalay to the religious and neighborhood groups we talked to in south Los Angeles, keeping confrontation manageable means turning the global back into the local. Ordinary virtue means fighting the global clichés of civilizational and religious clash by creating the space to do real politics together. Real politics happens when ordinary individuals grasp, through common interaction, that they have interests—peace or just peace and quiet—that are not captured by the global clichés. These are the clichés—the generalizations my Bosnian translator spoke of—that turn neighbors into strangers, adversaries into enemies, friends into deadly rivals. Peacemaking in Mandalay, in Bosnia, in south Los Angeles meant creating networks from different faiths and creeds who might share nothing more than a common determination to keep violence from getting the upper hand. This was commonality enough. It is when there is no peace committee, no monk talking to an imam, no preacher talking to the enraged adolescents on the streets, when there is no local politics stitching different people into alliances, that the global hatreds can acquire the velocity and intensity that spins them entirely out of anyone's control, including those who started it all.

Outsiders and internationals can help the ordinary virtues to prevail. Yet we always need to remember the baggage of history that we carry with us. We are here, we say, to respect *your* self-determination, *your* right to decide for yourselves. But this post imperial humility lies in uneasy contradiction with our belief that our values are universal and that we have a commitment to defend them everywhere, even when, or especially when, the self-determining majority want to exclude a minority from their vision of a democratic future.

Human rights activists take it as a matter of professional honor that they don't "do" politics, yet human rights activism, for all its disclaimers, is viscerally implicated in the societies it watches over, especially those with complex transitions toward democracy. If human rights activism wills the end of a successful transition, however, it must also will the means—that is, the less than perfect political processes that make a democratic transition possible.

It is also a fact that outsiders do not have the power, if we ever did, to determine how fast or slow any local transition proceeds anywhere. We have no ultimate standing on the question of questions: Whose place is this? Who rules?

The morally problematic character of our standing always bears remembering. In all the places we have traveled—Bosnia, Myanmar, Japan, Brazil, and the inner cities of the United States—we were only passing through. The beginning of understanding was to grasp how much we might never fully enter into the moral and political dilemmas of others.

The moral imagination, we've found, is not always up to the challenge of solidarity, the demands of understanding the world as others see it. But we need to try. It is possible to feel for the lives and struggles of others, but we should also recognize the limits of fellow feeling. It is not a betrayal of solidarity, just an admission of its limits to accept that these are *their* struggles, not our own, and it is they, not we, who will live with the consequences. Furthermore, there is a dimension of moral hazard to all displays of human solidarity. Those who live in safety like us will take moral stands in favor of the human rights of victims on the other side of the world. Those who live in danger, on the other side of the world, usually are the ones who pay the price for *our* convictions. If they, not we, pay the full price of our commitments and the mistakes that sometimes follow from these commitments then we owe it to them to understand, as fully as we can, the dangers that lurk in our own certainties and convictions and avoid them as best we can.

6

Fukushima

Resilience and the Unimaginable

JAPANESE PRIME MINISTER NAOTO KAN WAS IN HIS OFFICE at the Diet when the glass ornaments in the chandelier above his head began to jingle, shake, then sway, ever more violently, side to side.[1] The tremor went on for four minutes. The prime minister took cover, expecting the chandelier to fall. When it was safe to stand, he went immediately to the emergency command center in the cabinet office to take charge of operations. The first reports were good: all of Japan's fifty-four nuclear reactors had scrambled, shutting down safely. An hour later the news suddenly changed: there had been a "total station blackout," a loss of electrical power, at Fukushima Daiichi.

In Minamisoma, a city twenty-five miles from Fukushima Daiichi, a fishmonger watching the sea from the windows of his plant on the town wharf thought it was just a beautiful wave, like the ones he used to surf, until he noticed that fishing boats out in the open water were being picked up and hurled toward the shore.

In the town of Namie, five miles from the nuclear plant, a young municipal worker was driving around the parts of the town close to the sea with a loudspeaker, shouting for people to get out ahead of the wave, when, glancing in his rearview mirror, he saw the waves, chest high, roaring up the blacktop behind him.

At an elementary school in Ishinomaki, seventy-four students obeyed instructions to remain in the schoolyard after the earthquake before the tsunami struck. Three teachers disobeyed the order and escaped to higher ground with thirty-four students. Those who followed orders were swept away.[2]

After the tsunami, a shopkeeper from one of the coastal communities went to volunteer that night at the fire station. He spent the next six hours, till it got too dark to see, pulling bodies out of rice paddies, out of upturned cars and boats tossed into the fields, and realizing, as he did so, that they were his friends.

Inside the control room at Fukushima Daiichi, the plant superintendent, Masao Yoshida, and his team first thought the plant had survived the earthquake. It was after the tsunami struck and the lights overhead dimmed and the vast instrument panel in front of them went dark that they understood they were faced with a situation their instruction manuals never prepared them for: total power blackout.[3]

For these people—a prime minister, a fishmonger, a shopkeeper, primary school teachers, a municipal worker, and a nuclear plant superintendent—2:46 p.m. on March 3, 2011, was the moment when they entered the realm of the unimaginable. The unimaginable is not the unthinkable. Each separate element of the triple disaster—a major earthquake, registering 9.0 on the Richter scale, a tsunami of fifteen meters in height, and a nuclear accident—was thinkable. It was the three of them happening together that went beyond what anyone thought was possible and tipped the experience into the unimaginable.[4]

Traditional societies like tenth-century Japan, which suffered devastating tsunamis a thousand years ago, had expansive and capacious categories of fate that provided frames of meaning for the experience of the unimaginable. Ordinary people had plenty of experience with moments beyond their comprehension: besides flood, there was famine, pestilence, and premature death. Faced with such scourges, they might be angered by the hard cruelty of God's inscrutable will, but they did not suppose it was within their power to figure out the meaning of terrible events, still less to anticipate or prevent them. Courage in the face of disaster consisted of resilience born of stoic acceptance. The Shinto shrines built a thousand years ago on the bluffs above the sea on the coasts of Fukushima, the stone markers indicating where the waters reached in 917 AD, were an ancient society's warning to a modern one, a warning that went unheeded. The shrines are also a testament to a kind of resilience, a submission to the inscrutable, that is hard to imagine today.

The modern experience of the unimaginable is in a different register altogether. Our expectations are shaped by centuries of science, of accumulating knowledge about natural phenomena like earthquakes and tidal waves, and by the confidence we have acquired, through modern life, in the capacity of the modern state to harness this knowledge to protect us.

When the unimaginable strikes, our question is not What has God done? but Why was no one looking after us? Why did no one predict this? Why did the guarantees of the modern state prove useless?

Nothing has done more to sap confidence in the modern state, and in the predictive professions that provide expertise to the state, than our recurrent experience of the unimaginable. The unimaginable has become the face the future presents to us in the twenty-first century.

Fukushima recalled the breaching of the levees in New Orleans's ninth ward in September 2005, in the full pitch of Hurricane Katrina. Survivors asked why the Army Corps of Engineers hadn't built the levees to withstand a force 3 hurricane, just as Japanese evacuees bunked down in school gyms asked why the government and the nuclear operator had failed to anticipate a fifteen-meter tsunami. Both in New Orleans and in Fukushima the contract of trust between citizen and public institutions was ruptured by the unimaginable.[5]

When BP's Deepwater Horizon platform blew up and oil gushed into the Gulf of Mexico in 2010, shrimp fishermen, hotel owners, and coastal residents couldn't understand how a global corporation operating in the world's most advanced economy under a complex system of government regulation could have failed to prevent oil spilling out from a broken well head on the ocean floor for eighty-seven consecutive days.

In September 2008, after the sudden collapse of the financial services firm Lehman Brothers, millions of people around the world found themselves asking how it was that all the experts in risk management, all the economists with their models, all the regulators could have been so drastically wrong. Now as ordinary people struggle to rebuild, paycheck by paycheck, they are told by the same authorities they trusted to regulate mortgage and real estate markets that it cannot happen again. But we all suspect it can and it will.

The unimaginable is a constructed reality, one that becomes so because risk professionals, insurance companies, bankers, regulators, and governments lay down a deep structure of reassuring expectations that deny the unimaginable is even possible. They all tell us: be responsible for the risks you take, but leave the public risks—the systemic shocks—to us. We'll be there for you.

Only they weren't.

So now, in the wake of hurricanes, environmental disasters, and financial catastrophes, we face the future with the sense of having been deceived by governments and by experts who had no more idea than we did of what risks were headed our way.

The unimaginable has a dimension that goes beyond the idea of unthinkable natural, environmental, or financial risk. It also comprises the idea that we no longer can be sure what our fellow human beings might do to us. Prediction, after all, depends on some stable set of expectations about what our fellow human beings are like. Yet the twenty-first century was ushered in with such an astonishing act of human barbarity that our frame of expectations is much less stable than it used to be. If you wished your wife or husband goodbye as they boarded a flight for New York on the morning of September 11, 2001, or if you saw them off at a commuter stop to the World Trade Center that bright sunny morning, you could not have imagined that you and your loved ones had been selected at random for an unfathomable exercise of human malignity. September 11 cracked the granite under our feet. It ushered us into a world in which the future could no longer be trusted because our fellow human beings had just given us such an unforgettable demonstration of ingenious and well-planned ferocity. Since 9/11, thanks to Islamic jihad, thanks to attacks in countless places, nothing has become a more global experience than surviving—and trying to understand—the unimaginable.

To counter the new threats, we have given our government powers that would have been inconceivable except in wartime, but the sacrifice of civil liberties does not give us confidence that we'll be any safer. We're still aware, as we walk to work, take our children to school, line up for a movie, or wait for a flight at the airport, that in each of these moments we've become "a soft target."

Instead of embracing the future, imagining radiant tomorrows, we now think of the future in the language of harm reduction, target hardening, and risk management.

The professions of risk management and prediction have proliferated. Banks and investors consult "country risk" professionals before placing their financial bets; architects and engineers consult with seismologists to ensure that their "design basis" anticipates future ground motion; engineers who build levees and seawalls consult with meteorologists about extreme weather events; actuaries calculate risk for insurance companies; the Centers for Disease Control patrol the global biosphere and the world's public health systems looking for potential epidemics. Every foreign ministry of any size has a policy-planning unit whose job is to sketch "over-the-horizon scenarios" for decision makers. Every country's intelligence agency tries to detect the signal in the midst of the noise, the gathering crescendo of impending attack.[6]

Unfortunately, we don't notice the risks these specialists avert, only the ones they fail to stop. Ironically, it is our residual faith in risk management that makes the unimaginable so dumbfounding when it occurs. The scientific and technical progress that has occurred is real enough—from cell phones to penicillin, our technologies do make us safer—but as a narrative about the future, the idea of progress is a lullaby. The very weapons that progress puts in our hands to face the future leave us disarmed when the unimaginable arrives.

Historians will remind us that the unimaginable is how the future has always arrived. Our anxieties about time are nothing new. The present has always been shapeless, strange, and frightening. It's only in retrospect, looking backward, that history ceases to be chaotic and assumes, through analysis and reflection, a discernible meaning.

What's new is this negative dialectic between the progress we have made in predictive technique and the helpless anger we feel when these techniques fail to avert harm. The increasing sophistication of our predictive techniques does not prevent the future from arriving in terrifying form. What's new, moreover, is that we are managing manmade risks that have never existed on a global scale before, nuclear meltdown, climate change, and extreme weather events, the terrorism of the global spectacular.

All of this is testing our resilience. The battering we have received at the hands of the unimaginable makes us more individualistic in a bad sense, fixated on ourselves, saving what we can for our families and those close to us. An individualistic culture is a less resilient one, less confident in its collective capacities to provide basic existential guarantees.

We are more individualistic in our approach to risk because the guarantees we once took for granted from the modern state no longer seem reliable. The "welfare state," that emerged after 1945, promised us social solidarity and collective protection, but in the long era ushered in by the conservative counter-revolution of the 1980s and in the age of mass terrorism and financial crisis that has followed since 9/11 we have revised downward our expectations and hopes for the modern state. A "risk society," as the German sociologist Ulrich Beck called it in the 1980s, is one whose political ambitions are reduced to preventing the worst.[7] A risk-averse political horizon promises security at a price: not only more surveillance, but also a loss of confident daring.

The global middle-class public may be larger than ever before. It may be living longer, but we do not feel more confident about the future.[8] Thanks to the unimaginable, a tone of cynical disbelief ripples through our politics and public life. We live in a faithless moral environment: deluged by alarming information but without the faith in science and politics to believe that public authority can prevent the worst. It is no wonder that resilience has become the necessary virtue of our time.

Japan knows about resilience. Since 1945, it has recovered from apocalyptic military defeat, the detonation of two nuclear weapons, a mass-casualty terrorist attack in a subway, and in 2011, a tsunami that killed nearly twenty thousand people and triggered a major nuclear accident.

The catastrophe of 2011 unleashed a heart-searching discussion in Japan about why, despite all this experience, key virtues in the society—order, discipline, obedience, respect, courtesy—worked against the society's capacity to anticipate the worst and take action in time.

These virtues, especially trust in the company and the regulators—conspired to make a nuclear accident seem unthinkable. The first lesson—hammered home in an angrily eloquent commission report, authored by a team led by professor Kiyoshi Kurokawa—is that taking refuge in the idea of the unthinkable is an alibi and an excuse.[9] When spokesmen for Japan's "nuclear village," the collusive tribe of regulators and operators who created Japan's nuclear industry, proclaimed that the nuclear accident was "*soteigai*"–unthinkable–the Japanese public reacted with fury.

The public realized, after the fact, that this was a disaster waiting to happen. There had been plenty of warnings. The Kobe earthquake of 1995 and the East Asian tsunami of 2004 should have made risk managers review every feature of a nuclear plant built at the water's edge, with its backup generators at sea level. The "design basis" of the plant was built to withstand a six-to-seven-meter tsunami, but when an in-house report in 2006 warned the Tokyo Electric Power Company (Tepco) what might happen if a bigger tsunami hit the plant, the company did nothing.[10]

A Tepco director I spoke to looked back on his own complacency with shame and astonishment: "What bothers me now, as I look back, is that I didn't even know what a 'station blackout' was. Nobody that I knew in the company did. We didn't even know what the words meant. No one even had the concept."[11] Given the reach of the human imagination, nothing should be strictly unimaginable. That's what prophets of doom are for, and a leader's job is to know when to heed them. The Cassandra myth, however, is there to warn us just how rarely we do.[12]

The Kurokawa report called Fukushima a disaster "made in Japan," and it spread the blame far and wide, condemning "the ingrained conventions of Japanese culture: our reflexive obedience; our reluctance to question authority; our devotion to 'sticking with the program'; our groupism; and our insularity." The report blames so many people that the buck never stops anywhere.

When I visited Professor Kurokawa, in his Tokyo office, he himself admitted the truth of this. "People thought I was saying everyone was responsible, and therefore no one was. Actually I was saying we have to be responsible for decisions taken in our country. This was the 'inconvenient truth' I addressed to the elite of my society."[13]

Establishing individual responsibility for a disaster has to mean some people go to jail—and it's striking that no one has done so thus far, though three senior Tepco officials have been prosecuted.[14] The most visible casualty was prime minister Naito Kan himself, who was forced to resign five months after the disaster. The experience, Kan now says, has turned him into an antinuclear activist. The only safe energy strategy for Japan, he believes, is one without nuclear power at all.

Both Kurokawa and Kan take the long view: the only way to manage high-risk technology is to revive democracy. In Kurokawa's words, we can't be safe with high-risk technologies unless we have "the muscles of a vibrant civil society: diligent regulators, honest bureaucrats serving for the people of Japan, activist prosecutors, alert legislators, courageous whistle-blowers, relentless journalists, independent academics, thriving NGOs, and above all, ordinary people who vote."[15]

If renewing democracy is the answer, it's going to be a long haul before Japan's institutions are up to the task. The disaster itself inflicted long-term damage on the public's trust in their institutions. Spokesmen contradicted each other, national government did not communicate to local government, officials charged with reassuring the public in the irradiated zones were told nothing by regulators or by Tepco.[16]

After all this the Japanese public don't know whom to believe. Achieving democratic consensus about whether to restart Japan's existing nuclear plants is going to be difficult. Unable to decide who's right and who's wrong, the public have gone back to their own lives, leaving the power to decide still in the hands of the nuclear village, the tight circle of bureaucrats, politicians, and corporate directors who have decided Japanese energy policy since the 1950s.

Even so, the catastrophe has shifted the balance in the nuclear debate. Fukushima has conferred standing—the right to be heard—to "counter experts."[17] The counter-experts have won temporary injunctions to prevent the startup of local reactors, and leaders of the campaign have made no secret of their ultimate strategy: to use legal challenges to delay the return to nuclear for long enough—a decade perhaps—to force Japan's big companies to move away from nuclear into renewables. The counter experts point out that since 2011 Japan has been producing baseload power entirely without nuclear, and they are hoping that the more open the debate, the more public the discussion, the less likely Japan will decide to remain on the nuclear road.[18]

Under the pressure of these counter experts, Japan has moved to create regulators independent of politicians and operators alike; has imposed mandatory redesign of nuclear facilities to guarantee that loss of power can never happen again; has made a public commitment to smart grids; has broken up regional energy monopolies; and has created incentives for a more balanced energy portfolio, with less nuclear and more renewables.[19]

Despite all this, it seems hard to imagine how a heavily populated, highly industrialized island, totally dependent for all of its fossil fuels on imports from the volatile Middle East and dependent on safe transit of this oil through shipping lanes as dangerous as the Strait of Hormuz and the Moluccas Straits, can do without nuclear power for the production of baseload electricity.

There are 438 nuclear plants in operation worldwide, with sixty-seven more under construction. Even after the accidents at Three Mile Island, Chernobyl, and now Fukushima, global energy systems remain committed to nuclear.[20]

What no one now believes, as they once did, is that there is such a thing as a 100 percent safe nuclear reactor.

Fukushima has given us yet another lesson in the limits of our technologies of risk management and prediction. It is a lesson we keep having to re-learn. What human beings create is bound, sooner or later, to go wrong. As the American sociologist Charles Perrow argued in the 1980s, in a path-breaking study of the Three Mile Island accident, such incidents are "normal" occurrences in any advanced and complex technological system.[21] The unimaginable, therefore, remains permanently on the human horizon.

All the Japanese reports identify the root cause of the nuclear disaster in "the mindset" that prevented regulators and operators from predicting risk accurately; the "conceptual wall" that separated those in the routine present from imagining an apocalyptic possibility; the collusive mental atmosphere of the nuclear village; the stove-piping that prevented experts in seismology from grasping warnings from experts in tsunamis; the deep reluctance to ask "what if" questions; the rigidly binary fashion in which regulator and operator understood risk, according to which, plants were either safe or unsafe, and since no one could admit that there might be degrees of safety, both regulator and operator convinced themselves that the plants were 100 percent safe.

This pattern of conceptual denial and group thinking is a recurrent factor in major disasters. In the official report on the space shuttle Challenger disaster of 1986, Richard Feynman, a Nobel-prize-winning physicist and member of the Rogers Commission of Inquiry, identified a similar habit of mind in which, under the pressure of launch schedules and cost, engineers persuaded themselves that erosion in the O-rings, seals that if ruptured would cause catastrophic hydrogen leakage, was an acceptable risk.[22]

In his concluding thoughts on the Fukushima disaster, Yokara Hatamura, chairman of one of the Investigative Committees, echoed some of Feynman's conclusions, but with haiku-like concision: "Possible phenomena occur. Phenomena that are considered impossible also occur." "You cannot see things you do not wish to see. You can see what you wish to see."[23]

According to the cognitive psychologists Daniel Kahneman and Amos Tversky, we are error-making machines, constitutionally disposed to misprice risk, to nod off when we should be paying attention, to hope for the best when we should be planning for the worst.[24] Our "risk management" protocols are there to protect us against our own wishful thinking or carelessness.

Yet risk protocols and procedures can also entrench the kind of routinized thinking that leads to neglect of unexpected signals. What remains essential is the specifically human capacity for restless vigilance and improvisation. Robots will take over any risk management function that can be automated, but only human beings know how to improvise when the rulebook is gone, procedures no longer work, technologies no longer respond to instrumentation, or systems fail to reboot—when, in other words, the unimaginable hits us in all its dumbfounding force.

Ryusho Kadota's marvelous book on Masao Yoshida, site superintendent at Fukushima Daiichi, is a study of resilient improvisation when the known world has been swept away.[25] In darkness, with no electric power, cut off from their families and the rest of the world, with no functioning instrumentation, the core operating staff of eleven men, led by Yoshida, had to figure out what was wrong with three reactors, each with its own separate system failures. They had little or nothing to go on: the manuals had been washed away. They made sense of a senseless situation, drawing on decades of work in the plant, team loyalty, and a capacity to improvise. To get the water onto the fuel rods, they had to enter the containment building and expose themselves to radiation in order to open critical valves by hand. They sent older men, who'd already had their children, in to face the higher levels of radiation, protecting the younger ones from potentially cancer-causing doses. When one measure failed, they tried another; when hydrogen explosions brought roof paneling down onto their heads, they kept working, for forty-eight hours without a break. When they received ill-conceived orders from the prime minister's office in Tokyo to stop sluicing seawater over the fuel rods, Yoshida, the plant superintendent, pretended to obey, but ordered his men to continue anyway. They made mistakes, but they did not panic, they did not desert their posts; they worked as a team, they did not quarrel, they improvised solutions as best they could, and in the opinion of most experts, they did their best. They could not prevent the hydrogen explosions in three of the plants or the radiation leak that followed, but, in the words of the National Academy of Sciences, they did "reduce the severity of the accident and the magnitude of the offsite radioactive material release."[26]

The men in the Fukushima control room recall the extraordinary virtue of the men and women trapped in the World Trade Center's twin towers who did not panic, who assisted others to safety; they bring to mind the doctors and nurses at Memorial Hospital in New Orleans in 2005, who provided care for patients in a facility cut off by the flood without electric power.[27] People in extreme situations do not always panic; they do not desert their posts, betray their colleagues, abandon the suffering. Instead they seek to do their best in impossible situations. Since there are ultimately no fail-safe systems, no robotic substitutes, no procedures that can prevent the unimaginable, when all else fails, we are left with the virtue of resilience.

The word "resilience" is like a coin rubbed bare by overuse. So we need to do some work to recover what the word actually means. The American Heritage Dictionary lists two: first, "the ability to recover quickly from illness, change, or misfortune"; to which is added the idea of "buoyancy," the capacity to bob to the surface after being submerged. Second, in the language of metallurgy and materials science, resilience refers to "the property of a material that enables it to resume its original shape or position after being bent, stretched, or compressed."

The key feature of a resilient material is elasticity. The most resilient materials are alloys, combinations of elements acting together, rather than elements acting alone. New "memory alloys" developed in Germany, for example, can be bent and resume their shape millions of times. The metaphorical implications are obvious: we are more resilient when we act together, as a forged unit, a combination of skills under single leadership, than when we try to act alone.[28]

The metaphors, however, also point away from cooperation. They identify a resilient person as a pliable, shape-shifting individualist. Normally we don't think of such people as morally praiseworthy. They are Charles Dickens's "artful dodgers." Resilience may be an antiheroic disposition, a capacity to bend without breaking, to spring back after being knocked down.[29]

Child psychologists tell us that the best predictor of whether a person will develop resilience in adulthood is whether he or she has benefited from a reliable, long-term, enduring relationship with an adult in early childhood. It appears that children who grow up without a frame-creating adult presence are less resilient: major setbacks or misfortunes unravel their capacity to cope.[30]

The Japanese language has an especially resonant vocabulary of resilience. In Japanese, one word is frequently used after disaster: *ganbaru*. From the dictionary, I learn that *ganbaru* means "working with perseverance," "toughing it out." After the Kobe earthquake, *Ganbaru Kobe* became a slogan of the recovery.

A related term, derived from Zen Buddhism, is *gaman*, meaning "enduring the seemingly unbearable with patience and dignity." Another related term, *gamanzuyoi,* means "suffering the unbearable." Linked to this idea is the word *shoganai*, "acceptance of your fate."

From this we learn that resilience is both active and passive. The passive meaning may be the one we have inherited from Buddhist, Jewish, and Christian traditions, the ones that tell us resilience consists in reconciliation with force majeure, submitting to God's will. Modern resilience, by contrast, is active, springing back into shape like an industrial alloy.

Is it possible to combine the passive and active meanings of resilience—that is, to bring the acceptance of force majeure together with determined will to overcome? Again the Japanese language is helpful. The literal translation of resilience is *kaifuku-ryoku*. *Kaifuku* means returning to the original condition, and *ryoku* is the word for power. A Japanese student of mine suggested to me that *kaifuku-ryoku* does not capture the idea that those who are resilient possess "an iron core." So for her, the right translation in Japanese is *orenai-kokoro,* which means "an unbroken heart."

This is a beautiful possibility, the one I want to adopt, but it sets the moral bar very high. When we praise someone for resilience, we may not actually realize the harm we are doing.

Volunteers who went north to assist survivors after the earthquake and tsunami quickly learned never to use the word *ganbare* because, when people were praised, they felt they were being told "you're on your own." while those not receiving praise felt they were being condemned.[31] In an insidious if unintended way, praise for resilience did not bring zones of safety and zones of danger together: moral approbation became a way for the unharmed to wash their hands.

Praise for resilience can become an exercise in moral cruelty. It can make survival seem like an achievement, when in fact survivors know just how much their survival depended on chance. Praising resilience as if survival depends on personal qualities also neglects the crucial role of public leadership: how community leaders and government officials responded, whether they did their jobs. For many experts, focusing on resilience after disaster encourages fatalism instead of preventing it in the first place. Training programs to make people more resilient propel us, these experts argue, "onto a slippery slope towards learning to live with risks that are actually intolerable."[32]

We are not condemned simply to meet the unimaginable with resilience.[33] We can prepare for it, price the risk, budget for its eventuality. What was unimaginable today can be made fully preventable tomorrow. The levees that broke in New Orleans have been rebuilt to a higher standard; the backup power of nuclear reactors, everywhere, has been moved to higher ground. In the words of the U.S. Government Accountability Office, all of the world's nuclear regulatory bodies have taken some steps to focus on "previously unimagined accident scenarios," particularly the loss of electric power.[34] In the wake of the 2008 financial meltdown, banks have been banned from risk taking that might damage the global economic system. We can learn from our mistakes. We are not condemned to repeat them.[35] Even so, when all else fails, we need to learn how to be resilient. No place on earth has more to teach about resilience than Fukushima.

When the bullet train from Tokyo pulls into Fukushima City, everyone getting off the train is greeted by retirees holding banners that say Welcome to Fukushima! The stationmaster and his team also raise their white gloves and wave genially. Those who are disembarking, all Japanese except us, mostly look away and hurry down the stairs to the street.

When four of the six nuclear reactors at Fukushima Daiichi blew their stacks, one after another, in March 2011, they released a plume of radioactive caesium, strontium, plutonium, and iodine that the wind and rain then settled in a flame-shaped plume, north by north-west, over an area about fifty kilometers long and ten wide. One hundred thousand people living in that zone were evacuated, and four years later they still can't return. Fukushima farmers complain that no one in Tokyo will buy their soya or their canola oil. The fishermen say no one will buy their fish. The whole prefecture of Fukushima still lives under the pall of fear and suspicion, and that is why anyone who comes here gets a greeting at the station.

The government has divided the irradiated zone into three: green, yellow, and red. In the southern green zone the government is trying to convince people that it's safe to go back to their homes; in the yellow zone people can go in and out to check on their houses by day, but they can't stay there at night. In the red zone there are checkpoints manned by police wearing masks that bar entry to anyone who doesn't have a permit.

As we travel north, passing through the red zone, we monitor our own radiation exposure with Safecast radiation monitors, circuit-laden plastic boxes developed by American and Japanese engineers, a crowd-sourced response to public belief that the government wasn't telling them the truth about radiation levels. The radiation monitor is linked to a computer and a GPS, so that real-time data on dosages can be uploaded to a server and shared with everyone who has a monitor. Safecast provides a real-time profile of radiation levels throughout Japan that rivals the data provided by the police and the government.[36]

By the roadside, decontamination crews are at work in masks, boots, helmets and gloves, all skin completely covered, bent over in the rain, scraping centimeters of soil into large plastic bags and carting them away for eventual storage on the site of the decommissioned plant itself. The decontamination teams are tested after every shift and if their radiation levels are too high, they are taken off the job, critics say, fired without compensation.

You'd think that science had settled the issue of what constitutes safe exposure. The Chernobyl standard for safe return of people from a radiated zone is 1 millisievert per hour, while in Japan the government has set the standard at 20. Antinuclear forces and environmental lobbyists—two of them are traveling with us on the bus—insist the government standard isn't safe.

One sievert—a thousand millisieverts—gives you a 5.5 percent chance of developing cancer or genetic damage to tissue. Those who were exposed at Hiroshima and Nagasaki to exposures in the 4,500 sievert range died of their exposure within a month.[37]

In the Fukushima Daiichi plant, at the height of the emergency, plant workers were exposed to radiation in the 170 to 180 millisievert range. Four years later, radiation levels there are still so high that only robots and remote-control devices can be used in decommissioning work.

To date, all the deaths in the Fukushima disaster—nearly twenty thousand—were caused by the tsunami, none by exposure to radiation. The doctors have examined three hundred thousand patients in Japan looking for thyroid cancer, and they've found eighty-eight cases so far, but no conclusive evidence that radiation was the cause.[38] It will take decades before we know Fukushima's true cost.

In an irradiated zone, it is easy to feel a certain uneasiness stealing over you. You expect the foliage to be bare, the rice paddies dry, the trees skeletal. In fact, the leaves are as shiny, the rice shoots as spiky green, and the big trees as heavy with foliage as anywhere else. The sheer normality is unsettling.

After ninety minutes on the bus, wending our way through the heavily forested valleys, we reach the coastal fishing port of Minamisoma and head to a fish processing plant that replaces one on the oceanfront site that was washed away four years earlier. The sea is visible at the exit to the harbor channel, gray and soundless through the rain and mist.

The fishmonger, Nagamasa Takahashi, wears a white bandana on his head, a yellow windbreaker, and knee-high boots. His face is pockmarked and wet with rain, and his muscular body is soaked through his jeans. He was born in Soma City, saw the tsunami wipe out his factory and his home. Now he's rebuilding a new fish processing plant, but not in Fukushima.

In the fish plant, a few workers in masks, white coats, boots, and plastic gloves are processing piles of gray octopus on metal tables, cutting them up and throwing the pieces into white plastic boxes for freezing or onward shipping. Every shipment gets scanned through a radiation detector and is certified safe, but Tokyo shoppers still won't touch anything sourced from here.

When I ask him what it was like right after the earthquake on March 11, he laughs and shakes his head ruefully. In a police photograph, taken from a helicopter about a minute before the tsunami hit, you get an idea of what the fishmonger would have seen: majestic white waves, cresting from one end of the horizon to the other, lit in a radiant March afternoon light, moving with awe-inspiring speed toward the shore.

When he realized the white line on the horizon was an incoming tsunami, he ran for safety to the sandy, pine-covered bluffs just behind the town. He watched as the wave, cresting higher than the light poles, swept over the plant, picked up boats out at sea and flung them back into the fields, demolished sheds, houses, decking, roads, shops, cars, and people running for their lives.

On the sandy bluffs above town, survivors of tsunamis centuries before had built a Shinto shrine; the shrine survived intact, while everything else below it, the modern plants, houses, dockyards, boat slips, were ripped apart in less than a minute.

At first light, the fishmonger returned to the lower ground and wandered among the debris. His friends' boats were lying in the streets and fields, upside down, on their sides, hulls out, masts down, and bodies still lay unrecovered here and there in the streets and the wharves.

Some bodies were never recovered, washed away into the sea, or buried so deep in the mud they could never be found. To this day, volunteers scavenge the beaches around town and occasionally find a wristwatch or a bone fragment, buried in the sand. Then followed months of clearing away debris, pulling boats out of fields, turning cars upright, getting the wreckage carted away, figuring out what could be saved and what had to be thrown away.

"We're a small community. Neighbors are friends. Everyone lost somebody."

He doesn't remember much about the long period afterward except the day, two months later, when he was in a local restaurant and they served him sashimi—a normal midday meal, in a normal place—and he began to cry.

In another district of Minamisoma we meet Shinoya Wakamatsu outside his miso and soy sauce shop. The tidy, bare shop is piled high with bags of soya, miso paste, and gallon jars of soya sauce. He is thirty-eight years old, the tenth generation of his family to make miso. He is wearing a blue apron over jeans and a white windbreaker. His hair is cut short. He is tall, thin, stooping, a seemingly nervous figure, with a large engaging smile. He has come out to speak to us, with the diary he kept of 2011 tucked under his arm. "If I didn't have this diary," he says, "I wouldn't believe what happened."

Right after the quake, a friend on the coast road phoned him and shouted that a tsunami was on its way. He had to drag his father to the car—frozen with disbelief and fear—but he managed to move the whole family to a local gymnasium where they slept on the floor. Then he went to the fire station to help out. "I remember," he says, "how they told us to be strong." He worked until the next morning, mostly digging dead bodies out of the debris. Some of them were his friends. The memory weighs on him. He came back to the gym at 4:00 a.m. and went to bed. "I deeply appreciated being alive."

Now he is worried about the future of his business. In times past, he explains, local farming families would bring their soya, and his family would make batches of miso for them. Now—and this trend has accelerated since the tsunami—there are fewer farmers. Many can't bring their soya anymore because their fields are contaminated. Others have given up and moved away. But his family keeps going. In the shed behind the house, miso is fermenting in vats, each one marked in chalk with a date and batch number.

I ask him about how he manages to carry on. We have been here for ten generations, he says, like the horse festival. I don't know what he means. He pauses, looks down at his miso vats, and then suddenly clenches his fists together, stiffens momentarily, and says, "We will persevere—*ganbare* is the word he uses—"like the samurai."

The horse festival, I later understand, is held at the end of July every year, commemorating a thousand-year-old tradition of the Soma clan of warrior samurai, renowned for their horsemanship. Their leader trained his men by letting wild horses loose and rewarding the warrior who could catch a wild one with bare hands and bring it safely to the temple. This feat is reenacted every year. Thousands of people line the streets of Haramachi and Minamisoma to watch the samurai riders, who come from all over Japan, parade through the city. The traditional head of the Soma clan, astride the lead horse, initiates the competition by blowing on a large conch shell. Temple streamers are launched into the sky, and as they tumble to earth riders and horses jostle each other to be the first to seize the yellow streamer and carry it in triumph.

When the tsunami hit, the horse festival was devastated. Stables were washed away, horses were drowned, and those that survived were found wandering among the wreckage, starved and dehydrated.

In the first summer after the tsunami, the festival was canceled, but in 2012 it returned. One twenty-year-old worker at Fukushima Daiichi who fled with his family to Chiba, south of Tokyo, told a reporter that the festival was his "motivation in life." If there were no festival, he said, "I would have abandoned my hometown." An older man had come back from living elsewhere in Japan as an evacuee. He told the journalist, "I will return as a descendant of Soma samurai, at any cost. My will is unshakable."[39]

The miso soup maker, I realized, had been telling me that if the horse festival had survived, they would survive too. It was as if he were reaching back, deep into time, to find an anchorage that he and his family could stand on, that could not be swept away by the waves. For him and for the people raised by the sea, the horse races were a vital symbol of continuity. They were still going on and always would, twenty miles from the reactor and half a mile from a sea that had turned ferocious and would, most certainly, do so again.

From Minamisoma we head south down coastal highway 6 after passing through a checkpoint manned by a police officer in a white helmet and mask, who looks over the bus driver's permission to enter and then waves us into the red zone.

In Namie, five miles from Fukushima Daiichi, everything is as it was seconds after the earthquake: a three inch fissure in a wall; a vase in pieces on the floor of a sitting room; the windows of a sunroom collapsed in shards; a store sign in English, "Suzuki watch, jewelry, optical," collapsed on the sidewalk; the bus shelter where the municipal buses turned around, empty; a sign saying "Louer: Total Beauty Salon" over a shuttered shop; and at the crossroads, the single streetlight blinking red, yellow, and green, on and off.

This part of town was damaged by the earthquake but spared by the tsunami. We get back into the bus and drive to the lower town on the coast road, where the sea becomes visible in the distance, white breakers pounding into the sand dunes, their sound faint and muffled.

In the photographs taken on this spot by the police days after the tsunami, there is nothing but wreckage as far as the eye can see: wooden houses pulverized so that nothing is recognizable except a door and here and there a fishing boat, hurled out of the ocean. Police in turquoise gloves, white decontamination suits, and goggles are poking the ruins with sticks in search of bodies. In Namie, 586 houses were washed away and a further sixty-five collapsed. One hundred and eighty-two people died. Thirty-two bodies were washed away and never recovered.

Now the plain is bare, empty, desolate, the wreckage carted away, and no sign that ten thousand people lived here except the straight lines where streets used to run, before the black wave ripped off all the road surface.

One of the two town officials who accompanies us, Masami Nakagawa, was not born here, but after the tsunami she left her private sector job in Tokyo to work here. People like her dropped what they were doing and volunteered with the Japanese Reconstruction Agency. Why? "Nothing seemed so worthwhile," she says quietly, and we stand together for a moment, looking across a bleak, wet landscape, under gray clouds, at the far end of which, about five miles away, we can see six bare concrete smokestacks of the Fukushima plant itself.

Does she still feel this way? Yes, she says, it was the best move she ever made.

People like her, she says, aren't the ones who deserve praise. The "invisible heroes," as she calls them, were the municipal officials who had to evacuate their citizens in the panic and chaos that followed and who have stuck with the evacuees in years since dealing with compensation, housing and rehousing, and the endlessly repeated question, which never gets a straight answer: When, if ever, will the 21,434 people who lived in the township be able to return?

The municipal workers in Namie faced excruciating tests of their own resilience in the immediate aftermath of the earthquake and tsunami. What should they do while waiting for orders that didn't come? What should they do when orders were contradictory or couldn't be carried out? How could they stick to the rules when desperate people, people they knew, neighbors, friends, relatives, pleaded that they were a special case?

When order began to collapse, the full brunt of chaos fell on the municipal workers. They had little preparation—a few evacuation drills no one could remember—and absolutely no information, except what they heard, like everybody else, on the car radio. It is their resilience that turns out to be the least noticed but the most important element in the Namie story.

Naoki Kobayashi was in a municipal car with a loudspeaker, going up and down the streets, telling people to escape when the tsunami hit. Now in his early thirties, he is a quiet, mild man, a town official who gives an impression of deep fatigue. "I can't really remember how it was," he says. "There was panic everywhere." All he will say is that had he been any closer, further out on the coast road, closer to the sea, he wouldn't have made it. He was driving back to higher ground when he saw, in his rearview mirror, the wave roaring up behind him, chasing him like a pack of black dogs.

His family's house was washed away, and for hours, until his mother showed up at the town hall, he didn't know where she was. He is still angry at the operating company, Tepco, for keeping them in the dark. Tepco evacuated two of their company towns, but left

Namie, five kilometers away from the nuclear plant, to fend for itself. The municipal workers took the decision to evacuate the town on their own. They used the community wireless system to contact mayors forty kilometers away to ask if they could evacuate their people there, and then they loaded them onto buses. Sometimes it took four successive evacuations before the evacuees found a permanent place to stay.

The memories of that time, which stretched on for weeks, then months, then years after the disaster, weigh on him. "The worst of it was being asked questions by our people and having no answers, absolutely no information. We felt the responsibility." It fell to these municipal workers, young, without instructions, to face tired, frightened neighbors and friends.

"We felt lonely and depressed," he says. "We were evacuees ourselves and separated from our families most of the time. We suffered very much from stress."

The rules were breaking down, the chain of command was inconstant—sometimes he'd get an order, sometimes he had to decide for himself—and as for procedures to follow, there was little if anything to go on. It was just the pressure of people's needs, their stark individuality, that he remembers: toothless old women in the gymnasium shouting at him that the rice balls the municipal soup kitchen were offering them were too hard for old people to eat, and the shame he felt—still feels—that he answered them harshly.

We inspect the gymnasiums, now empty, where the families of Namie stayed for months until temporary housing could be found. The gymnasiums were cold, unheated; families slept on the floors; the food was basic; the toilets were what you'd expect from a gym; in the photographs they show me you can see families clustering together on mats, with their shoes neatly lined up alongside, many of them wearing masks on their faces, some sitting quietly, cross-legged, hands over their ears to block out the noise, staring downward.

There were twenty-one thousand people in the town before the tsunami; the evacuees are now scattered throughout Japan, and in a recent survey nearly half said they will never return. So the town is planning for only five thousand inhabitants to return when the evacuation orders are lifted. No one knows when this will happen, perhaps after 2020 when the radiation hazard—and the half-life of caesium 137—begins to decay. I ask Naoki Kayobashi, now thirty-one, still unmarried, still working in a temporary office, thirty kilometers from his hometown, whether he will ever go home. He pauses. "That's what they say."

We have to leave Namie at dusk. The town officials stand in a little line and wave to us until we pull out of sight. We are left with our thoughts. I think of the improvised shrine to the dead on the bare blacktop that leads to the power plant: the plaster Buddhas, the wilting flowers, the Japanese sticks that families left with the names of the dead on them, the unopened beer cans the decontamination workers left around it as an offering, the burned-out candle ends. I think also of the new municipal graveyard, on the height of land where the school children of Namie fled to safety, the height of land that overlooks the desolate plain, now scraped bare of soil and signs of life, where people used to live, and now among the sandy bluffs filled with pines, where those who were claimed by the tsunami have been laid to rest.

The unimaginable is a fact of life, but it is also an alibi. We are bound to be taken by surprise by fate and the future, but we do learn how to cope. Resilience takes many moral forms, from the "artful dodgers" to the inspired teamwork of a group under pressure. It can be active, passive, selfish, and selfless; it can be learned, but it cannot be taught.

When we put together what we learned from the people who survived Fukushima, we could say that they taught us to understand resilience as a latent inner resource: tacit, bodily, physical, beyond words, instinctual, yet at the same time metaphysical, a belief that we can handle whatever the future holds in store. Resilience is also social and political: it depends on faith in public authorities, social networks, friends and family. All of this—instinctual, metaphysical, political—creates the confidence that generates the simple expectation that you will survive today and begin to recover tomorrow.

Resilience depends critically on institutions. The national government in Japan failed; so did Tepco. The institution that continued to function was municipal government. It was the untold resilience of the municipal workers who organized the evacuations and then stood by the evacuees that kept the tent pole of order above everybody's head.

Resilience rises to virtue when it expresses itself as responsibility for others. If we become capable of this virtue it is because we retain hope in the future of such a community. There is an unseen metaphysics at work here.

Resilience depends on some shared belief in a collective future worth fighting for. If there were no such hope, what would the point of resilience be? What would you want to survive for? No one wants to survive alone: that, surely, was the lesson of Robinson Crusoe.

There are varieties of hope, from "hoping for the best" to "hope against hope" to "radical hope," the capacity to believe in a future when all hope seems gone.[40] There are so many examples from the twentieth century—from Primo Levi to Nadezhda Mandelstam and Nelson Mandela—we have plenty of evidence that human beings can cling to hope and survive in even the darkest circumstances.[41]

The connection between hope and resilience is easily mocked, and no one did a more loving job of mockery than Charles Dickens in his depiction of the eternally foolish but eternally optimistic Wilkins Micawber, the character in *David Copperfield* who, whenever faced with difficulty, liked to say, "Something will turn up."[42] Micawberish is still the word we use for the form of hope that never rises above hopefulness.

The hope I am talking about is an ordinary virtue: it is free of hubris, and so it takes for granted, that we will not always be able to avoid the worst. At the same time, it is not misanthropic: it prepares for the worst but does not think the worst of human beings. It is anti-utopian: while it believes that over time we get better at learning from our mistakes, it does not have any faith that we can fundamentally change; it is rationalist but questions that History, with a capital H, is knowable. It draws faith from the past, from the memory of the samurai, but it also knows that sometimes all you can do is to keep moving, keep going toward the future, no matter how uncertain the destination. But resilience has an unshakeable, physical element of faith. It affirms that we do learn and that we are not condemned to endless repetition of our folly. This complex hope is, I believe, what underpins human resilience. It is more than a disposition, more than an inheritance, more than an attitude of responsibility toward others. It is also a metaphysical commitment, deep inside, usually left unspoken, to the future continuity of human life itself, no matter what, a commitment best expressed by the belief that we will not only survive but prevail.[43]

7

South Africa

After the Rainbow

IN THE BATTLE AGAINST THE STRONG, VIRTUE IS A MORE POTENT weapon for the weak than violence. In any trial of strength, the strong will prevail if force is the arbiter. The weakness of the strong lies in the moral domain. In the battle of ideas, those with virtue may have more legitimacy than those with weapons. The virtue we are talking about here is the rare kind, the one prepared to sacrifice for an ideal. Ordinary virtue can only knuckle down and endure oppression, but the extraordinary kind can bring tyranny to its knees. In sentencing Nelson Mandela to life in prison, the apartheid regime thought they were marooning him on Robben Island forever. Instead his imprisonment drained power from his captors. When he walked into freedom in 1990, he did so as a symbol of virtue triumphant. In Myanmar Aung San Suu Kyi achieved power through the same dynamic.[1]

The South African regime had no difficulty containing the violent threat from the MK, the African National Congress's armed guerrillas.[2] The challenge they could not turn back was virtue, in the form of an ANC diplomatic strategy that turned the regime into a moral pariah. The moral appeal of the ANC rested on two rival visions, the first enshrined in the African Charter, of a South Africa belonging to "all who live in it"—white, black, colored, and Asian—and the Pan-Africanist ideal of black self-determination and majority rule.[3]

What made Mandela's inclusive vision prevail after 1994 was its stark necessity. After his release, the country teetered at the edge of civil war. White elites and the ANC leadership alike were forced into partnership negotiations to move the country back from the brink. Both understood there was too much to lose. Thanks to this mutual recognition of the necessity of avoiding further bloodshed, the ANC became the first national liberation movement to take power in an advanced economy, with concentrated, capital-intensive industries dependent on foreign markets for sales and capital.[4]

These extraordinary conditions and the joint recognition that neither minority nor majority could prevail through violence help explain the further paradox that an African liberation movement with Marxist tendencies ended up creating a liberal democracy anchored in the most advanced liberal constitution anywhere in the world. The constitution promised property and security for the minority and political power and economic justice for the majority.

The ANC leadership's own experience of the law under apartheid helped them accept a liberal constitution.[5] Mandela came to understand, from his experience as both a lawyer and then as a defendant in apartheid-era courts, that law could sometimes protect the weak. This is why the ANC accepted an independent judiciary, rights of appeal, and the rule of law in the new constitution and why, when the Constitutional Court challenged one of Mandela's early decisions as president, he complied instantly.

Once the battle against apartheid was won, the alliance of virtue that brought it down began to fragment. To empower blacks, affirmative action had to send whites home. To empower blacks, Indians and Coloreds were left behind. The virtue of justice—which held the transition-era coalition together—now became the wedge that drove the races apart. The white minority accepted the new dispensation because it had nowhere else to go and because so many knew that apartheid was unsustainable.[6] Although black empowerment policies drove many whites out of the public realm, they soon found their feet in the private sector. Whites accepted minority status in politics in return for liberal constitutional guarantees. Afrikaners who had once withheld these guarantees from the majority now became the most passionate defenders of human rights and the rule of law.[7]

But the bargain was fragile. Property rights protected a distribution that left whites in possession of more than 90 percent of the arable land and most of the mines and mineral resources. Sooner or later, the rights that protected this distribution would come under challenge.

This was not the only dynamic slowly dissolving the 1994 settlement. The South African liberation movement conceded liberal checks and balances in order to secure power. Once in power, they resented institutional obstacles to their authority, like a free press, independent courts, and opposition parties.[8] In power, the ANC set out to tame independent institutions and to treat the opposition in parliament not as adversaries but as enemies. Within a short period of time, under President Thabo Mbeki and still more under President Jacob Zuma, the new elite justified their own corruption as the long-denied rights of the majority to their share of the spoils.

Mugabe's Zimbabwe showed the way to this new pattern of rule. In Kenya, likewise, the liberationists used power to enrich their own ethnic elites. In Rwanda, the victor of the liberation struggle has entrenched himself and his cadre in perpetual power. Across Africa, with exceptions such as Ghana, the pattern repeats itself. Why should South Africa's liberation movement not succumb to the same dialectic? President Zuma has appropriated millions in state funds to equip his private estate in his Zulu homeland; ANC cronies have siphoned off commissions from deals for weapons that South Africa neither needs nor can afford; state-owned airways, electric utilities, and power companies have all been pillaged by their new leadership.[9]

Western criticism goes unheeded because African dictators can always turn to China instead. China's loans and grants come with no human rights strings attached.[10]

So the question that anyone traveling to South Africa, twenty-five years after liberation, will ask is whether a story that began with virtue overcoming tyranny will end with tyranny's insidious return.

I first went to South Africa in September 1997 to report on the amnesty hearings of the Truth and Reconciliation Commission (TRC) in Port Elizabeth, an industrial town on the shores of the Indian Ocean.[11] The hearings were held in Centennial Hall in the heart of the black township of New Brighton. For a week I sat in the packed hall as white policemen, who had terrorized the community for decades, appeared on stage before a panel of three commissioners and pleaded for amnesty in return for full disclosure of beatings, torture, and extrajudicial killings of black dissidents, going back to the 1970s.

The listening audience, many wearing earphones so that they could hear English or Afrikaans testimony translated into their native Xhosa, were deeply attentive, and when a particular crime was described, a sound like the swell of an ocean wave would sweep across them, as they all let out a murmur of anger or pain.

The TRC was established to find truth, not only about the crimes of apartheid, but also about those of the liberation movement. Blacks resented the implied equivalence between the violence of a hated regime and the violence of a liberation struggle, but they accepted the TRC's jurisdiction over both because Mandela had asked them to. The township community was told that there was no chance to send people to jail for these crimes: the offenses dated back decades, the evidence had been destroyed, the South African deep state was impenetrable, and the loyalty of the ANC to its own perpetrators was unbreakable.[12] So amnesty was the bait the commission used to lure the perpetrators from their lair of silence.

At the time, I was impressed by the willingness of a whole society—the hearings were broadcast every night on South African television—to undergo the catharsis of truth in the name of what they called "reconciliation." It was never clear, however, what reconciliation meant exactly: being reconciled *to* the facts of apartheid? Being reconciled *with* the perpetrators? Reconciled to the fact that the liberation movement had "necklaced" opponents? Reconciliation meant these things, and all of them were hard work. Even then it was obvious that the work would take generations.

In the hall in New Brighton in 1997, I sat beside an implacable woman named Joyce Mtimkulu as she listened to two cops describe how they kidnapped her activist son Siphiwo in a Port Elizabeth street in 1982, threw him into the trunk of a car, drove him to a remote location, drugged him, shot him in the back of the head, then burned his body on a bonfire while they drank beer, finally collecting his cinders in a black garbage bag and tossing his remains into a nearby river. I went home to her tiny, neat-as-a-pin house in

New Brighton township and asked Joyce whether it was good to know the truth at last. Joyce had a regal presence and a queen's disdain. She scoffed: "What truth? They didn't tell the truth. That story—how they gave him drugs so he wouldn't feel the pain—that was a lie." To Joyce, it seemed a loathsome form of bad faith for the cops to have claimed they wanted to spare her son a final moment of suffering. This bad faith tarnished whatever truth the promise of amnesty had been able to extort from them. She wanted every last drop of truth, and she was furious that she had been shortchanged in the most important moral transaction of her life.[13]

Joyce was reconciled to the facts, such as they were, but how could she be reconciled to her son's killers? What cruel moral perfectionism, on the part of outsiders, could ever ask her to forgive them?

The virtues of truth, on the other hand, were easier to grasp. Establishing the cold facts, it seemed to everyone then, was vital for any political transition. If all sides failed to accept certain brute realities as a baseline, they could not create a common political future: instead, they would keep fighting over the past. That had been the pattern in Bosnia.

While no society ever lives in truth, just as no individual ever does, there is a small set of impermissible lies that can wreck a society's chances of transitioning from tyranny to freedom. For example, when I was in South Africa in 1997, it was easy to imagine that at some time in the future, when things got hard for the minority, some aging veterans of the apartheid era or even their children might be tempted to say the old days weren't so bad. Likewise, when things got hard for the ruling majority, they might be tempted to say: we are the heirs of a just war of liberation. All is permitted to us.[14]

Eighteen years later, in December 2015, I revisited the Centennial Hall in New Brighton to see whether the truth that the Truth and Reconciliation Commission had fought so hard to establish had vanquished the impermissible lies of apartheid and the liberation struggle alike. I was accompanied by Janet Cherry, a professor at the local university, who had attended the same amnesty hearings, working as a researcher for the commission. She is a white-haired, fine-featured woman in her fifties, born into a liberal academic family in Cape Town and committed all her life to the black struggle. We had both followed the Mtimkulu case, but she had a disorienting sequel to tell me. The police had testified that they had dropped the remains of Joyce's son in the Fish River, but later investigations showed that they had even lied about this: his bones were found at the bottom of a septic tank near the spot where they killed him. Why, we wondered, did they persist in lying about this? It was as if a tiny crack had appeared in the truth that the TRC had tried to establish as common ground under the feet of all South Africans.

And what about the impermissible lies? Yes, Janet Cherry said, in the white suburban gardens, there was plenty of nostalgia for the good old days, but at least nobody tried to pretend that apartheid wasn't built on torture and killing, just as none of the victors in the liberation struggle would still claim that the struggle was blameless.

Janet took me downtown to the Sanlam Building, a dark, derelict, hulk of a place, where she was interrogated several times in the 1980s. We stared upward at the stairway ascending into the dark, the long walk that so many took to the notorious sixth floor where the interrogations were held. This was where, in 1978, the black activist Steve Biko was beaten so badly that he died of his injuries.

Janet is proud, in an unassuming way, of her defiant younger self. She did not break under the interrogations at Sanlam, but keeping faith with the liberation struggle since then has never been easy. She cannot have been happy when the ANC went to court to try to prevent the TRC from reporting its findings about ANC torture of informers and terrorist attacks on civilians.[15]

As an activist proud of the broad alliance that defied apartheid in Port Elizabeth in the 1980s, Janet is dismayed at the way the ANC now claims that it was the only progressive force leading the struggle. The ANC were in guerrilla camps, in jail on Robben Island, or overseas. The actual struggle in Port Elizabeth, she remembers, was led by a local coalition of activists from all the races. Only now, the ruling ANC claims it led the struggle all the time in her town.

The ANC's re-writing of the history of the struggle in Port Elizabeth goes hand in hand with clumsy attempts to dominate local politics. This was on display later that afternoon. Janet took me to a demonstration against violence toward women on the seafront at Port Elizabeth. Levels of violence against South African women of all races are disturbingly high.[16] So we were marching in a vital cause, though the numbers who turned out on a fine December afternoon in the fading sunlight were disappointingly small. We set out, about a hundred strong, along the promenade in Port Elizabeth. Although the demonstration had not been called by the ANC, it was led by the head of the ANC women's league. The ruling party is everywhere, "hegemonic," taking over demonstrations, leading them from the front, insisting that the banners flown must be the green, yellow, and black of the ANC.

Janet and I watched as a trio of immaculate late-model white Mercedes sedans followed behind the marchers and gathered in the parking lot. At the end of the demonstration while the rest of us straggled home on foot, the heirs of the liberation struggle slid into their three luxury cars and were borne swiftly away.

In 1997, South Africans watched the Truth and Reconciliation hearings on television. In 2012, they watched the proceedings of the Marikana inquiry, held after a police shooting at which thirty-four miners were killed. The contrast between the two illuminates the road South Africa has traveled since liberation.

Marikana is a platinum mine, northeast of Johannesburg, owned by Lonmin, a London-based company with prominent figures on its nonexecutive board, including Cyril Ramaphosa, deputy president in the ruling ANC government.

On August 10, 2012, the rock drillers at Marikana walked off the job, demanding a pay increase. When their union, the National Union of Mineworkers (NUM), refused to take their claim to the management, the strikers marched in protest to the NUM offices. There they were met with gunfire, apparently from the union offices. Two strikers died. The next day, union officials were found dead at the mine site. The wildcatters, armed with spears and knives, then marched on the Lonmin offices, where they were met with tear gas and rubber bullets. In the melee that followed, two Lonmin security guards were killed. Police then surrounded the strikers, now led by a young rock driller nicknamed Mamboush.[17] In negotiations with the police, Mamboush, wrapped in a bright green blanket, agreed that his men would disarm if they were allowed to march to the "mountain," an outcrop of barren red rocks in the middle of the mine area. Instead of respecting this agreement, the police fired tear gas to disperse them, and two policemen were killed. Over the next two nights, the strikers, now numbering three thousand, camped out around the mountain. They were now fully armed with spears, knives, and pangas—and equipped with charms provided by traditional healers, the Sangoma, that the strikers believed would turn police bullets into water. Lonmin, represented by a black vice president, refused to negotiate, and attempts by others to intercede came to nothing. Meanwhile, Cyril Ramaphosa, working on behalf of the Lonmin, appealed to the police and the ANC government to use force to end the strike.

When the end came on the afternoon of August 16, 2012, it was sudden and brutal. As Mamboush led a group of armed strikers down the mountain, the police opened fire. In the initial fusillade sixteen were killed, including Mamboush, who dropped to the dust at the policemen's feet, still wrapped in his green blanket, with fourteen bullets in his body. In the subsequent twenty minutes, the police clambered among the rocks on the mountain and shot sixteen more strikers, some as they tried to surrender, others in the back of the head. It was the worst police killing since the Sharpeville massacre of 1960 under apartheid.[18]

When the head of the South African police appeared before the press the day after the killings, she praised her force for doing a good job.[19] Her police commander that day—a black woman—had learned her trade under apartheid. It was shocking for South Africans to discover that apartheid methods had worked their way into the muscle memory and moral instincts of the police of the new South Africa.

Marikana is more than a fable about the deadly persistence of human contempt from one regime to another. It is also a devastating story of the failure of South African institutions: a union so alienated from its own workforce that its stewards chose to fire on their own strikers; a black executive of Lonmin so subservient to his London bosses that his only instinct was to use violence against fellow citizens; a vice president of the country pleading that blacks like him had no real control over "the system"; a judicial commission of inquiry so timorous about taking on the ANC that it never attributed criminal responsibility to anybody; a prosecution service that initially charged the strikers, not the police, with murder and then abandoned prosecutions altogether, so that three years later no one has been held responsible for shooting fleeing strikers in the back.

Why did liberal institutions all fail to protect a group of poor and unschooled miners in the country's key industry? Certain realities become clear when you listen to the female chief of the South African police service as she gives testimony in the Marikana inquiry. Her sullen and contemptuous gaze makes it obvious she knows she is inviolable. In a one-party state, as long as she pleases the ruling clique, who can touch her?

Deserted by the institutions of their own country, the strikers reverted to long-buried traditions of their rural homelands, putting their faith in healers who gave them charms to ward off bullets, and so they advanced, in warrior style, bending low and clashing their weapons together, trusting in their own strength but still unable to conceive that the police created to serve a free society would shoot them down like dogs.

It took nine seconds of indiscriminate shooting plus twenty minutes of targeted assassination to crush the strikers and to send a message to every worker in South Africa: if you challenge your employers, challenge your unions, the black South African state will crush you just as surely as the white apartheid state once did.

Janet Cherry teaches history and development studies to black students at the Nelson Mandela University campus situated in the heart of New Brighton. The social landscape of apartheid is still visible outside: a hundred yards away is an informal settlement, a straggling cluster of tin and wattle-and-daub shacks. Down the hill, however, change has come, new concrete and brick houses built by the national housing agency.

Janet teaches the "born frees," students born after apartheid and now entering the once all-white universities of South Africa in record numbers. They are the generation who launched the campaign

Rhodes Must Fall that took down the statue of Cecil Rhodes from its plinth at the University of Cape Town in April 2015. This victory helped launch a second campaign in the fall of 2015, Fees Must Fall, which spread across all South African universities. They sought pay increases for the largely black ancillary staff, as well as an end to Afrikaans as a language of instruction, arguing that the nine African languages—Xhosa, Zulu, and the others—were not taught equally. These demonstrations brought South African universities to a standstill that continued throughout 2016.[20]

Why, one wonders, should "born frees" be so deeply alienated from a society whose institutions, at least nominally, were built to empower them? In conversations with students over the next few days, several themes became clear. For black students, gaining access to white universities was not liberating, just intimidating and finally infuriating.[21] White students took laptops and cell phones for granted; black students might not have electricity at home; white students were nonchalant about student debt, while black students could be crushed by it. In class, white students could show off the head start that private schools were giving them, while black students struggled to catch up. Most of all, born-free black students felt marooned: no longer assured of a place in a prosperous future yet unable to return to rural homelands where there was no work.[22] For this generation, then, liberation left them betwixt and between, at home nowhere.

What frightened the government was how rapidly the student protest spread, how little control ANC student organizations had over the protests, and how openly scornful the students were of the president, his party, and its record in government. Within weeks, President Zuma capitulated, though nobody believes he would keep the promises he made to end the crisis.[23]

Zolisa Marawu, a hulking twenty-four-year-old sociology student, with "Death by Fees" chalked on his T-shirt, was one of the protest leaders in Port Elizabeth. He lives with his mother, a schoolteacher, in a nearby township and is studying educational sociology. He leans back in his chair, languid, bulky, and bitingly articulate. Zolisa's contempt for the ANC is visceral:

> For me, the ANC is a little mafia; to get services you have to be connected to certain people; it is a network of privilege similar to apartheid; it exploits you and then oppresses the people. It is not my government. My people are sitting at home for five to ten years, and the ANC will bring in some kind of corporate program to pick up trash and they will promote that as "job creating" just to get votes. So they create dependency. It is a way to prolong the power of the ANC, not the power of the people.

You might assume that he would be lapping up the message from Julius Malema and his Economic Freedom Fighters, anti-ANC populists who are campaigning for white expropriation, but Zolisa is just as scathing about Malema.

So where do you go if you are trying to free yourself from the shadow of Mandela and the false promise of his heirs? Zolisa wants to follow in his mother's footsteps and become a teacher. Every schoolteacher in the township, he's learned from his mother, has to be a social worker, going into the homes, working with the parents, solving family crises, finding jobs for kids, helping them when they lose heart. He talks about creating schools that would be centers for community organization and mobilization. "We aren't making political agents; we are making dependents."

Here Zolisa—and the born-free generation for which he speaks—touches a core irony of liberation: the ANC set out to raise millions out of poverty, and more than 16 million South Africans now receive some kind of welfare benefit.[24] Like the Bolsa Familia in Brazil, these payments kept a promise of liberation, but they also create dependency, cementing the ruling party's grip on a grateful, patient, but submissive electorate.

I talked next to Khrusta Mtsila, a thin and wiry union official from the National Union of Metalworkers of South Africa (NUMSA), a left-wing breakaway union, part of an emerging anti-ANC movement. Mandela was always too eager to accommodate the whites, he says. The whole point of liberation was to transfer economic power to the black majority. That never happened. "People are fed up with corruption and stagnation. People have lost faith." The time has come, Khrusta said, for expropriation of the land held in white hands and its redistribution to poor blacks.[25] What about the constitution, I ask? Don't the rights of owners have to be protected? Khrusta replies: "The poor do not have any access to justice. They can't get justice because they don't have the finances."

Even so, I ask, is radical land redistribution the answer? What about Zimbabwe? There the so-called veterans of the liberation struggle took over prosperous white-run farms and in a few years had run them down to ruin. Is that the model he wants to follow? Khrusta stiffens: Zimbabwe's reform was not "an outright failure," he says with irritation. It's a media exaggeration.

The reluctance of South African leaders to criticize Mugabe and his disastrous land reform starts at the top, with Mandela and Mbeki, who rebuffed all Western efforts to enlist them to put pressure on their liberator brother.[26] Yet the same reluctance to criticize Mugabe is all too evident in the ANC's fiercest critics.

Another student, Quama Zondani, has been listening to my exchange with the union leader. Quama is twenty-three, round-faced, wearing a bright yellow T-shirt. "Maybe Zimbabwe was not radical enough," he says.

The issue here isn't really Zimbabwe or land reform, but the South African constitution and the 1994 settlement that protected the property rights of the whites. Quama warms to his subject:

> A constitutional crisis is coming.... The constitution seeks to protect the oppressor. It is an obstacle to liberation. My ancestors did not take up arms to share a toilet with a white man or woman. We will have to revolt. We see the constitution as going out of its way to protect private property claims that were gotten in dubious ways.

When I say the same constitution that protects white property protects black property too, against seizure by an ANC government perhaps, Quama's eyes narrow.

It's hard to listen when the born frees praise Mugabe's land seizure program, which reduced the breadbasket of Africa to ruin.[27] But later, when we travel through Kwazulu Natal province, I see why the land issue is so aggravating. It is as if the very landscape of their country screams at the younger generation: you own nothing. As you travel north from Durban, up the highway to the Mozambique border, you pass intensively farmed sugar cane estates on both sides of the highway, owned by multinationals, followed by forests of eucalyptus, also owned by the same multinationals; in the distance are the huge mines of Richard's Bay and the long lines of freight cars carrying coal for shipment to China. After the multinational holdings, the road traverses the traditional tribal homelands, run by tribal rulers, some of whose cows wander across the roads. There seem to be few, if any, small-scale African farmers: the homelands that apartheid forced them onto was the worst land, suitable only for grazing; and what wealth does accumulate there ends up in the hands of the chiefs, whom the regime pays off with cars and bribes.

In the homelands you do see a few new roofs, electricity lines, and concrete paths between the huts, but apart from this, liberation has brought little change. About twenty miles from the Mozambique border we gave a lift to the local health worker, wearing his government ID badge on his dirty blue coat. He goes from house to house taking swabs and samples to check for malaria. There's been none in his village for ten years, but down the road, five villagers had died in the past year. When I ask him whether anything's changed in the past twenty years in his village, he thinks, looks out at the forest, then into my eyes, and slowly shakes his head.

So when you hear this, when you notice the way South African cities empty out at Christmas, as the black men and women who work in the restaurants, hotels, and factories head back to their rural homelands, to places where little if any has changed for the better you begin to see why radical redistribution of land might be deeply appealing. The constitution will allow white owners to stage a long opposition—and like all such struggles for justice, it will divide, dismay, and discourage international investors, but the coming confrontation is looming.

For the generation that inherited Mandela's settlement, the very institutions of the new South Africa entrenched inequality. As the transition disappoints, as growth slows, as black empowerment fails to meet the needs of a young generation, the search for someone or something to blame narrows to one scapegoat: white privilege.

The phrase is on everyone's lips. Angry black students tell me they are tired of having to educate their white colleagues that such privilege exists. Whites reply that it is less and less plausible to blame all of South Africa's woes on less than 10 percent of the population. A South African journalist, Ferial Haferjee, has grown so perplexed by this discourse that she has written a book, *What If There Were No Whites in South Africa?*, that points out, tartly, that South Africa's problems would not be solved even if all white wealth were handed to blacks. She writes:

> Everywhere I turn a generation born free is in chains. Everywhere I turn, a generation born free is talking as if it is at once obsessed by and imprisoned by whiteness and white supremacy. The black obsession with whiteness and white privilege is all, it seems, we ever talk about in sustained ways in our national conversation.[28]

Janet Cherry is troubled by the revival of the rhetoric of white privilege. It means that the born frees she teaches have given up on the coalition that brought apartheid to its knees.[29] It depresses her, after thirty years of fighting side by side with black activists, to hear her students say that the problems in South Africa could be solved through expropriations. She believes the real problem is economic. When the local Volkswagen factory advertises a single job, thousands queue up. It makes no sense to denounce Volkswagen as an instrument of white domination. The company is not blameless, it is not a charity, but it has provided the best jobs in town for seventy years. The tragedy, the real one, is that there just aren't enough jobs to go around.[30]

Then there is Zama Zama: an informal settlement where about nine hundred people live in the middle of the bare and rocky veldt about half an hour's drive from Pretoria. In the Zulu language, Zama Zama originally meant someone who scavenges illegally for ore in mineshafts, but the definition has widened to describe anyone trying to achieve something against the odds.[31] The odds to be overcome in Zama Zama are terrifyingly steep. Informal settlements exist by the thousands in South Africa: they are in a zone of exclusion and desperation all their own. Townships like New Brighton and Kwa-zikele may be poor, but like the favela of Santa Marta in Rio, they have policing, services, municipal government, hospitals, combi taxis to shuttle workers to jobs, and social workers to look after mothers with children. Informal settlements like Zama Zama have nothing at all: no heat, light, sewers, sanitation, police, transport, or governance. The ANC state has abandoned them as completely as the apartheid regime ever did.

It is a straggling warren of tin, cardboard, plywood, and wattle shacks in the rocky red-brown veldt by the side of the road, the kind of place you might not even notice as you drive past. The people who live there are from Limpopo, a poor northern province; others are migrants from Zimbabwe, driven south by the wreckage Mugabe has made of his economy. About a third of the men manage to find some work, but most of the women have just ended up there, living day to day, month to month, year to year. They may have come because an aunt, a mother, a sister, or a brother had come there trying to get work in Johannesburg or Pretoria, but when no work could be found they ended up here, on welfare if they can get it, living in shacks open to the winds, the rains, the mud, and the freezing cold. The police drive by but don't stop; a municipal water truck occasionally shows up; there is a school an hour down the road, but it is full and can only take a child from Zama Zama when a vacancy opens up. Apart from a tired white social worker and her eager young black assistant, the South African state is nowhere to be seen.

We've been brought here by a Christian charity named after a verse in the Bible—James 1:27. If you look it up, it says,

> Pure and undefiled religion before God the Father is this:
> to care for orphans and widows in their misfortune and to
> keep oneself unstained by the world.[32]

The charity's director is Robert Botha, a South African diplomat in Paris who heard the call and turned his life upside down in obedience to the scriptural injunction that gives his charity its name. He is a large, anxious, driven man who serves his faith with a certain blunt realism. He tells me that working in Zama Zama is chaotic. Criminals and drunks prey on the women at night, people make promises to turn their lives around and just can't; almost everyone is damaged, by idleness and unemployment, by drugs, alcohol, HIV, and abuse going back to their childhood, for which, he says, there is only one possible cure: unconditional love, if only he, or someone, could provide it. For all the difficulties, he can point to the results that come from faith: the school, run by a Zimbabwean woman, provides three meals a day to fifty children in a pair of shipping containers; behind the container is a vegetable patch which provides tomatoes and zucchini for the school soup; and the settlement doesn't have to wait for the water truck because they can now get a trickle of water from a new well.

We are delivering diapers, food, and baby clothes to a particular shack in the middle of the settlement. It is a baking Saturday afternoon, the radios in the *shebeens* are blaring, and the men there are sitting in the shade, drinking, arguing, and playing cards. We find the shack we're looking for, a tiny, neat structure of white plaster board, without windows, marked off from next door by an immaculately swept dirt yard, fenced off by interwoven branches. A two-year-old boy is playing in the yard, and in the doorway stands a smiling, long-haired girl, who must be between eighteen and twenty, holding a tiny baby boy swaddled tightly in a blanket. Inside, in the darkness, are two more tiny baby boys, also tightly swaddled despite the stifling heat and laid out on a single bed in a scene that combines neatness and exemplary domestic care with absolute destitution. There are no windows, no light, no heating in the winter, a cardboard box for a night table: the mother and the little boy will sleep in a single bed, and the triplets will sleep in a makeshift cot. We hold the babies one by one: they are thin little creatures, eyes closed, struggling in the heat. Robert Botha says if they don't gain weight soon they will have to go to the regional hospital. We lay the diapers down, the plastic bag with the water and the groceries, and the mother smiles broadly. She is so young it is painful to imagine how she copes, how she keeps the yard swept, how she makes sure her little boy doesn't run away and get himself hurt; how she gets enough nourishment herself to suckle three tiny, desperate mouths. Yet she is unafraid, unabashed, unfazed by it all, grateful for the groceries and happy to hear that Robert and his team will be back the following week. One of Robert Botha's donors has promised to keep up the support, who knows for how long. As we leave her, I think to myself that we have been in the presence of ordinary virtue that is somewhere between brave and desperate.

We return to the school, and sitting on children's chairs in the middle of the single classroom we talk to several young women—Ophelia, Mpo, Portia, and Shelly—who work there, helping out with the children or preparing food. They all have dreams—Portia says shyly it is the idea of becoming a "financial lawyer"—and then came Zama Zama. They all have children, but there do not seem to be men with whom they could have a family. They live with an aunt, or their mother, or a grandmother, and one day follows another, in the same unchanging rhythm. "I get up in the morning," Ophelia says, "I clean the house and feed the children and then I sit and think about life. Later I play cards with Shelly. We go to the *shebeen*. We drink, then we do some *jiga jiga,* then go home to sleep, wake up the next day, same thing." They laugh shyly about the *jiga jiga,* the transactional sex with the men who have jobs and some money, the sex that provides them with a cell phone, a hat, or a pair of shoes.

They speak in their native language, and Andrew, the young trainee social worker, who is also from Limpopo, translates for us. When the girls are finished talking and sit quietly looking at the floor, or playing with their cell phones, I ask Andrew why he wants to be a social worker here. He says, in a whisper, that he lost his mother to Aids and he does not want people to get sick like she did. He came from a poor village, he said, where the old people did not know how to write their name. He looks at me shyly and says the word "empower"; yes, he wants to empower these young women so that their lives do not end as his mother's did, so that before they die they can at least write their own names.

Liberation was supposed to reach Zama Zama, to sweep those shacks and *shebeens* away, to make it possible for Portia to become the "financial lawyer" she dreamed of being. Only now, twenty years on, she and her friends live disempowered to a degree that makes the idea that they are equal citizens of a free country a cruel illusion. The political elites in their white Mercedes sedans have given up on Ophelia, Mpo, Portia, Shelly, and the young mother with triplets in the shack. Informal settlements are problems easily pushed into a file labeled too hard to solve. It's so much easier to blame it on white privilege or the apartheid legacy.

South Africa was supposed to be different. The constitution promised all citizens a right of access to housing. In 1998 a group of poor people in an informal settlement decided to take their constitution at its word. One winter morning, municipal bulldozers in Wallacdene, a settlement outside Cape Town, crashed through the shacks and bulldozed them into a big pile, leaving about five hundred people suddenly homeless. One of the settlers, Irene

Grootboom, found a lawyer, and he took their case right up to the Constitutional Court. Amazingly, the Court found in their favor. No, the poor people didn't have a right to a house–if the court granted that right, millions of people would start clamoring for one too–but the people in an informal settlement did have the right to have "access" to housing, meaning that the municipality couldn't just bulldoze them out of their homes: their government had to help them find permanent shelter. The court ordered the government to find a way to meet the people's needs. Months later, the ANC government came back and dumped a pile of paper on the judges' desk. Arthur Chaskalson, the chief justice of the Court, a man who had represented Nelson Mandela during the Rivonia trial, went through the papers, and when it came time to ask the authorities a question, his was simple: "Could you show me the page where it tells Irene Grootboom how she gets a house?"[33] The authorities had no answer. Eight years later, having won her victory in a case about economic and social rights that law schools around the world assign to their students, Irene Grootboom died of cancer. When she died, she was still living in a shack. The new South Africa never did find her–and the people in her informal settlement–a home.[34] The lesson–which they need to teach in law schools–is that the best constitution in the world won't give poor people their rights unless elites, especially elected officials, feel a daily obligation, and political pressure too, to make constitutions deliver what they promise.

Four of the countries–Brazil, Myanmar, Bosnia, and South Africa–that we visited on this journey are living through transitions to liberal democracy that never seem to arrive at their destination. The stakes are moral as well as material: to find justice for the poor and excluded of the favelas of Rio; in Myanmar to return a country to the community of nations; in Bosnia, to find reconciliation among peoples who invented the term "ethnic cleansing"; and in South Africa to build a political community of citizens that would end the crippling poverty of the Zama Zamas.

In Brazil, Myanmar and South Africa, the transitions were driven by political pressure from within. Only in Bosnia was freedom imposed by external force, which may explain why Bosnians never felt they owned their institutions or the freedom those institutions conferred. In the three other cases, the challengers for power were successful because they used virtue as a weapon. They delegitimized the existing class in control and sapped their moral right to rule.

In all four countries the pressure of expectation and frustration is high, and in all four the goal remains distant. In Bosnia, twenty-five years since Dayton, the three peoples have still not moved beyond a zero-sum politics of ethnic competition and elite corruption. In Brazil, even after more than a decade of the workers' party in power, economic exclusion remains the fate for millions of the marginalized poor; in Myanmar, the National League for Democracy will have to figure out how 135 different ethnicities and religions can now join together, under the Lady's leadership, to build a country that can return to the world.

The question for South Africa is whether liberal democracy can escape the iron law of oligarchy, the ineluctable tendency of newly empowered elites to degrade the institutions explicitly created to put limits on their corruption. The portents are not favorable, and in the new generation there is something ominous for the ANC: a scathing contempt for their moral mandate, for the very claim that, having endured Robben Island, they are entitled to rule forever. After the Rhodes Must Fall campaign, Sisonke Msimang a young blogger, directly challenged the historical core of the ANC's moral authority:

> Your role in the revolution will not save you. Your history of speechmaking and sleeping in a cold detention cell will not save you. Not even backbreaking labor on Robben Island will spare you the skepticism of today's champions of freedom.[35]

The municipal elections of 2016 administered a withering rebuke to the ANC, and now the question becomes whether the opposition parties, given the chance to govern in Port Elizabeth and Pretoria, can demonstrate that the voters' faith in them was not misplaced.[36] If they can create a reputation for honest administration, it will serve the opposition parties well when they confront the ruling ANC in national elections.

One lesson to take home after visiting all four countries in transition, but especially South Africa, is that transitions are not redemption dramas. Instead of seeing transition as a tough struggle between elites determined to use power for their own purposes and a populace struggling to get their hands on at least some of the fruits of democracy, outsiders fall prey to the illusion that transition is a redemption story in which good triumphs over evil. For a global audience South Africa offered this fantasy in its purest form. This is why the global identification with the rainbow nation was so strong and why disillusion with it now is so intense. Today, after twenty years of disillusion, official South Africans still talk about "radical transformation" as if it is the next step. You see the phrase inscribed on the backs of the yellow T-shirts worn by ANC supporters. Transformation is yet another redemption fantasy, deployed by an ANC leadership desperate to conjure up the fading magic of the Mandela legacy. Yet the path that Mandela took was not the path of redemption, but something much more modest and attainable: the path of liberal freedom, enshrined in the 1994 Constitution. In politics, as he understood better than his successors, there is no redemption, only a struggle for power in which the best hope of an equilibrium lies in an institutional settlement that rewards the virtues of restraint and duty.

There is a wider lesson to be drawn from the four transitions we have studied and from the illusions and disillusions that they engendered both inside and outside. All of these transitions, after all, sought to achieve democracy grounded in liberal constitutionalism. They all sought to make liberal freedom possible for millions of people who had never known it before.

The point about liberal freedom is that it is non-redemptive. It is not visionary and does not seek to transform anyone or anything, still less human nature; it has no project of salvation. It has humble but precise ambitions: to protect human beings from themselves, from our own lust for domination and our inveterate taste for cruelty. Liberal freedom protects human beings by means of institutions.[37] Limited government, countervailing power, constitutional rights, markets regulated by law: liberal freedom uses these institutions in order to enable the ordinary virtues to flourish among free citizens.

Liberal freedom has its own epistemology: the belief that public truth is found in competitive debate. With that epistemology comes a moral corollary: that no citizen has a monopoly on truth and that the very purpose of politics is to shelter and protect the conditions of free debate. With this comes a further corollary: that in the community of free citizens there are no enemies, only adversaries, and that opposition is a precondition for any successful search for collective truth.

A regime of liberal freedom is not everyone's cup of tea. It is not attractive to religious or secular ideologues who believe they have privileged access to the truth. It is downright repulsive to populists who believe that democracy is simply majority rule. So liberation movements and populist democrats chafe against its restrictions; majorities resent the rights that keep minorities safe.

Liberal freedom is not even egalitarian. It believes that the question of justice in a society is about whether everyone has enough—down there in Zama Zama, or in the Rio favela—not whether the rich have too much. Liberal freedom believes law is there to keep markets honest and competitive, not to determine what a just distribution of income should be.[38]

So, roughly speaking, it is a political ideal that socialists and communists do not like because it contains no redemptive promise of egalitarian justice; conservatives like it even less because its primary concern is with the freedom of individuals, not with the preservation of tradition, religion, or communal values.

When global audiences invested the South African transition with redemptive hope, they misconceived what liberal freedom is. They also succumbed to the illusion that liberal freedom comes with guarantees and that good institutions can always save a country from bad rulers.

It should not be a surprise, in fact, that power corrupts liberators. Redemption stories carry with them the illusion that countries can escape this iron law, just as redemption carries the fantasy that countries can escape their history.

In the primal redemption narrative in all politics—Moses and the Israelites fleeing the land of the Pharaoh, the Old Testament tells us that Moses himself never secured redemption. He never lived to see the Promised Land. He did not cross "over Jordan" as the American slave spirituals once sang. As he lay dying, the Bible says, with cruel precision, he could actually see the Promised Land from his deathbed (Deuteronomy 34).

Let's remember what we *can* see from where we stand in the midst of these transitions that have no end. No one is in jail because of their race or their political opinions in South Africa—that is progress. Every black child born in the country knows that they have the right to vote and choose their rulers. That is progress. More people have roofs over their heads than they did in 1994, and more have electric light and a toilet. This is progress. Progress is progress. It's just not redemption or reconciliation. But it is something.

At a beach restaurant in Port Elizabeth we eat our lunch—beside a deafening class of forty or so primary school boys and girls, all in uniforms, from every race, on an outing on the last day of class before summer break. They are eight-to-ten-year-olds, the girls working on their coloring books, a black girl and a white girl side by side in rapt concentration, while the boys rush about, pushing each other, teasing, goofing around. You feel that the future of a country is prefigured here in this ordinary scene. It will be thirty years before we know how the story turns out. Will the old aversions revive, the old apartness reinstate itself, as these children become adults and compete for mates and positions and jobs? These questions have no answer, but looking at these children you have to believe that the answers are not already given and that the possibilities before them remain open.

In the late afternoon I return for a walk on the beach and come upon a group of teenagers, from a local high school, collecting their towels, their boards, their flip flops and T-shirts, preparing to head home. A ruggedly built black teenager, chest bare, and a dark-haired white girl wearing a shirt over her bikini linger behind. They might be sixteen. They are entwined: she has her arms around his neck and her leg wrapped around one of his. They stand motionless, looking out at the tide coming in: their heads incline and touch as they watch the waves. They are still for minutes. Then they come out of their trance and run to catch up to the others.

In South Africa the virtues at work in this simple scene—the trust and the desire—are not yet ordinary. The fact that young men and women of different races meet, fall in love, live together registers differently here than in other places. Inter-racial sex and inter-racial marriage were banned, and even under freedom they remain rare.

As incomes in South Africa rise, races do interact more frequently, and then over time they invite each other into more intimate domestic spaces.[39] The wealthier people are, the less suspicious of other races they turn out to be, the more they desire to interact. A lot turns on whether South Africa can grow an economy that makes racial concord a little easier.

As inter-racial contact becomes "ordinary," South Africa could enter a "normal" world where attraction is individual, singular, never race-meeting-race, just one soul and body desiring another. Consciousness of difference would never disappear, but over time, with decent politics, inclusive public goods, and social peace, individual characteristics—physical traits, ethical character, personal history, and moral behavior—would supplant race as the basis of human relations. Then inter-racial sex and marriage become ordinary, and it is their ordinariness that would be progress.

When one tries to peer into South Africa's future, a lot turns on what happens to that black boy and that dark-haired white girl who held each other on the beach and looked at the sunset together. A lot turns on how, in years ahead, they will remember that moment, whether they subsequently rejected being together in a return to their own race or whether that moment allowed them to see each other just as two people, figuring out what it means to desire another, free to choose or reject, link or break apart, as they wished. What you want for those young people, on the brink of adult life, is simply that being together would be ordinary, not a statement, not a heroic act, just one moment of attraction in a fulfilled life for both of them. That would be freedom. The whole point of a liberal society is to create laws and institutions that make virtue ordinary. In a decent society, love should not require anyone to be a hero.

Conclusion

Human Rights, Global Ethics, and the Ordinary Virtues

IN A SPEECH GIVEN AT THE UNITED NATIONS IN 1958 TO commemorate the tenth anniversary of the Universal Declaration of Human Rights, when she was already seventy-four years old, Eleanor Roosevelt took stock of the progress that human rights had made in the preceding ten years. The president's widow didn't measure its progress by the number of human rights treaties that had been negotiated or ratified. Instead she asked what difference human rights had made in the moral lives of ordinary people. After all, she asked, where do universal human rights begin? Her answer, apparently extemporaneous, has become one of the most frequently quoted remarks she ever made:

> Where, after all, do universal human rights begin? In small places, close to home—so close and so small that they cannot

be seen on any maps of the world. Yet they are the world of the individual person; the neighborhood he lives in; the school or college he attends; the factory, farm, or office where he works. Such are the places where every man, woman, and child seeks equal justice, equal opportunity, equal dignity without discrimination. Unless these rights have meaning there, they have little meaning anywhere. Without concerted citizen action to uphold them close to home, we shall look in vain for progress in the larger world.[1]

For Mrs. Roosevelt the test of human rights' historical impact was whether human rights as law had strengthened the virtues of ordinary human beings. If not, law acted in vain.

Mrs. Roosevelt's question is a way of drawing together our conclusions about the question that this book has explored: whether moral globalization, in particular the spread of human rights, has changed the ordinary virtues, whether the new global ethics of our time have made people more tolerant, trusting, and assertive of their rights in daily life.

The first thing to notice is how rarely we ask Mrs. Roosevelt's question. Those who study the human rights revolution since 1945 measure its progress using metrics like state ratification of conventions, state compliance with human rights pressure, the variable incidence of human rights abuses, and so on.[2] Those who tell the story of the human rights revolution as a story of progress have been quick to assume that once human rights was promulgated as the official discourse of states it must have had some influence on the ordinary virtues. Human rights scholars are only just beginning to measure, in any serious way, whether it actually does.

Our journey for the Carnegie Council gave us some evidence that Mrs. Roosevelt's rights revolution has been part of a long-prepared and momentous change in the rules of moral standing. Everywhere we went, whether it was in the doorway of a favela, a tin shack in South Africa, or a dusty street in Mandalay, everyone we talked to took it for granted that their voice counted for something. In three years of journeys across four continents, we never encountered anyone who did not meet our gaze, who averted their eyes and looked away in shame at their own moral status. Everyone simply took it for granted that they had the right to engage with, disagree with, joke with us, the curious strangers from far away. Of course, Mrs. Roosevelt's human rights revolution is not the only reason why, everywhere we went, ordinary men and women met our gaze. The rights revolution of the post-1945 era is only one moment in the much longer history that created the modern idea of human equality. Centuries of struggle against the commerce in human beings universalized the norm, already proclaimed in the world's great religions, that all human beings have a protected moral status. Since 1945, this consciousness, once confined to religious egalitarians, revolutionaries, and antislavery campaigners, has come to shape the moral thinking of billions of people around the world. The tumultuous struggles against empire abroad and racial discrimination at home affirmed the equality of all peoples and their right to rule themselves. After the fall of the Soviet Union in 1989, liberal constitutions entrenched democratic equality as a worldwide norm.

Let us not be so naïve as to suppose that the liberal revolution has carried all before it. Equality in law and ethics may be the new norm in constitutions and moral discourse alike, but inequalities of power and status, of voice and entitlement, remain everywhere. At the same time, every person we met on our journeys simply took for granted their right to speak and be heard. Moral globalization, when considered as a long struggle for equality, has resulted, everywhere we went, in a new norm of equal voice. Obviously, equality meant more than voice rights to the people we spoke to, but since we were in dialogue, voice to voice, it was the importance they attached to their own voice that signaled a wider and deeper sense of their own moral significance.

In our dialogues—with desperately poor people in Zama Zama, street demonstrators in Rio, displaced Japanese farmers—our humblest interlocutors took it for granted that there was no hierarchy of race or class or expertise that could deny them the right to speak their piece. Equally, they took it for granted that they could make their case to foreigners like ourselves. Our interlocutors, in other words, accorded to us the same voice rights we accorded to them. Neither they, nor we, assumed we were in self-enclosed, self-justifying moral universes. We both accepted an obligation to explain ourselves to each other.

This is the core of a global ethic: thanks to the democratic revolution that began in 1789, the decolonization of the world after 1945, the battles for racial equality everywhere, the fight of gay men and women to be heard, the Western world at least and much of the world besides have adopted a rule of equal moral standing for our conversations about ethical matters.

Now a norm honored as much in the breach as in the observance is still a norm. A person silenced on grounds of race now has recourse in a language of rights that other citizens must recognize as legitimate. A woman who stands up for her rights may have to fight for them, but except in those countries where sharia or customary law still rules, she does not have to fight to secure the equality norm in the first place. That work has now been done.

Everywhere, however, a gap remains between what the norm prescribes and what social life allows. Legal equality before the law coexists with customary codes, in villages and rural areas, where women remain in subordination. In India, the untouchables are accorded rights but still face stubborn discrimination when they raise their voice. Everywhere, the voices of the rich and propertied have greater weight than the poor, and everywhere, especially in politics, money's voice is loudest of all. All this merely tells us that the human battle for equality is not over.

Notice too that equality of voice is a procedural ethic—no one can be left out of the discussion—but it makes no presumption that we will agree on very much beyond that. Saudi Arabia is an equal member of the family of nations, and her peoples nominally enjoy the right of self-determination, yet authorities in Saudi Arabia will continue to deny that women should get the vote. Elsewhere, among the faithful in Christian, Muslim, Buddhist, and other faith communities, believers will continue to claim that their faith gives the only true answer to moral questions; some true believers will continue to argue that abortion is murder, while others will believe otherwise. Equality of voice does not create a chorus singing in harmony.

Nonetheless, in the global conversation, across cultures and national boundaries, authorities that were unquestioned when the Universal Declaration on Human Rights was drafted no longer enjoy the power to impose their view on moral questions. The privileges that once attached to race, gender, and religion may not be gone, but their moral authority is contested everywhere.

The individuals we talked to make up their moral life as they go along, with fewer authorities to guide or coerce them. We never heard anyone argue as if moral choice was a matter of simply following what some priestly or political authority told them to think. Doctrine, dogma, formal teaching, and generalized rules have become less salient to moral decision making itself. The very purpose of moral life is less about obedience than about affirming the self and the moral community to which one belongs. This in turn helps to reinforce the sense in which, when we make choices, we are not obeying time-honored universal commands, but rather thinking through, for ourselves, what our situation demands.

Even the most doctrinaire of our interlocutors turned out to be ingeniously individualistic manipulators of doctrines to suit their own political purposes. Only in an individualistic modernity of the kind that has suddenly descended upon Myanmar does an entrepreneur like Ashin Wirathu, the radical monk, become possible. Everyone else we spoke to took it for granted that they were the ones who would have to make up their own minds.

So equality of voice and moral choice as an individual responsibility were the two new expectations we observed everywhere. This is the great achievement of Mrs. Roosevelt's revolution, but it left most of our interlocutors restless, uncertain, and unsatisfied with the results. For there is a dialectic of insatiability at work here. The moral equality already achieved shows up the inequalities of privilege, power, income, and fate that remain.

In the habitations of the poor and dispossessed, we also began to see the limits of Mrs. Roosevelt's revolution. Among the very poor, human rights and global ethics were terms most had never heard of. They never used such language in our hearing. Instead we heard a deeper and more primal register: "You can't treat us like garbage. We're human beings." This was how the claim to belong to the human family was articulated to us by the poorest of the poor.

Abstractions of any sort—and human rights is one—were of little use to these people. This observation confirmed the research of other academics, but it raised another question: so what discourses *did* they use to make sense of their existence? At first, this question seemed superfluous. Isn't it supposed to be true that life at the bare minimum is a battle for survival, not a struggle for meaning? On the contrary, it was soon obvious that even in the most desperate shantytown or illegal settlement, the most crime-ridden housing project, life remains a search for moral order of some sort.[3]

From the most hard-pressed people we met we learned that moral order is a necessity of life and that the battle for it must be waged, even if it cannot always be won. Especially if you are poor, it is vital to believe that there is a community of a kind and not just a jungle ruled by predators. For with order there is hope, even if the hope is of escape.

What human beings share, everywhere, is not a language of the good or a global ethic, but instead a common desire, in their own vernacular, for moral order, for a framework of expectations that allow them to think of their life, no matter how brutal or difficult, as meaningful.

As we listened to favela dwellers, inhabitants of informal settlements, farmers in their fields, monks in their places of worship, we began to see that ordinary people do not generalize or systematize their thinking. A global ethic, applicable to all mankind, is essentially unimaginable and irrelevant. This is not because ordinary people don't reflect, and often deeply, about the injustice of the world and imagine a better one. It is because the validity of a moral proposition for them does not turn, as it does for philosophers in the Kantian tradition, on whether it can be universalized or generalized. Its validity turns instead on whether it is true for them and their immediate community, whether it makes sense, even provisionally, of their specific context and situation.

In every one of our settings, people were struggling to make sense of convulsive, destabilizing change. The anxieties of the people we talked to were focused on where their country was headed and how to make sense of its chaotic history. Indeed, what made their search for moral order so stressful was that people doubted that they had any control over a careening public domain.

The secular narratives—the inevitability of technical progress, the spread of democracy, the triumph of liberalism—that provided an illusion of control for elites mean little to the poor and dispossessed. Even the cosmopolitan elites seemed to be losing faith in grand narratives. In Los Angeles and New York, triumphalism about the superiority of the United States in particular, and liberal democracy in general, had been replaced by a more self-critical register that questioned whether America and other such democratic experiments could deliver on their promise. Lurking just beneath the anxieties left in the wake of Fukushima, likewise, was a questioning of faith in technology, expertise, and scientific rationality.

Everywhere we went the secular narratives that make sense of public life were in crisis. Hence the heightened and highly polarized competition to fill public space with new narratives, whether it be the populism of the left or of the right. When faced with these disintegrating narratives, when assailed by polarized public competitors on all sides, the people we met could only suspend judgment on larger social meanings and get on with the one exercise that did provide reassurance and order—namely, the daily practice of the ordinary virtues.

The colleague who shared the entire journey with me came back with a different conclusion. Devin Stewart, who directs programs for the Carnegie Council, came home with the view that everywhere we went we were witnessing a recognizably universal search to define, affirm, and defend human dignity.[4]

It was less obvious to me that there was one virtue at stake in all the moral affirmations we heard. For one thing, dignity might be too focused on the self and fail to address the situations in which the moral problem was how to make sense of a collapsing or disintegrating public world. Dignity is a defense of "me," or my group's claims, but other virtues on display were about solidarity with others. Dignity itself also turned out to be contested ground. In Bosnia, for example, to be dignified could mean either forgiving your enemies or blaming them forever for their crimes. Because the claims of dignity pulled in opposite directions, at least in Bosnia, the people we talked to remain paralyzed twenty years after the formal end to the war.

So instead of one virtue, I saw a cluster of them in the essential work of all our informants, which was to make a life that was both bearable and meaningful.

A further conclusion we drew from our travels is that the reaction against the forces of globalization is not a passing discontent, but an enduring element in ordinary people's defense of their identities. Everywhere, people were struggling to have it both ways at once: to benefit from globalization, from cheap communications and transport, from new goods and new opportunities, without having their jobs, communities, and settled values swept away.

Everyone we met understood that globalization was impinging upon the local frameworks within which they made their choices, but everywhere too, people divided into whether they considered themselves beneficiaries of globalization or its victims. Educated elites with networks and mobility to profit from globalization often seemed to us to be in a different realm of discourse and expectation from those of their fellow citizens who felt left behind. Yet even those who saw themselves as victims were not seeking to wall themselves off, but simply to have some choice, agency, or control so that the globalizing forces of money and power would not destroy them. In this battle for control, the most powerful languages of resistance were not global but local: national pride, local tradition, religious vernacular.

Even as globalization divides the world into winners and losers, both have to live within the same complex moral universe where local and global claims collide. Even as local self-determination clashes with international human rights, both sides concede that there are no universally accepted rules for deciding the contest. To live in such a divided moral universe is to live in competing theaters of justification and to face demands to explain your choices that will succeed with one audience only to fail with another. Globalization means that it's no longer possible to live in a moral bell jar, safe from impingement. Devoutly religious persons will face demands to justify their choices, just as their secular challengers will be asked to justify theirs. The globally mobile elites face a barrage of justification from those left behind, while those left behind have to develop their own rhetoric of self-justification.

No wonder murderous fantasies of extermination are alive and well in a globalizing world. It is so much simpler to live only with those with whom you agree, to believe that the real task is to get rid of the infidels who stand between you and paradise. The latest, but surely not the last, example of the genocidal pursuit of moral purity is the terrorist state known as ISIS, currently battling for survival in the borderlands between Iraq and Syria. It may not survive, but the dreams of a holy caliphate are too deeply embedded in Islamic tradition to fade away with military defeat. Genocidal projects of this sort have a long history, and they are likely to be a permanent feature of our future. The murderous resort to violence is in service of a utopia: the fantasy of living without enemies, in concord with like-minded zealots just like you, free of the burden of justifying yourself to those who hold different views of life's meaning.[5]

Instead of confirming that we are living in a world where moral values are converging, our journeys demonstrated that we actually live in competing moral worlds—global and local—and must live with the demand of justifying ourselves to competing audiences. At the same time, our journey demonstrated just how easy it was, both for us and for our partners in dialogue, to recognize each other across our differences. The virtues we display are enduringly common because daily life throws up the same challenges: how much, if at all, to trust those who rule over us; how much, if at all, to tolerate those who are different; how much to forgive, if we can, those who have wronged us; and how to rebuild life when fate and misfortune sweep away what we have tried to accomplish.

It might be, as philosophers since Aristotle have argued, that when we recognize virtue across the differences of race, religion, language, and culture we are actually recognizing a universal Good, a common core of moral practice, grounded in our natures and shared by all human beings. Yet it seems equally plausible to think that what we were recognizing is not the Good, in its universal, unchanging form, but goodness, in all its astonishingly contextual singularity.[6]

In our journeys across cultures and nations it was easy for us and for our interlocutors to recognize each other as fellow human beings. We grasped the kinship between their local practices and our own. We recognized the goodness in each other, even if we couldn't understand the whys and wherefores of the behavior in front of us. But this does not mean that we all accept the same idea of the Good or the same grounds for moral authority.

Because human beings do not agree on the Good, even though they can recognize goodness, they also disagree about who has moral standing—in other words, who is to be trusted and believed on moral questions.

If globalization is putting into question so many sources of moral authority, it is surprising that international human rights activists should take their own standing for granted. They believe it is accorded them by the treaties and conventions that states have signed. But the standing of the promoters of moral universalism was contested everywhere we went. The moral standing of human rights was not self-evident to Burmese monks, ANC activists in South Africa, or Bosnian survivors of war any more than the authority of the European Court of Human Rights is evident to the majority of British citizens who voted to leave the European Union.

So the ultimate question in our journey slowly became: Of the three moral systems we examined—human rights, global ethics, and ordinary virtues—whose authority prevails in each situation?

We were struck, everywhere we went, by the primacy of the local. Even in a globalized world, local sources of moral life—our parents and siblings, our home, our place of worship, the local school, if there is one—are bound to be the primary shaping force of our ordinary virtues. In turn, the states that protect us will always exert a stronger moral influence over us than any external source, whether it be a UN agency, international NGO, or the international media. This is especially the case where the local state in question is democratic and can claim that it speaks in the name of the people.

While we once may have thought that democratic values and human rights advance hand in hand, we are learning that the contrary may be the case. Democratic sovereignty and the moral universalism of human rights are on a collision course everywhere. Democratic majorities have been rejecting universalist claims—the right of asylum in one place, the right of strangers to nationality in another—in the name of a democratic defense of local values.

What was striking too, on our journeys, was that local and global moral discourses argued from diametrically opposed ideas about the ultimate object of moral concern. For the human rights activist, for the global ethicist, the object of ultimate concern is the frail, vulnerable, universal human being. Human differences—of race, class, or situation—are secondary. The very nature of moral duty is to be impartial, to regard the distinction, for example, between a citizen and a stranger as morally irrelevant.

In the moral universe of the ordinary virtues, on the other hand, the citizen-stranger, the us-versus-them distinction, was the first consideration, the starting point for moral decision making. The universal human being was rarely if ever the object of ultimate concern. The most striking feature of the ordinary virtue perspective is how rarely any of our participants evoked universal principles of any kind—that is, ideas of general obligation to human beings as such—and how frequently they reasoned in terms of the local, the contingent, the here and now, what they owed those near to them and what they owed themselves.

The people we spoke to in favelas, illegal settlements, and villages all took their privileged status as human beings for granted; all assumed a right to equal voice, but surprisingly, it did not follow that they believed they had any universal obligations to others like themselves. It was as if they claimed equality for themselves, as individuals, without assuming that equality must imply duties to everyone else.

The audience ordinary people imagined, when justifying their behavior, was not the human race, some abstract standard, beyond the veil of ignorance or some set of principles written down in a human rights text, but themselves: their own reflection in the mirror. Beyond this, the audiences that mattered were their neighbors, their friends, their family, their significant others. They worried about how they would look to these local audiences and to themselves, not to a wider world. Virtue was local.

In the ordinary-virtue perspective, moral life is a continuous process of identity testing. We seek a path of action that will enable us to think well of ourselves and at the very least to ensure that others will not think too badly. We want to do the right thing, if we can, and we want to be able to live with ourselves afterwards. We are not trying to prove the validity of propositions, to live by a rule, or to conform our behavior to some system. We are always in a particular situation, a context, a moment—a place in space and time—and we are always with others, with people whose opinion shapes us and whose views we wish to shape.

To repeat, when we speak here of ordinary people, we are talking about ourselves, people like us. Wherever we went our subject was never "them," but rather what they had to teach us about the unseen biases of our own thinking. What we learned is that we do care about consistency, not alignment with general principle but consistency of our conduct over our own lifetime. We struggle to act well today as we acted well yesterday in order to maintain a coherent sense of ourselves through life.

When we have moral decisions to make we reason about the actual human beings before us—clothed, gendered, rich and poor, racially distinct—and our moral feelings about them depend utterly on their relationships to us, on whether they are neighbors or strangers, citizens or visitors, friends or foes, like us or like "them."

Here Hannah Arendt was surely right when she observed in *The Human Condition,* "Men, not Man, live on earth and inhabit the world."[7] The concept of Man, Arendt argued, is too hard for us to understand. The philosopher David Hume said much the same two hundred and fifty years earlier when he wrote that there was no such thing as "love of mankind merely as such," only love of this person for that, in this situation and no other.[8] It is impossible to think of human beings as such. Instead, we think about human beings we know. That is all we can do.

To return to Mrs. Roosevelt for a moment, she assumed, as most human rights activists have always done, that human rights universalism and the ordinary virtues are complementary and mutually reinforcing, but what if they are not? In human rights, it is assumed, as if it were a natural fact, that human beings recognize the universal human subject in every encounter we have with distinct human beings. This is the primary recognition that matters. Indeed, in human rights reasoning, there is no "other"; there is only us.

In the ordinary-virtue perspective, on the contrary, "otherness" is primary. We start where we are, with human beings as they actually present themselves to us, clothed, differentiated by skin color, gender, sexual orientation, and patterns of speech. Common humanity, in this perspective, is not what we see, only difference and otherness.

From the perspective of ordinary virtue, the first question we ask of another human being is always: Is he / she one of us or one of them? From this initial question everything follows, including whether we owe them anything. If they are citizens, depending on the type of regime we live under, we may owe them shelter, clothing, a hearing, health care, and other forms of assistance. If they are strangers, what we owe them ceases to be a duty and becomes, instead, a matter of pity, generosity, and compassion.

It is no surprise, therefore, that what claims citizens must accord to strangers—to refugees and migrants—has become the most contentious issue in a globalizing world. Not just in Europe, either, but in Zama Zama too, where Zimbabweans and Mozambicans languish on the outside of South African society. Here the human rights and the ordinary-virtue perspectives diverge radically. Where human rights sees asylum as a right that any stranger, with a well-founded claim of persecution, can claim against a citizen, from the ordinary-virtue perspective asylum is a gift that a citizen makes as a matter of sovereign discretion.

From an international rights perspective, provided a stranger meets the criteria for protection set down in international law, there is no upward limit to the number of people citizens are required to receive into their community. From an ordinary-virtue perspective, this idea removes from a political community its very sovereignty. It equalizes the citizen and the stranger, removes the power of the citizen to determine who is worthy of the gift. From the ordinary-virtue perspective, the claims of the citizen must trump the claims of the stranger or democratic self-determination has no meaning.

In her *Origins of Totalitarianism*, written after her own experience of being forced into exile from Nazi Germany, Hannah Arendt observed that it was an illusion to suppose that if a person were to lose his rights as a citizen, he could still claim his rights as a human being. As she bitterly but wisely remarked:

> If a human being loses his political status, he should, according to the implication of the inborn and inalienable rights of man, come under exactly the situation for which the declaration of such general rights provided. Actually the opposite is the case. It seems that a man who is nothing but a man has lost the very qualities which make it possible for other people to treat him as a fellow human being.[9]

It is when we have no particular claim to make on the solidarity of another—a claim of common citizenship, or race, or kinship, or shared language—that we are forced back, Arendt says, on the primal, the last claim of all, the claim of human solidarity, and it is then, she rightly says, that we are at our most vulnerable.

It follows from this idea that it is difference, not identity, that is primary in human recognition, that when citizens everywhere believe that asylum is a gift, not a right, they do so because they accord a natural priority to those who share their identity as citizens.

Human rights activists too easily regard this view as a form of racism masking itself as a claim about democratic rights. If this were true, the ordinary virtues would cease to be virtues at all. But there is also an ordinary-virtue perspective that is not racist. In our journeys many people were at home in a multicultural, multifaith global city. They accepted moral equality among the races, but they wanted to live with their own in communities of their own choosing. From an ordinary-virtue perspective there is no contradiction between believing that races and religions should "live together" in a global city while simultaneously choosing to live apart, but side by side, in residential communities self-segregated by race or religion. The paradox may be that living apart is what makes living together possible, and it is choice in the matter that renders the arrangement legitimate and possible.

This illustrates, again, the distinction between the moral perspective of the ordinary virtues and universal human rights.

Human rights enjoins us to be tolerant, to recognize the universal equality in all human beings. From an ordinary-virtue perspective, on the other hand, human beings do not appear clothed in what Marx called their "species being."[10] Ordinary virtue accepts no general obligation to tolerate anyone. Its motto is "Take people one at a time." It refuses the temptation of synecdoche—the metaphor in which we allow the part to stand for the whole. Prejudice and hatred are exercises in ferocious synecdoche, dire insistence that a particular individual represent all the projected generalities of prejudice.

In effect, tolerance as an ordinary virtue is a discipline of moral individualism, a decision formed by life experience, to suspend prior judgment, to take people as they come, to judge them on their merits, to bat away stereotypes and focus on the distinct reality of the person with whom you are dealing in a moral situation. You can only take people one person at a time. That is the wisdom of ordinary virtue.

Ordinary virtue, to be sure, has no monopoly on wisdom. Indeed, its preferences for the local and the familiar, for us rather than them, can easily be preyed upon and exploited, turned into an apologia for exclusion and cruelty toward strangers. The more distant the strangers, the weaker the bond that ordinary virtue is likely to feel. We are at our most abstract about human beings when we feel pity toward strangers—looking at a photograph of some destitute person, fleeing war or tyranny, stranded on a beach, semi-naked, desperate for help. We may feel an identifying sorrow on that person's behalf—but then we usually move on to the proximate business at hand, which is dealing with the human beings—our own family and friends—whom we actually know. If we do act on behalf of strangers—and we do—we call forth the extraordinary virtues: we put ourselves out, we make an extra effort, we go and help, or we simply write a check. Even then, what may drive us is not some abstract conviction that refugees have rights, but simple pity and compassion. Human rights universalism is contemptuous of pity because it is discretionary, emotional, and highly personal. Yet it is possible that pure pity has done more real work to save victims than the language of rights.

So it is not surprising, really, that while moral globalization and ethical convergence are occurring among cosmopolitan elites, human rights as law or ethics figures little in ordinary people's reckoning with the moral quandaries they face in everyday life. Eleanor Roosevelt had hoped it would, but it hasn't happened and is not likely to. We have more immediate things to worry about than the universal, and our moral life is an exercise in triage in favor of local priorities.

So what then might be the use of a universal ethic like human rights in a world where the moral perspective of most people is still determined by the ordinary virtues?

Universalising moral rhetoric like human rights is not best understood as deriving from our ordinary virtues, or indeed from any basic emotional intuitions about our shared identity as human beings. We have already said our sense of species being is weak. Instead human rights is best seen as a rational thought experiment, as a critical discourse whose purpose is to force the ordinary virtues to enlarge and expand their circle of moral concern. Just as civil rights function as a protection against the tyranny of the majority in domestic law, so international human rights function best as a challenge to majoritarian moral preference among democratic and nondemocratic states in the international arena. Human rights is the legal and moral structure that enjoins political leaders and their citizens not to give in to the exclusionary and restrictive preference of "us" versus "them."

Human rights and the ordinary virtues are thus in tension, just as law is in tension with moral feeling. It is the work of political wisdom to reduce the tension between law and ethics, and between law and popular sentiment, but the tensions will always remain. Human rights enjoins citizens to be morally consistent and universalistic in their perspective toward strangers in danger, but ordinary virtue will always pull them toward favoring citizens close to home. The meeting point between the language of rights and the ordinary virtues is actually the language of compassion, pity, and generosity. A prudent politician is likely to discover that maintaining public support to assist strangers and refugees is more likely to succeed if the appeal is cast in the language of the gift, rather than the language of rights.

Moral globalization ought to have had one key result: to make transnational solidarity between human beings easier now than it was in Mrs. Roosevelt's time. Universal languages of obligation exist to widen ordinary people's circle of moral concern. This widening of concern is in turn empowered by the technologies that are re-shaping our time. We can travel from zones of safety to zones of danger and back again in no time at all. We can donate to charities halfway across the world. Equally, if it is horror we wish to confront, it is all just a click away. But we should not announce a new age of global solidarity too soon. It would be difficult to argue that human rights have rooted transnational instincts of solidarity in us more deeply now than they were in Mrs. Roosevelt's time, or in times more distant to us. The feelings of solidarity, shame, and sorrow we feel when our technologies present us with the martyred child, the drowned grandmother on a Greek beach, the massacred innocent in a Nigerian schoolyard are not, I would argue, very different from those that Michel de Montaigne felt five hundred years ago, ob-serving the slaughter of Catholics by Protestants and Protestants by Catholics in the religious wars of the sixteenth century. He saw men leaving the dead bodies of their enemies to be devoured by pigs. It disgusted and repelled him as it disgusts and repels us. We agree with him when he says, "For this is the utmost point to which cru-elty can arrive—that a man should kill a man, not being angry, not in fear, only for the sake of the spectacle."[11] Our technologies now en-able us to make a spectacle of cruelty beyond anything he could imagine. But we remain his moral kin. He hated cruelty then, and if we hate it now, we do so just as he did. Our conscience may have a more global reach than Montaigne's, since we have more informa-tion about the moral harms we may be doing to others far away, but our conscience is no sharper. His conscience was local, and he blessed the ordinary virtues of his fellow French men and women as the saving graces of a savage time. We should too. Our conscience remains local because our ultimate loyalties are local: to kith and kin, our own, our people, our community. The human rights revolution has changed what we believe about the duty of states. I doubt it has changed *us*.

Indeed, one could go further and say that we are living a genuine crisis of the universal amidst a return of the sovereign. Everywhere sovereign states are pushing back against universal obligations, whether it be the refugee convention, the laws of war, or the human rights covenants. It is not just China and Russia who insist on their sovereignty. Ordinary citizens in democratic states too, faced with the claims of refugees and desperate migrants at their borders, fearful of terror attacks, are telling their leaders: protect us from strangers. In an age of fear, the ordinary virtues can't function without security, and it is doubtful that human rights can turn back this tide. In a global age of threats, from enraged fanatics, the sovereign returns and the universal loses its grip, not just on rulers but also on those they rule.

So two claims converge here: that human rights play only a limited role in structuring the ordinary virtues of most people despite the rights revolution; and that states increasingly are pushing back against any universal claim that diminishes their sovereignty.

If the sovereign has returned, then the question becomes how the sovereign can guarantee security and justice for its own people without extinguishing the virtues of generosity and hospitality toward desperate and defenseless people at its gates. Acknowledging that such people have rights based in international law is a necessary condition for decency, but it is not sufficient to sustain a public culture of welcome. Such a public culture must replicate the virtues of the private realm, the virtues of compassion and generosity, so that citizens see, in the actions of their government, a version of their better natures.

It cannot be accidental that the most politically popular program of refugee settlement in the world, Canada's, maintains its popularity because it appeals specifically to the hospitality and generosity of ordinary Canadian families and depends on their willingness to sponsor individual refugees.[12] This one-to-one, family-to-family relationship has proved more successful and more enduring than state sponsorship, suggesting that states need to do as much to encourage the gift relationship as they do to respect rights obligations. Indeed they cannot sustain public consent for human rights unless they also appeal to and cultivate the virtues of generosity and compassion.

The ordinary virtues depend on public evocation and on public cultivation. They may be local and personal, but they are dependent on public choice, on whether leaders appeal to the best, rather than the worst, in their citizens; whether public leaders practice generosity instead of preying on fear; whether there are decent schools, safety in the streets, police who arrest for good cause not for bad, judges who don't take bribes, municipal institutions that rally when disaster strikes, and so on. The World Values Survey shows that in societies where public trust is weak, where citizens have little faith in their police, judges, or politicians, they also turn out to have little trust in each other.[13] In other words, ordinary virtue in private life is dependent on trustworthy public institutions. It is a fantasy to believe that if only the fetters of the state could be removed from daily life, ordinary virtue would flourish. The contrary is the case. Only when citizens feel they are treated with minimum decency by their own public institutions can they be expected to treat strangers with equal decency.

Ordinary virtues can endure in tyrannies, oligarchies, and authoritarian regimes, but they have to battle to preserve decency against a public realm which rewards venality, oppression, and cruelty. It is easier for the ordinary virtues to flourish in conditions of liberal freedom: where there is consent of the governed, rule of law, an independent judiciary, freedom of assembly and expression, majority rule and minority rights, and competitive markets. These institutions empower moral individuals, enable them to pry themselves loose from the carapace of class, faith, religion, and caste and live as free moral agents. To say this, however, is immediately to bring rights back as the essential institutional safeguards required for ordinary virtue to function. But these are not universal human rights, rather the rights enshrined in national laws and constitutions, the ones that traditions of local struggle and national history have rendered dear to those who defend them.

Liberal freedom has proved its worth, over many centuries in the North Atlantic world, as a reliable system for keeping abuse of power in check. It would be fanciful to claim that liberal freedom has made the human beings who enjoy it less venal and more humane than peoples raised under different systems of rule. It is doubtful that liberal freedom has improved the ordinary virtues. The most that we can say is that liberal freedom has set up some time-tested barriers against the inveterate tendency of human beings to abuse power and oppress others. But these tendencies remain, and they are constantly at work, challenging the controls that good institutions try to impose on human proclivities to abuse power. When institutions fail, as they often do, ordinary virtues can survive, but they struggle because a corrupted public world seems to reward only venality, selfishness, and personal enrichment. Liberal democracies have often failed to protect the ordinary virtues, but it does not follow that they are fated to decline and fail altogether. That assumption would underestimate the capacity of ordinary citizens to rally for the restoration of lost liberties and lost decencies. It is always premature to pronounce either the death of virtue or the death of liberal freedom.

If ordinary virtue is social—that is, if it requires tolerably good institutions in order to flourish—there isn't a place on earth, not even those societies that originated liberal freedom, where these institutions are in good health. Just as ordinary virtue, as Montaigne said, is in constant struggle with the ordinary vices, so liberal institutions are constantly at risk from corruption, predation, and abuse.

It is a comforting illusion to divide the world into secure liberal democracies that have a mutually enabling relation between institutions and virtue and those that are still struggling to create this virtuous upward spiral. One striking result of our journey, in fact, is that despite enormous advantages—constitutional stability, high per capita wealth, and global power—a liberal order in the United States is still struggling to deliver on its basic premise of due process to millions of its people, especially its black citizens. The moral operating system of global cities depends, above all else, on rule of law, fair policing, and due process in the criminal justice system. Who could say the ordinary virtues receive adequate institutional support in America? Japan, likewise, thinks of itself as the most stable of the liberal democracies, but what Japanese citizen can still trust that the nuclear regulators and operators will keep them safe? Fukushima was many things, but it was also an indictment of the liberal state.

Even in developed liberal democracies the ordinary virtues struggle wherever honest, non-collusive, responsive institutions are lacking. Ordinary virtue cannot flourish in an environment of organized injustice toward immigrants, minorities, and the poor. If poor and disadvantaged families cannot count on equal protection of the laws, their private virtues will languish.

Developing and developed societies alike are struggling against the iron law of oligarchy, against the inveterate temptations of power, against the ordinary vices of human indifference and greed.

No society approaches full legitimacy in the eyes of its citizens. At all times there will be abuses and injustices that awaken their anger. The question is when citizens snap. The tipping point, we discovered on our journeys, is moral: that is, when an abuse long tolerated suddenly becomes seen as an expression of moral contempt by an elite toward its people. At this point when injustice is too flagrant, contemptuous, indifferent to dignity, the coping that ordinary virtue makes possible simply breaks down.

Conversely, where institutions function, where officials do their jobs, ordinary virtues can revive because public institutions also display resilience and public officials shoulder duties of care.

I am joining all those—the development economists, for example—who say that good institutions matter, but I am saying they matter because they empower the virtues that are essential both to the cohesion of these societies and to the survival of the institutions themselves.[14] In a world divided between authoritarian capitalist regimes and liberal democratic ones, believers in liberal freedom should worry not whether their regime can prevail in competition with authoritarian ones, but whether they can prevail against their own forms of institutional entropy: elite capture, corruption, and inequality.

In all these situations, the virtues struggle with their opposites, with avarice and corruption, intolerance, hatred, and desire for vengeance. It is exactly as Michel de Montaigne said in his essay "On Cruelty," "The very name of virtue presupposes difficulty and contention and cannot be experienced without an opponent." Ordinary virtues are in a lifelong battle with ordinary vices. Without the constant inner temptation of the ordinary vices—cruelty, hatred, power-lust—virtues would not be what they are, a victory, however temporary, of the best in us over the worst in us.

Ordinary virtues can handle the struggle with ordinary vices, but they may well be helpless in the face of barbarism. The best they can do is hunker down, shelter their own, and wait for the horror to pass. In one of the Paris cafés where nineteen people died in the attacks of November 2015, the owner was Jewish, his wife of Muslim heritage, the staff included Muslims, the manager was from Tunisia, and nobody cared about this or thought their diversity was any kind of moral gesture. Working together across difference just happened, because people were attracted to each other and liked to be together. In this Paris café there was no politics, no ideology, no "commitment to diversity," and no arms for people to defend themselves when barbarians burst in upon a peaceful Friday night and sprayed the place with gunfire and a young Muslim woman was among those who died with a bullet in her back.[15]

So yes, ordinary virtue is helpless before the extraordinary vices, but then if you ask how life in that quarter of Paris, in that small café, will be rebuilt, how the café will reopen and people will gather again, it is the ordinary virtues that will have to do the work: resilience, reconciliation with the facts, trust in strangers, more limited now than in the past, but still defiant, and as always anti-ideological, without theory, not interested in generalizing beyond what you actually know, just an inchoate, unformulated, but stubborn commitment to live together again.

Terrorism has taught us to acknowledge the dividedness, the radical antagonism in globalized modernity. We are a single species, but we do not live in a single moral world. It is our dividedness that defines the human race. We cannot get beyond our skins, our history, our races, our genders, all the distinguishing differences that are the source of pride and shame, status and power. The hatreds and follies that drive people to kill others are not always susceptible to "development," "meliorism," understanding, or good will. Sometimes, violence cannot be resisted with argument: it must be met with force.

Globalization of our economies does not produce globalization in our hearts and minds. The geography of our virtues has changed, yes: we now play out local conflicts before the whole world, and when we justify ourselves we do it to strangers linked to us by new media. That is what moral globalization means, the steady enlargement of the audiences before which we feel we must justify ourselves. Perhaps, over time, as our local justifications fail, we may begin to be ashamed of our provincial convictions and begin to enlarge our conscience, but moral change, in the deepest realms of our hearts, will always be slow. We are always locked in a battle with ordinary vices. In the public realm, our conflicts over power, resources, standing, and significance are inveterate, and many of these conflicts will not be settled by argument but with blood and fire. Our moral languages do not share the same history, and they are very slow, as they should be, to forget the humiliation and injustice that one moral system, in its pride, has visited on those who adhere to other systems.

But it is also the case that we share the same biology, the same body, and the same eventual fate. We also share the ordinary virtues, and we recognize them across all our differences. They are ordinary because they are concerned with the recurrent essentials of our common life, because they express our learned instincts about what moral life requires of us if we are to survive and reproduce the life of family, neighborhood, kith and kin. We are moral beings because we have no choice—our survival and our success as social beings depends on virtue. It is not an option, but a necessity. We are not required to be heroes, but we do want to be adequate fathers and mothers, sons and daughters, neighbors and friends. We want, through these experiences, to be able to return our own gaze in the mirror.

The test of public institutions is whether they make it possible for us to behave decently toward each other. I have nailed my colors to the mast with the claim that the institutions most likely to foster these virtues are liberal democratic ones, but there are, as we have seen, no societies that have freed themselves from the toils of oligarchy, corruption, and injustice; and if that is so, there are no guarantees of any kind, only our constant, recurrent, never-ending struggle to live by the ordinary virtues.

Notes

INTRODUCTION

1   Kate Hallgren, *Toward Peace with Justice: One Hundred Years of the Carnegie Council* (New York: Carnegie Council, 2014).

2   Andrew Carnegie, *The Autobiography of Andrew Carnegie and the Gospel of Wealth* (New York: Signet Classics, 2006); David Nasaw, *Andrew Carnegie* (New York: Penguin Press, 2006).

3   Jonathan Spence, *The Memory Palace of Matteo Ricci* (London: Penguin, 1985).

4   Michel de Montaigne, "Of Cannibals," in *The Complete Works*, ed. Donald M. Frame (1948; repr., New York: Everyman's Library, 2003), 31, 182-194.

5   "Uncontacted Tribe: Extraordinary Aerial Footage," Survival International, www.survivalinternational.org.

6   Joseph Conrad, *Heart of Darkness* (1899; New York: Norton, 2006).

7   Karl Popper, *The Open Society and Its Enemies* 5th ed. (1945; London: Routledge, 2002).

8   Isabel Hilton, "China's Economic Reforms Have Let Party Leaders and Their Families Get Rich," *The Guardian*, October 26, 2012, https://www.the

guardian.com/commentisfree/2012/oct/26/china-economic-reforms-leaders
-rich. Eva Pils of King's College London pointed out to me that the official
Communist Party version of what Deng Xiaoping said is, "Let some people
get rich first."

9   Svetlana Alexievich, *Second-Hand Time*, trans. Bela Shayevich (London:
    Fitzcarraldo Editions, 2016).

10 Albert O. Hirschman, *Exit, Voice and Loyalty* (Cambridge, MA: Harvard
    University Press, 1970).

11 Francis Fukuyama, *The End of History and the Last Man* (New York: Avon
    Books, 1992).

12 Emrah Sahin, "Ottoman Institutions, Millet System: 1250 to 1920: Middle
    East," in *Cultural Sociology of the Middle East, Asia, and Africa: An
    Encyclopedia*, ed. Andrea L. Stanton, Edward Ramsamy, Peter J. Seybolt,
    and Carolyn M. Elliott (New York: Sage, 2012).

13 Karl Marx and Friedrich Engels, *The Communist Manifesto* (1848).

14 "Breakthrough Innovation for the SDGs," UN Global Compact, https://www
    .unglobalcompact.org; John Ruggie, *Just Business: Multinational Corporations
    and Human Rights* (New York: Norton, 2015).

15 "The 0.7% ODA / GNI Target: A History," Lester B. Pearson Partners in
    Development–Report of the Commission on International Development
    (New York: United Nations, 1970), http://www.oecd.org/dac/stats/the07
    odagnitarget-ahistory.htm.

16 Michael Ignatieff, *Human Rights as Politics and Idolatry* (Princeton, NJ:
    Princeton University Press, 2000); Samuel Moyn, *The Last Utopia:
    Human Rights in History* (Cambridge, MA: Harvard University Press,
    2012).

17 I have borrowed the idea of vernacularization from Sally Engle Merry,
    *Human Rights and Gender Violence: Translating International Law into
    Local Justice* (Chicago: University of Chicago Press, 2006).

18 Robert McCrum, Robert Macneil, and William Cran, *The Story of English*,
    3rd rev. ed. (London: Penguin, 2002).

19 Michael Ignatieff, *The Warrior's Honor: Ethnic War and the Modern
    Conscience* (New York: Metropolitan, 1998).

20 "The History of Earth Day," Earth Day Network, http://www.earthday.org /about/the-history-of-earth-day/.

21 Pope Francis, "Laudato Si: Encyclical Letter of the Holy Father Francis on Care for Our Common Home" (2015), http://w2.vatican.va/content/fran cesco/en/encyclicals/documents/papa-francesco_20150524_enciclica -laudato-si.html.

22 Thomas Nagel, *The View from Nowhere* (New York: Oxford University Press, 1989).

23 The veil of ignorance, of course, refers to the famous heuristic employed by John Rawls in *A Theory of Justice* (Cambridge, MA: Belknap Press, 1972). For the global application of his theory of justice, see John Rawls, *The Law of Peoples* (Cambridge, MA: Harvard University Press, 1999).

24 Thomas Hurka, "The Justification of National Partiality," in *The Morality of Nationalism,* ed. Robert McKim and Jeff McMahan (New York: Oxford University Press, 1997), 139-157; Joseph Carens, "Aliens and Citizens: The Case for Open Borders," *Review of Politics* 49, no. 2 (1987): 251-273; Michael Blake, "Distributive Justice, State Coercion, and Autonomy," *Philosophy and Public Affairs* 30, no. 3 (2001): 257-296; and Michael Walzer, "The Distribution of Membership," in *Boundaries,* ed. Peter Brown and Henry Shue (Totowa, NJ: Rowman and Littlefield, 1981), 1-35.

25 Henry Shue, *Basic Rights: Subsistence, Affluence, and U.S. Foreign Policy* (Princeton, NJ: Princeton University Press, 1980); Thomas Pogge, "Assisting the Global Poor," in *The Ethics of Assistance,* ed. Deen K. Chatterjee, (Cambridge: Cambridge University Press, 2004), 260-288; and Peter Singer, "Famine, Affluence, and Morality," *Philosophy and Public Affairs* 1, no. 3 (1972): 229-243.

26 Peter Singer, *One World: The Ethics of Globalization,* Terry Lectures (New Haven, CT: Yale University Press, 2002).

27 Isaiah Berlin, "Two Concepts of Liberty," in *The Proper Study of Mankind: An Anthology of Essays,* ed. Henry Hardy and Roger Hausheer (London: Chatto and Windus, 1997), 191-243. For a disagreement with Berlin, see Ronald Dworkin, *Justice for Hedgehogs* (Cambridge, MA: Harvard University Press, 2011).

28 James Ron and David Crow, "Who Trusts Local Human Rights Organizations? Evidence from Three World Regions," *Human Rights Quarterly* 37, no. 1 (2015): 188–239.

29 Pierre Rosanvallon, *La Crise de l'Etat Providence* (Paris: Seuil, 1981).

30 Julia Annas, *Intelligent Virtue* (Oxford: Oxford University Press, 2011); Clifford Williams, ed., *Personal Virtues: Introductory Essays* (London: Palgrave Macmillan, 2005); Onora O'Neill, *Towards Justice and Virtue: A Constructive Account of Practical Reasoning* (New York: Cambridge University Press, 1996).

31 Montaigne, "Of Cruelty," in *Complete Works*, 372–386; see also Judith N. Shklar, "Putting Cruelty First," in *Ordinary Vices* (Cambridge, MA: Harvard University Press, 1984), 7–45.

32 Daron Acemoglu and J. A. Robinson, *Why Nations Fail: The Origins of Power, Prosperity, and Poverty* (New York: Norton, 2012); Dani Rodrik, *The Globalization Paradox: Democracy and the Future of the Global Economy* (New York: Norton, 2011); *One Economics, Many Recipes: Globalization, Institutions and Economic Growth* (Princeton, NJ: Princeton University Press, 2009); Dani Rodrik, Arvind Subramanian, and Francesco Trebbi, "Institutions Rule: The Primacy of Institutions over Geography and Integration in Economic Development," NBER Working Paper 9305 (Cambridge, MA: National Bureau of Economic Research, 2002).

1. JACKSON HEIGHTS, NEW YORK

1 Our site visit to Queens would not have been possible without the assistance of Dr. Kavitha Rajagopalan, who provided research, contacts, and insight throughout. Thanks also to professor Nancy Foner of Hunter College for invaluable scholarly advice on the literature about immigration.

2 Roger Sanjek, *The Future of Us All: Race and Neighborhood Politics in New York City* (Ithaca: NY: Cornell University Press, 1998), 20–21.

3 Thomas Nail, "Migrant Cosmopolitanism," *Public Affairs Quarterly* 29, no. 2 (April 2015): 187–199.

4 A. P. Lobo and J. J. Salvo, "A Portrait of New York's Immigrant Melange," in *One Out of Three: Immigrant New York in the 21st century*, ed. Nancy Foner (New York: Columbia University Press, 2013), 41.

5 "Quick Facts," United States Census Bureau, http://www.census.gov/quick facts/table/POP645214/36081.

6 Steven Vertovec, "Super-diversity and Its Implications," *Ethnic and Racial Studies* 30, no. 6 (2007): 1024–1054; Fran Meissner and Steven Vertovec, "Comparing Super-diversity," *Ethnic and Racial Studies* 38, no. 4 (2015): 541–555. Hyper-diversity is the term used by Timothy Garton Ash, Edward Mortimer, and Kerem Oktem in "Freedom in Diversity: Ten Lessons for Public Policy from Britain, Canada, France, Germany and the United States" (Oxford: St. Antony's College, 2013). See also Saskia Sassen, *The Global City: New York, London, Tokyo* (Princeton, NJ: Princeton University Press, 1991); R. Scott Hanson, *City of Gods: Religious Freedom, Immigration and Pluralism in Flushing Queens* (New York: Fordham University Press, 2016).

7 New York's tenement museum, a monument to Lower East Side migration in the nineteenth century, is located on Orchard Street; see https://www.tenement.org.

8 Nancy Foner, "Immigration Past and Present," *Daedalus* 142, no. 3 (Summer 2013): 16–25.

9 Nancy Foner, "Models of Integration in a Settler Society: Caveats and Complications in the U.S. Case," *Patterns of Prejudice* 46, no. 5 (2012): 486–499.

10 Marc Fisher, "Open Doors, Slamming Gates: The Tumultuous Politics of U.S. Immigration Policy," *Washington Post,* January 28, 2017, https://www.washingtonpost.com/politics/open-doors-slamming-gates-the-tumultuous-politics-of-us-immigration-policy/2017/01/28/b646ea48-e57a-11e6-a453-19ec4b3d09ba_story.html?hpid=hp_hp-top-table-main_refugeeshistory-730pm%3Ahomepage%2Fstory&utm_term=.d67d300d6ba6.

11 Sanjek, *The Future of Us All,* 367.

12 The community is celebrated in Frederick Wiseman's lyrical and compassionate film *In Jackson Heights* (Cambridge, MA: Zipporah Films, 2015).

13 On sanctuary cities, see Ohio Jobs and Justice Political Action Committee, "The Original List of Sanctuary Cities, USA," http://www.ojjpac.org/sanctuary.asp.

14 Foner, "Immigration Past and Present."

15 Steven Vertovec, "The Political Importance of Diasporas," Migration Policy Institute, June 1, 2005, http://www.migrationpolicy.org/article/political -importance-diasporas; Gabriel Sheffer, *Diaspora Politics* (Cambridge: Cambridge University Press, 2003).

16 Susanne Wessendorf, "Commonplace Diversity and the 'Ethos of Mixing': Perceptions of Difference in a London Neighborhood," *Identities: Global Studies in Culture and Power* 20, no. 4 (2013): 407–422.

17 Richard Alba and Nancy Foner, *Strangers No More: Immigration and the Challenges of Integration in North America and Western Europe* (Princeton, NJ: Princeton University Press, 2015), chap. 4.

18 Douglas S. Massey, Jonathan Rothwell, and Thurston Domina, "The Changing Basis of Segregation in the United States," *Annals of the American Academy of Political and Social Science* 626 (November 2009): 74–90; Camille Zubrinsky Charles, "The Dynamics of Racial Residential Segregation," *Annual Review of Sociology* 29 (2003): 167–2007.

19 The phrase "global neighborhoods" is used by M. C. Waters, P. Kasinitz, and A. L. Asad in "Immigrants and African Americans," *Annual Review of Sociology* 40 (2014): 369–390.

20 John Kucsera and Gary Orfield, "New York State's Extreme School Segregation: Inequality, Inaction and a Damaged Future," Civil Rights Project, University of California, Los Angeles, March 2014, http:// civilrightsproject.ucla.edu/research/k-12-education/integration-and -diversity/ny-norflet-report-placeholder/Kucsera-New-York-Extreme -Segregation-2014.pdf.

21 "The Rise of Intermarriage," Pew Research Center, http://www.pewsocialtrends .org/files/2012/02/SDT-Intermarriage-II.pdf; Zhenchao Qian and Daniel T. Lichter, "Changing Patterns of Interracial Marriage in a Multiracial Society" *Journal of Marriage and Family* (October 2011); "Households and Families: 2020 Census Brief," http://www.census.gov/population/www/cen2010 /briefs/tables/appendix.pdf; Roland G. Fryer Jr., "Guess Who's Been Coming to Dinner? Trends in Interracial Marriage over the 20th Century," *Journal of Economic Perspectives* (Spring 2007), http://pubs.aeaweb.org/doi /pdfplus/10.1257/jep.21.2.71.

22 Anthony Appiah, *The Ethics of Identity* (Princeton, NJ: Princeton University Press, 2005), 230: "Equality wasn't what morality demanded of us as individuals: it denotes a regulative ideal for political, not personal conduct. We go wrong when we conflate personal and political ideals."

23 Nancy Foner and Roger Waldinger, "New York and Los Angeles as Immigrant Destinations: Contrasts and Convergence" in *New York and Los Angeles: The Uncertain Future*, ed. David Halle and Andrew Beveridge (New York: Oxford University Press, 2013).

2. LOS ANGELES

1 Steven Vertovec, "Super-diversity and Its Implications," *Ethnic and Racial Studies* 30, no. 6 (2007): 1024–1054; Fran Meissner and Steven Vertovec, "Comparing Super-diversity," *Ethnic and Racial Studies* 38, no. 4 (2015): 541–555; Timothy Garton Ash, Edward Mortimer, and Kerem Oktem, "Freedom in Diversity: Ten Lessons for Public Policy from Britain, Canada, France, Germany and the United States" (Oxford: St. Antony's College, 2013); Saskia Sassen, *The Global City: New York, London, Tokyo* (Princeton, NJ: Princeton University Press, 1991).

2 "The World's Cities in 2016" (New York: United Nations, 2016), http://www.un.org/en/development/desa/population/publications/pdf/urbanization/the_worlds_cities_in_2016_data_booklet.pdf.

3 Enoch Powell, "Speech to the Birmingham Conservative Association," April 10, 1968, http://www.telegraph.co.uk/comment/3643826/Enoch-Powells-Rivers-of-Blood-speech.html.

4 The visit of the Carnegie Council team to Los Angeles was made possible by the cooperation of the following institutions at the University of Southern California: the Levan Institute for Ethics and the Humanities, the Center for the Study of Immigrant Integration, the Center for the Study of Religion and Civic Culture, the Shoah Foundation, the Office of Immigrant Affairs of the City of Los Angeles, the Los Angeles Police Department, and the Annenberg School. I am grateful to Dr. Lyn Boyd Judson of the Levan Institute for invaluable assistance and to Hebag Farrah of the Center for Immigrant Integration for bibliographic research.

5 David Halle and Andrew A. Beveridge, *New York and Los Angeles* (New York: Oxford University Press, 2013), 4.

6 See Edward Thompson, "The Moral Economy of the English Crowd in the 18th Century," *Past and Present* 50 no. 1 (1971): 76–136. See also Sam Bowles, *The Moral Economy: Why Good Incentives Are No Substitute for Good Citizens* (New Haven, CT: Yale University Press, 2016).

7 Will Kymlicka, *Multicultural Citizenship* (Oxford: Clarendon Press, 1995); Kwame Anthony Appiah, *The Ethics of Identity* (Princeton, NJ: Princeton University Press, 2005); Charles Taylor, *Multiculturalism: Examining the Politics of Recognition,* ed. Amy Gutmann (Princeton, NJ: Princeton University Press, 1994).

8 Adam Smith, *The Theory of Moral Sentiments,* intro. Amartya Sen, ed. R. P. Hanley (1759; London: Penguin, 2009).

9 These figures are in Los Angeles 2020 Commission, "A Time for Action" (Los Angeles, 2014), http://clkrep.lacity.org/onlinedocs/2014/14-1184_MISC _b_8-25-14.pdf; see also Roger Waldinger, "Not the Promised City: Los Angeles and Its Immigrants," *Pacific Historical Review* 68, no. 2 (May 1999): 253–272; Harry W. Richardson and Peter Gordon, "Globalization and Los Angeles," in *Globalization and Urban Development,* ed. Harry W. Richardson (Berlin: Springer, 2005), 197–209.

10 Anthony Damasio, *Descartes' Error: Emotion, Reason, and the Human Brain* (New York: Penguin, 2005); Joshua Greene, *Moral Tribes: Emotion, Reason, and the Gap between Us and Them* (New York: Penguin, 2013); Steven Pinker, *How the Mind Works* (New York: W. W. Norton, 1997).

11 Robert Behn, "Some Thoughts on the Five Challenges that Tacit Knowledge Creates for Public Management" (conference paper presented at St. Gallen University, Switzerland, June 2016).

12 Susanne Wessendorf, "Commonplace Diversity and the 'Ethos of Mixing': Perceptions of Difference in a London Neighborhood," *Identities: Global Studies in Culture and Power* 20, no. 4 (2013): 407–422; Amanda Wise, "Hope and Belief in a Multicultural Suburb," *Journal of Intercultural Studies* 26, nos. 1–2 (2005): 171–186.

13 On thick and thin theories of the moral good, see Michael Walzer, *Thick and Thin: Moral Argument at Home and Abroad* (Notre Dame, IN: University of Notre Dame Press, 1994).

14 Website of the *Boyle Heights Beat,* www.boyleheightsbeat.com.

15 Manuel Pastor and Chris Benner, *Just Growth: Inclusion and Prosperity in America's Metropolitan Regions* (London: Routledge, 2012).

16 Website of A Better LA, http://www.abetterla.org/programs/.

17 Aquil Basheer and Christina Hoag, *Peace in the Hood: Working with Gang Members to End the Violence* (Los Angeles: Hunter House, 2014).

18 Kristy Hang, "The Seoul of LA: Contested Identities and Transnationalism in Immigrant Space" (PhD diss., School of Cinematic Arts, USC, 2013).

19 R. T. Schaefer, "Placing the LA Riots in their Social and Historical Context," *Journal of American Ethnic History* 16, no. 2 (Winter 1997): 58–63; M. Herman, "Ten Years After: A Critical Review of Scholarship on the 1992 Los Angeles Riots," *Race, Gender and Class* 11, no. 1 (2004): 116–135; Paul J. Kaplan, "Looking through the Gaps: A Critical Approach to the LAPD's Rampart Scandal," *Social Justice* 36, no. 1 (2009): 61.

20 Christopher Stone, Todd Foglesong, Christine Cole, "Policing Los Angeles Under A Consent Decree: The Dynamics of Change at the LAPD," *Harvard Program in Criminal Justice Policy and Management,* May 2009; see also L. D. Gascon, "Policing Divisions: Race, Crime and Community in South LA" (PhD diss., UC Irvine, 2013).

21 Richard Flory, Brie Loskota, and Donald Miller, "Forging A New Moral and Political Agenda: The Civic Role of Religion in Los Angeles, 1992–2010" (unpublished paper, Center for Religion and Civic Culture, USC, 2011).

22 Paul F. Diehl, Charlotte Ku, and Daniel Zamora, "The Dynamics of International Law: The Interaction of Normative and Operating Systems," *International Organization* 57 (Winter 2003): 43–75.

23 Manuel Pastor and Enrico A. Marcelle, "What's at Stake for the State: Undocumented Californians, Immigration Reform, and Our Future Together" (Los Angeles, Center for the Study of Immigration Integration, University of Southern California, 2013), http://csii.usc.edu/undocumented CA.html.

24 Roger Waldinger, "Not the Promised City: Los Angeles and Its Immigrants," *Pacific Historical Review* 68, no. 2 (May 1999): 253–272; Philip J. Ethington, "Into the Labyrinth of Los Angeles Historiography: From Global Comparisons to Local Knowledge," Los Angeles and the Problem of Urban Historical

Knowledge, A Multimedia Essay, http://www.usc.edu/dept/LAS/history
/historylab/LAPUHK/Text/Labyrinth_Historiography.htm.

25 Waldinger, "Not the Promised City"; see also Greg Hise, "Border City: Race
    and Social Distance in Los Angeles," *American Quarterly,* 56, no. 3
    (September 2004): 545–558, http://www.jstor.org/stable/40068233.

26 See "Los Angeles 2020"; Scott Kurashige, "Crenshaw and the Rise of
    Multiethnic Los Angeles," *Afro-Hispanic Review* 27, no. 1 (Spring 2008): 41–58.

27 Raphael J. Sonenshein, "The Dynamics of Biracial Coalitions: Crossover Politics
    in Los Angeles," *Western Political Quarterly* 42, no. 2 (June 1989): 333–353.

28 Bruce Katz and Jennifer Bradley, *The Metropolitan Revolution: How Cities
    and Metros Are Fixing Our Broken Politics and Fragile Economy* (Washington,
    DC: Brookings Institution Press, 2013).

29 See Richardson and Gordon, "Globalization and Los Angeles."

30 "Los Angeles 2020."

31 Karl Marx and Friedrich Engels, *The Communist Manifesto* (1847).

32 Mike Davis, *City of Quartz: Excavating the Future in Los Angeles* (London:
    Verso, 1990).

33 John Stuart Mill, *Considerations on Representative Government* (1861),
    chap 4: "Under What Social Conditions Representative Government Is
    Inapplicable."

34 Jeffry Frieden, "Will Global Capitalism Fail Again?" (Brussels: Bruegel
    Essay, 2009), fig. 1; Dani Rodrik, *The Globalization Paradox: Democracy
    and the Future of the World Economy* (New York: Norton, 2011); Joseph
    Stiglitz, *Making Globalization Work* (New York: Norton, 2007); *Globalization
    and Its Discontents* (New York: Norton, 2003).

3. RIO DE JANEIRO

1 Mario Pezzini, "An Emerging Middle Class," *OECD Observer,* 2012, http://
   www.oecdobserver.org/news/fullstory.php/aid/3681/An_emerging_middle
   _class.html.

2 Jonathan Watts, "Voices of Brazil: The Police Chief Pioneer," *The Observer*
   (London), January 26, 2014; Donna Bowater, *Daily Telegraph* (London),
   October 19, 2013.

3 World Bank, World Development Index, Brazil, http://wdi.worldbank.org /table/2.9.

4 Human Rights Watch, "Good Cops Are Afraid: The Toll of Unchecked Police Violence in Rio de Janeiro," *Human Rights Watch,* May 2016.

5 Clarissa Huguet and Ilona Szabó de Carvalho, "Violence in the Brazilian Favelas and the Role of the Police," *New Directions for Youth Development* 119 (2008): 93–108; Rogerio F. Pinto and Maria S. Do Carmo, "The Pacifying Police Units of the State of Rio De Janeiro: Incremental Innovation or Police Reform," *Public Administration and Development* 36 (2016): 121–131; Erika. R. Larkins, "Performances of Police Legitimacy in Rio's Hyper Favela," *Law and Social Inquiry* 38, no. 3 (2013): 553–578; Suketu Mehta, "In the Violent Favelas of Brazil," *New York Review of Books,* August 15, 2013, http://www.nybooks.com/articles/2013/08/15/violent-favelas-brazil/ ?pagination=false.

6 M. Alves and P. Evanson, *Living in the Crossfire: Favela Residents, Drug Dealers and Police Violence in Rio de Janeiro,* (Philadelphia: Temple University Press, 2011), 113–133.

7 Bianca Freire-Medeiros, Márcio Grijó Vilarouca, and Palloma Menezes, "International Tourists in a 'Pacified' Favela: Profiles and Attitudes. The Case of Santa Marta, Rio de Janeiro," *Die Erde* (Berlin) 144, no. 2 (2013): 147–159.

8 Janet Tappin Coelho, "Brazil's 'Peace Police' Turn Five. Are Rio's Favela's Safer?," *Christian Science Monitor,* December 19, 2013.

9 Natalia Viana, "Brazil's Security Plans for the Olympics Raise Eyebrows," *Open Society Foundations,* August 5, 2016; Anna Jean Kaiser and Andrew Jacobs, "Security Force of 85,000 Fills Rio, Upsetting Rights Activists," *New York Times,* August 7, 2016, http://www.nytimes.com/2016/08/08/world /americas/rio-olympics-crime.html?_r=0.

10 Michael Clausen, "Corruption and Democracy in Brazil: An Interview with Timothy Power," *Brasiliana: Journal for Brazilian Studies* 1, no. 1 (September 2012); Carlos Pereira, Timothy J. Power, and Eric D. Raila, "Coalitional Presidentialism and Side Payments: Explaining the Mensalão Scandal in Brazil," Occasional Paper BSP 03-08 (Oxford: Brazilian Studies Programme, Latin American Centre, University of Oxford, 2008).

11 Marcus Tullius Cicero, *De Officiis* (*On Duties*), ed. M. T. Griffin and E. M. Atkins (Cambridge: Cambridge University Press, 1991); under Justinian was issued the Corpus Juris Civilis, between 529 and 534 CE, the foundation of modern civil law.

12 Manuel Balan, "Surviving Corruption in Brazil: Lula's and Dilma's Success despite Corruption Allegations and Its Consequences," *Journal of Politics in Latin America* 6, no. 3 (2014): 67–93.

13 Our participants included professor Roberto Kant de Lima, Dr. Michel Misse, Dr. Gláucia Mouzinho, Abel Gomes, Odilon Romano Neto, Arthur Gueiros, Jean Wyllys, Rafael Iorio, and Dr. Fernanda Duarte, a Carnegie Global Fellow.

14 Amaury de Souza, "The Politics of Personality in Brazil," *Journal of Democracy* 22, no. 2 (2011): 75–88.

15 *Soccer Politics,* "Corruption and the 2013 Protests in Brazil," blog entry by Vishnu Kadiyala, 2013, http://sites.duke.edu/wcwp/world-cup-2014/politics -in-brazil/corruption/.

16 Monica Arruda de Almeida and Bruce Zagaris, "Political Capture in the Petrobras Corruption Scandal," *Fletcher Forum on World Affairs* 39, no. 2 (Summer 2015): 87–97; Monica Arruda de Almeida, "Managing Public Perceptions: New Wealth and Corruption in Brazil," *Fletcher Forum on World Affairs* 36, no. 2 (Summer 2012): 51–55; E. E. Dellasoppa, "Corruption in Brazilian Society: An Overview," in *Policing Corruption: International Perspectives,* ed. R. Sarre, D. K. Das, and H. J. Albrecht (Oxford: Lexington Books, 2005); see also Kurt Weyland, "The Politics of Corruption in Latin America" (conference paper presented at the University of New Mexico, September 1997); Michael Clausen, "Corruption and Democracy in Brazil: An Interview with Timothy Power," *Brasiliana: Journal for Brazilian Studies* 1, no. 1 (September 2012), 107–120; Pereira, Power, and Raila, "Coalitional Presidentialism and Side Payments."

17 Daniel Gallas, "Brazil's Odebrecht Corruption Scandal," BBC News, March 7, 2017, http://www.bbc.com/news/business-39194395.

18 Brad Brooks, "Rio's Slum 'Pacification' Effort Stalls as Killings Tick Up," Reuters News, August 4, 2016.

4. BOSNIA

1 Michael Ignatieff, *Blood and Belonging: Journeys into the New Nationalism* (London: Chatto and Windus, 1993); see also Michael Ignatieff, *The Warrior's Honor: Ethnic War and the Modern Conscience* (New York: Metropolitan, 1998); and Michael Ignatieff, *Virtual War: Kosovo and Beyond* (Toronto: Penguin Canada, 2000).

2 David Rieff, *Slaughterhouse: Bosnia and the Failure of the West* (New York: Touchstone, 1995); Samantha Power, *A Problem from Hell: America and the Age of Genocide* (New York: Basic Books, 2002); Roger Cohen, *Hearts Grown Brutal: Sagas of Sarajevo* (New York: Random House, 1998); Zlatko Dizdarevic, *Sarajevo: A War Journal* (New York: Fromm, 1993).

3 Kathryn Sikkink, *The Justice Cascade: How Human Rights Prosecutions Are Changing World Politics* (New York: Norton, 2012); Ruti G. Teitel, *Transitional Justice* (New York: Oxford University Press, 2000); Richard J. Goldstone, *For Humanity: Reflections of a War Crimes Prosecutor* (New Haven, CT: Yale University Press, 2000); Louise Arbour, *War Crimes and the Culture of Peace* (Toronto: University of Toronto Press, 2002); Gary J. Bass, *Stay the Hand of Vengeance: The Politics of War Crimes Tribunals* (Princeton, NJ: Princeton University Press, 2002); Rory Stewart and Gerald Knaus, *Can Intervention Work?* (New York: W. W. Norton, 2011); Martha Minow, *Between Vengeance and Forgiveness: Facing History after Genocide and Mass Atrocity* (Boston: Beacon Press, 1998); Martha Minow and Antonia Chayes, eds., *Imagine Coexistence: Restoring Humanity after Violent Ethnic Conflict* (San Francisco: Wiley, 2003).

4 Christopher Clark, *The Sleepwalkers: How Europe Went to War in 1914* (New York: Harper Collins, 2012).

5 Noel Malcolm, *Bosnia: A Short History* (London: Macmillan, 1994); Ivo Banac, *The National Question in Yugoslavia: Origin, History, Politics* (Ithaca, NY: Cornell University Press, 1988); Jacques Rupnik, ed., *International Commission on the Balkans, Unfinished Peace* (Washington, DC: Carnegie Endowment, 1996); Jacques Rupnik, *Le Déchirement des Nations* (Paris: Seuil, 1996).

6 Richard Holbrooke, *To End a War* (New York: Random House, 1998).

7   Carnegie Council on Ethics in International Affairs, Sarajevo Symposium,
    June 28, 2014, https://www.carnegiecouncil.org/programs/archive/sarajevo
    /index.html.

8   Margaret MacMillan, *The War That Ended Peace: The Road to 1914* (New
    York: Random House, 2013), 333.

9   Jorge Luis Borges, "Legend," in *Collected Fictions,* trans. Alan Hurley
    (London: Allen Lane, 1999).

10 International Commission on Missing Persons, http://www.icmp.int.

11 Leo Tolstoy, "The Kreutzer Sonata" (1889), in *The Kreutzer Sonata and
    Other Short Stories* (New York: Dover, 1993).

12 J. W. Honig and N. Both, *Srebrenica: Record of a War Crime* (New York:
    Penguin, 1996).

13 Swanee Hunt, *This Was Not Our War: Bosnian Women Reclaiming the Peace*
    (Durham, NC: Duke University Press, 2004).

14 Roy Gutman, *A Witness to Genocide* (New York, Macmillan, 1993); Ed
    Vulliamy, *Seasons in Hell: Understanding Bosnia's War* (New York:
    St. Martin's Press, 1994).

15 Michael Ignatieff, "When a Bridge Is Not a Bridge," *New York Times Magazine,*
    October 27, 2002, http://www.nytimes.com/2002/10/27/magazine/when-a
    -bridge-is-not-a-bridge.html?pagewanted=all.

16 Azra Hromadzic, "Bathroom Mixing: Youth Negotiate Democratization in
    Postconflict Bosnia and Hercegovina," *Polar: Political and Legal
    Anthropology Review* 34, no. 2 (2011): 268–289.

17 Joe Sacco, *Safe Area Gorazde: The War in Eastern Bosnia, 1992–1995*
    (Seattle, WA: Fantagraphics Books, 2000).

5. MYANMAR

1   J. S. Furnivall, *Colonial Policy and Practice: A Comparative Study of Burma
    and Netherlands India* (Cambridge: Cambridge University Press, 1948 / New
    York: New York University Press, 1948). A plural society "is in the strictest
    sense a medley, for they [ethnic groups] mix but do not combine. Each
    group holds by its own religion, its own culture and language, its own ideas

and ways. As individuals they meet, but only in the market place,…
[and]… with different sections of the community living side by side, but
separately, within the same political unit. Even in the economic sphere
there is division of labor along racial lines, Natives, Chinese, Indians and
Europeans all have different functions, and within each major group
subsections have particular occupations." Julie Pham, "J. S. Furnivall and
Fabianism: Reinterpreting the 'Plural Society' in Burma," *Modern Asian
Studies* 39, no. 2 (May 2005): 321–348; UNFPA, Myanmar Census, 2014.
United Nations Population Fund Myanmar: Country Profile, 2016,
http://myanmar.unfpa.org/en/country-profile-0.

2 George Orwell, *Burmese Days* (1934; New York: Harcourt, 1974).

3 Michael W. Charney, *A History of Modern Burma* (Cambridge: Cambridge
University Press, 2009).

4 Thant Myint U, *The River of Lost Footsteps: A Personal History of Burma*
(New York: Farrar, Straus and Giroux, 2006); Martin Smith, *Burma–
Insurgency and the Politics of Ethnicity* (London: Zed Books, 1991).

5 Author interview with U Hlaing Bwa, Myanmar Institute of Theology,
Yangon, June 15, 2015.

6 Ian Holliday, "Ethnicity and Democratization in Myanmar," *Asian Journal
of Political Science* 18, no. 2 (August 2010): 111–128.

7 "When the Lid Blows Off: Communal Violence in Myanmar," *The Economist,*
March 30, 2013, http://www.economist.com/news/asia/21574506-sectarian
-violence-was-not-supposed-be-part-myanmars-bright-new-direction-when
-lid-blows; Nehginpao Kipgen, "Conflict in Rakhine State in Myanmar:
Rohingya Muslims' Conundrum," *Journal of Muslim Minority Affairs* 33,
no. 2 (2013): 298–310, DOI: 10.1080/13602004.2013.810117; Akm Ahsan
Ullah, "Rohingya Refugees to Bangladesh: Historical Exclusions and
Contemporary Marginalization," *Journal of Immigrant and Refugee Studies*
9, no. 2 (April–June 2011): 139–161; Joshua Kurlantzick, "Myanmar: The Next
Failed State?" *Current History* (September 2011): 242–247, http://www.cfr
.org/burmamyanmar/myanmar-next-failed-state/p25710; Greg Barton and
Virginie Andre, "Islam and Muslim–Buddhist and Muslim–Christian
Relations in Southeast Asia," *Islam and Christian–Muslim Relations* 25,
no. 3 (2014): 281–285; Azeem Ibrahim, *The Rohingyas: Inside Myanmar's*

Hidden Genocide (London: Hurst, 2016); S. K. Kosem and A. Saleem, "Religion, Nationalism and the Rohingya's Search for Citizenship in Myanmar," in *Muslim Minority State Relations: Violence, Integration and Policy,* ed. R. Mason (London: Palgrave Macmillan, 2016), 212–224.

8 "When Buddhists Go Bad," *Time,* July 1, 2013.

9 Tin Maung Maung Than, "Myanmar in 2013: At the Halfway Mark," *Asian Survey* 54, no. 1 (January / February 2014): 22–29; see also Nick Cheesman and Htoo Kyaw Win, eds., *Communal Violence in Myanmar* (Yangon: Myanmar Knowledge Society and Australian National University, 2015).

10 "Buddhism in Myanmar," http://www.buddhanet.net/e-learning/buddhist world/burma-txt.htm; Ranga Sirilal and Shihar Aneez, "Hardline Buddhists in Myanmar, Sri Lanka Strike Anti-Islamist Pact," Reuters, September 30, 2014.

11 "When Buddhists Go Bad."

12 Michael Ignatieff, *Blood and Belonging: Journeys into the New Nationalism* (New York: Farrar, Straus and Giroux, 1993), chap. 1; Michael Ignatieff, *The Warrior's Honour: Ethnic War and the Modern Conscience* (Toronto: Penguin Canada, 1998), chap. 3.

13 Mong Palatino, "The Meaning of the Mandalay Riots in Myanmar," *The Diplomat,* July 12, 2014; Soe Zeya Tun, "Myanmar Police Arrest 5 as Calm Returns to Mandalay after Riots," Reuters, July 3, 2014.

14 Author interview with U Tin Htut, Daw Win Mya Mya, and Nan San Moon, Mandalay, National League for Democracy headquarters, June 15, 2015.

15 For a wonderful discussion of Yangon traffic, the taxi system, and the market in cars, see Ardeth Maung Thawghmung, "The Politics of Everyday Life in Twenty-First Century Myanmar," *Journal of Asian Studies* 70, no. 3 (August 2011): 641–656.

16 Jane Perlez, "For Some, Daw Aung San Suu Kyi Falls Short of Expectations in Myanmar," *New York Times,* November 12, 2014, http://www.nytimes .com/2014/11/13/world/asia/for-some-daw-aung-san-suu-kyi-falls-short-of -expectations-in-myanmar.html.

17 Tim Hume, "Aung San Suu Kyi's 'Silence' on the Rohingya: Has 'The Lady' Lost Her Voice?," CNN, June 1, 2014.

18 Kenneth Roth, "Rights Struggles of 2013," in *Human Rights Watch World Report*, 2014 http://www.hrw.org/world-report/2014/essays/rights-struggles -of-2013.

19 "The Arakan Project," *Insight on Conflict*, https://www.insightonconflict.org /conflicts/myanmar/peacebuilding-organisations/arakan-project/.

20 Author interview with Myat Thu and Myo Aung Htwe, Yangon School of Political Science, Yangon, June 19, 2015.

21 Author interviews on background, U.S. embassy, Yangon, June 19, 2015.

22 Aung San Suu Kyi Tells UN That the Term Rohingya Will Be Avoided, *The Guardian*, June 20, 2016, https://www.theguardian.com/world/2016/jun /21/aung-san-suu-kyi-tells-un-that-the-term-rohingya-will-be-avoided; "Joint Press Availability, U.S. Secretary of State and Aung San Suu Kyi," Naypyidaw, May 22, 2016.

23 Thomas P. (Tip) O'Neill and Gary Hymel, *All Politics Is Local: And Other Rules of the Game* (Holbrooke, MA: Bob Adams, 1994).

6. FUKUSHIMA

1 Author interview with Naoto Kan, Tokyo, June 6, 2015, plus author interviews with citizens and officials in Fukushima Prefecture, June 9–11, 2015.

2 "Kin Sue over Tsunami Deaths of 23 Kids at Miyagi School," *Japan Times*, March 20, 2014, http://www.japantimes.co.jp/news/2014/03/10/national /kin-sue-over-tsunami-deaths-of-23-kids-at-miyagi-school/#.VZqqy0sVpuY.

3 Elsa Gisquet and Malka Older, "Human and Organizational Factors Perspective on the Fukushima Nuclear Accident: March 11–March 15, 2011" (Paris: IRSN, 2015).

4 Government of Japan, Cabinet Office, Nuclear Emergency Response Headquarters, "Current Status and Challenges of Evacuation Areas in Fukushima," June 2015; author interviews with Hiroo Inoue and Nobuaki Arima, Support Team for Residents Affected by Nuclear Incidents, June 2015.

5 Michael Ignatieff, "The Broken Contract," *New York Times Magazine*, September 25, 2005, http://www.michaelignatieff.ca/assets/pdfs /TheBrokenContract.2005.pdf.

6 David A. Moss, *When All Else Fails: Government as the Ultimate Risk Manager* (Cambridge, MA: Harvard University Press, 2002).

7 Ulrich Beck, *Risk Society: Towards a New Modernity* (London: Sage, 1992).

8 Steven Pinker, *The Better Angels of Our Nature: Why Violence Has Declined* (New York: Viking, 2011).

9 National Diet of Japan, "The Fukushima Nuclear Accident Independent Investigation Commission: Executive Summary" (Tokyo, 2012).

10 Richard J. Samuels, *3.11: Disaster and Change in Japan* (Ithaca, NY: Cornell University Press, 2013); "Nuclear Power in Japan," World Nuclear Association, http://www.world-nuclear.org/info/Country-Profiles/Countries-G-N/Japan/; Executive Summary of the Interim Report of the Japanese Investigatory Commission on the Fukushima Disaster, December 2011, http://www.cas .go.jp/jp/seisaku/icanps/eng/120224SummaryEng.pdf; Final Report of the Japanese Investigatory Commission on the Fukushima Nuclear Power Stations of Tokyo Electric Power Company, http://www.cas.go.jp/jp /seisaku/icanps/eng/final-report.html; National Diet of Japan, Official Report of the Fukushima Nuclear Accident Independent Investigation Commission (The Kurokawa Report), 2012, http://warp.da.ndl.go.jp /info:ndljp/pid/3856371/naiic.go.jp/wp-content/uploads/2012/09 /NAIIC_report_hi_res10.pdf.

11 Author interview with Eiju Hangai, Minamisoma, June 16, 2015.

12 Executive Summary of the Interim Report of the Japanese Investigatory Commission; see also Final Report of the Japanese Investigatory Commission.

13 Author interview with Kiyoshi Kurokawa, Tokyo, June 18, 2015.

14 Jake Adelstein, "Trial in Japan Will Delve into 'the Hidden Truths' of the Fukushima Nuclear Meltdown," February 29, 2016, http://www.latimes.com /world/asia/la-fg-japan-tepco-fukushima-20160229-story.html.

15 Kiyoshi Kurokawa, "Speech at GRIPS Commencement," National Graduate Institute for Policy Studies, San Diego, CA, September 17, 2013.

16 Author interview with Yukiko Fukui, Nippon TV, Tokyo, June 17, 2015.

17 One characteristic example of Japanese counterexpertise is the film directed and produced by the Tokyo lawyer Hiroyuki Kawai, *Nuclear Japan: Has Nuclear Power Brought Us Happiness?* (2015).

18 On the concept of standing, see Michael Ignatieff, *Fire and Ashes: Success and Failure in Politics* (Cambridge, MA: Harvard University Press, 2013).

19 Matthew Bunn and Olli Heinonen, "Preventing the Next Fukushima," *Science* 333, no. 6049 (September 2011), 1580–1581.

20 Chatham House Asia Programme, "The Role of the Nation-State in Addressing Global Challenges: Japan-UK Perspectives," Conference Report (London, March 2015).

21 Charles Perrow, *Normal Accidents: Living with High-Risk Technologies* (New York: Basic Books, 1984).

22 Richard Feynman, "Volume 2: Appendix F–Personal Observations on Reliability of Shuttle," in *Report of the Presidential Commission on the Challenger Disaster* (NASA, 1986), http://history.nasa.gov/rogersrep /v2appf.htm; see also Richard Feynman, *What Do You Care What Other People Think?* (New York: Bantam, 1988).

23 Final Report of the Japanese Investigatory Commission.

24 Daniel Kahneman, *Thinking Fast and Slow* (New York: Farrar, Straus and Giroux, 2013).

25 Ryusho Kadota, *On the Brink: The Inside Story of Fukushima Daiichi* (Tokyo: Kurodahan Press, 2014).

26 National Academy of Sciences, *Lessons Learned from the Fukushima Nuclear Accident for Improving Safety of U.S. Nuclear Plants* (Washington, DC: National Academies Press, 2014).

27 Sheri Fink, *Five Days at Memorial: Life and Death in a Storm-Ravaged Hospital* (New York: Crown, 2013).

28 On the resilience of memory alloys, see Jonathan Webb, "Memory Alloy Bounces Back into Shape 10 Million Times," BBC News, May 29, 2015, http://www.bbc.co.uk/news/science-environment-32886000.

29 Charles Dickens, *Oliver Twist* (London, 1837–1839). For antiheroic examples of resilience after wartime, see Werner Sollors, *The Temptation of Despair* (Cambridge, MA: Harvard University Press, 2014); see also Ian Buruma, *Year Zero: A History of 1945* (New York: Penguin, 2013).

30 National Scientific Council on the Development of the Child, "Supportive Relationships and Active Skill-Building Strengthen the Foundations of Resilience," Working Paper 13 (Cambridge, MA: Center for the Developing Child, Harvard University, 2013). I am grateful to Stephen Lassonde for this reference.

31 I gratefully acknowledge the contribution of my Harvard Kennedy School student Ku Ka Tsai to this analysis.

32 Chiara de Franco and Christoph Meyer, eds., *Forecasting, Warning and Responding to Transnational Risks* (London: Palgrave Macmillan, 2011); see also Eva Illouz, "Ne déplaçons pas la source de la violence sur les victimes elles-mêmes," *Le Monde,* December 31, 2016.

33 Nicholas Nassim Taleb, *The Black Swan: The Impact of the Highly Improbable,* 2nd ed. (New York: Random House, 2010).

34 U.S. Government Accountability Office, "Nuclear Safety: Countries' Regulatory Bodies Have Made Changes in Response to the Fukushima Daiichi Accident," GAO-14-109, March 6, 2014.

35 Author interview with Kiyoshi Kurokawa, GRIPS, Tokyo, June 3, 2015.

36 Azby Brown, "Issues at Fukushima Daiichi Nuclear Power Plant (FDNPP)," *Safecast,* March 23, 2015, https://medium.com/safecast-report/safecast -report-part-2-7c6e644aae38. Accessed July 6, 2015.

37 Author interview with Hitoshi Aoki, Fukushima, June 19, 2015.

38 "Fukushima Child Thyroid Cancer Issue," *The Hiroshima Syndrome,* http://www.hiroshimasyndrome.com/fukushima-child-thyroid-issue .html; see also "30 Fukushima Children Diagnosed with Thyroid Cancer in Second Check but Radiation Said 'Unlikely' Cause," June 7, 2016, http://www.japantimes.co.jp/news/2016/06/07/national/30-fukushima -children-diagnosed-with-thyroid-cancer-in-second-check-but-radiation -said-unlikely-cause/#.V5hweGMq7dk.

39 "Historic 10th Century Japanese Wild Horse Chase Gets Back in the Saddle
     One Year On from Disaster That Crippled Nearby Nuclear Plant," *Daily
     Mail*, July 29, 2012, http://www.dailymail.co.uk/news/article-2180871
     /Historic-10th-Century-Japanese-wild-horse-chase-gets-saddle-year-disaster
     -crippled-nearby-nuclear-plant.html; Ayako Tanaka, "Japanese Horses
     Struggling in Wake of Disaster," June 7, 2011, http://www.chronofhorse.com
     /article/japanese-horses-struggling-wake-disaster.

40 Jonathan Lear, *Radical Hope: Ethics in the Face of Cultural Devastation*
     (Cambridge, MA: Harvard University Press, 2006).

41 Nadezhda Mandelstam, *Hope against Hope: A Memoir* (New York:
     Atheneum, 1970); Primo Levi, *The Drowned and the Saved* (New York:
     Vintage, 1989); "Living the Legacy," Nelson Mandela Foundation,
     https://www.nelsonmandela.org.

42 Charles Dickens, *David Copperfield* (London, 1850).

43 William Faulkner, winner of the 1949 Nobel Prize in Literature, speech at
     the Nobel banquet, December 10, 1950, http://www.nobelprize.org/nobel
     _prizes/literature/laureates/1949/faulkner-speech.html.

7. SOUTH AFRICA

1 Aung San Suu Kyi, *Freedom from Fear: And Other Writings*, foreword by
     Václav Havel, intro. Michael Aris (1991; London: Penguin, 2010); see also
     Václav Havel et al., *The Power of the Powerless: Citizens against the State in
     Central Eastern Europe*, intro. Steven Lukes, ed. John Keane (Armonk, NY:
     M.E. Sharpe, 1985).

2 Janet Cherry, *MK: Umkhonto Wesizwe* (Johannesburg: Jacana Publishing, 2014).

3 Steve Biko, *I Write What I Like: Selected Writings*, preface by Desmond
     Tutu (Chicago: University of Chicago Press, 1996).

4 Andrew Ross Sorkin, "How Mandela Shifted Views on Freedom of Markets,"
     New York Times, December 9, 2013.

5 Author interview with George Bizos, anti-apartheid lawyer, Johannesburg,
     December 2015.

6 Breyten Breytenbach, *Parool / Parole: Collected Speeches* (Cape Town:
     Penguin South Africa, 2015); see also Carmel Rickard, "The Judiciary and

the Constitution," in *Opinion Pieces by South African Thought Leaders,* ed. M. du Preez (Johannesburg: Penguin Books, 2011), 67–84.

7 Author interview with Roelf Meyer, National Party minister and negotiator at CODESA, the talks that led to the creation of the South African Constitution, Pretoria, December 2015.

8 Roger Southall, *Liberation Movements in Power: Party and State in Southern Africa* (Pietermaritzburg: University of Kwazulu-Natal Press, 2013).

9 Justice Malala, *We Have Now Begun Our Descent: How to Stop South Africa Losing Its Way* (Cape Town: Jonathan Ball, 2015); see also Susan Booysen, *Dominance and Decline: The ANC in the Time of Zuma* (Johannesburg: Wits University Press, 2015); Mark Gevisser, *A Legacy of Liberation: Thabo Mbeki and the Future of the South African Dream* (New York: Palgrave Macmillan, 2009).

10 Richard Dowden, *Africa: Altered States, Ordinary Miracles* (London: Portobello Books, 2011), chap. 18.

11 For the Truth and Reconciliation hearings and testimony, see the website of the Truth and Reconciliation Commission, http://www.justice.gov.za/trc.

12 Author interview with Glen Goosen, superior court judge, Eastern Cape, December 2015. Judge Goosen was a member of the TRC investigation team.

13 Michael Ignatieff, "Digging Up the Dead," *New Yorker,* December 10, 1997.

14 Jillian Edelstein, *Truth and Lies: Stories from the Truth and Reconciliation Commission in South Africa* (London, Granta Books, 2001), Introduction.

15 "Decision to Go to Court Was Sanctioned by Mandela: Motlanthe," South African Press Association, October 31, 1998, http://www.justice.gov.za/trc/media%5C1998%5C9810/s981031b.htm.

16 Author interview with Pamela Rubushe, social worker at Dora Nginza hospital, New Brighton, Eastern Cape, December 2015; see also Rachel Jewkes et al., "Why, When and How Men Rape: Understanding Rape Perpetration in South Africa," *South African Crime Quarterly* 34 (2014): 23–31, http://www.ajol.info/index.php/sacq/article/view/101459.

17 Mamboush's real name was Mocinemi Noki. He was thirty years old, with a wife and child, from a small village in the Eastern Cape. See Nick Davies,

"Marikana Massacre: The Untold Story of the Strike Leader Who Died for Workers' Rights," May 19, 2015, http://www.theguardian.com/world/2015 /may/19/marikana-massacre-untold-story-strike-leader-died-workers-rights.

18 For information about the Marikana Commission of Inquiry, presided over by Judge Ian Farlam, see http://www.marikanacomm.org.za.

19 *Miners Shot Down,* a film by Rehad Desai, Uhuru Productions, 2014, http://www.minersshotdown.co.za.

20 Rosa Lyster, "The Student Protests Roiling South Africa," *New Yorker,* October 21, 2016, http://www.newyorker.com/news/news-desk/the-student -protests-roiling-south-africa.

21 Author interview with professor Francis Wilson, University of Cape Town, December 2015; I am grateful to Fouad Cassim, adviser to the minister of finance, for providing background on the economic context of the student demonstrations in an interview in Pretoria, December 2015.

22 Author interview with student protest leaders, University of Pretoria, December 2015.

23 "Zuma Announces a 0% Increase in Tertiary Education Fees for 2016," RDM NewsWire, October 23, 2015, http://www.timeslive.co.za/politics/2015/10 /23/Zuma-announces-a-0-increase-in-tertiary-education-fees-for-2016.

24 Booysen, *Dominance and Decline,* 33.

25 On the legal issues relating to the land issue, I learned more from an interview with Janet Love, national director of the Legal Resources Center, Johannesburg, December 2015; see also http://www.lrc.org.za/law-policy -reform.

26 Mark Gevisser, *A Legacy of Liberation: Thabo Mbeki and the Future of the South African Dream* (New York: Palgrave Macmillan, 2009); on the land issue in South Africa more generally, see Ben Cousins, "Land Reform in South Africa," *Journal of Agrarian Change* 9, no. 3 (2009): 421–431.

27 Samantha Power, "How to Kill a Country: Turning a Breadbasket into a Basket Case in Ten Easy Steps—the Robert Mugabe Way," *The Atlantic,* December 2003, 86–89.

28 Ferial Haffajee, *What If There Were No Whites in South Africa?* (Johannesburg: Picador Africa 2015).

29 Janet Cherry, "Overcoming Oppression through Praxis: Non-Racialism as a Prefigurative Strategy" (unpublished paper, Nelson Mandela Bay University, 2015).

30 See "Corporate Citizenship," website of Volkswagen South Africa, http://www.vw.co.za/en/volkswagen-groupsouthafrica/corporate-citizenship .html.

31 For a definition of "Zama Zama," see http://www.oxforddictionaries.com /definition/english/zama-zama?q=Zama+Zama.

32 https://www.bible.com/bible/107/jas.1.27.net. Accessed August 12, 2016.

33 Author interview with George Bizos, Pretoria, December 2015.

34 Daniel Schneider, "The Constitutional Right to Housing in South Africa: The Government of the Republic of South Africa vs. Irene Grootboom," Harvard Kennedy School Case, Parts A and B (Cambridge, MA, 2001).

35 Sisonke Misimang, "The Old Is Dying and the Young Ones Have Just Been Born," *Africa Is a Country*, May 15, 2015, http://africasacountry.com/2015 /05/the-old-is-dying-and-the-young-ones-have-just-been-born/.

36 Joe Brock, "ANC Shaken to the Core as South African Voters Look beyond Race," Reuters, August 5, 2016, http://www.reuters.com/article/us-safrica -election-race-analysis-idUSKCN10G1BJ.

37 Two canonical versions of liberal freedom are to be found in Judith N. Shklar, *Ordinary Vices* (Cambridge, MA: Harvard University Press, 1985) and in Isaiah Berlin, *Four Essays on Liberty* (Oxford: Oxford University Press, 1969).

38 Harry G. Frankfurt, *On Inequality* (Princeton, NJ: Princeton University Press, 2015).

39 Jan Hofmeyr and Rajen Govender, "National Reconciliation, Race Relations, and Social Inclusion," South African Barometer Briefing Paper 1, December 8, 2015, https://www.scribd.com/document/292748740/South -African-Reconciliation-Barometer-2015.

CONCLUSION

1 Quoted in Church Peace Union, "In Your Hands: A Guide for Community Action on the 10th Anniversary of the Universal Declaration of Human Rights" (New York, 1958).

2 Beth Simmons, *Mobilizing for Human Rights: International Law in Domestic Politics* (New York: Cambridge University Press, 2009).

3 Katherine Boo, *Behind the Beautiful Forevers: Life, Death, and Hope in a Mumbai Undercity* (New York: Random House, 2012); Jonny Steinberg, *A Man of Good Hope* (New York: Knopf Doubleday, 2015).

4 Devin T. Stewart, "In Search of a Global Ethic," *Democracy,* April 18, 2016, http://www.carnegiecouncil.org/publications/articles_papers_reports /777.

5 Karl Popper, *The Open Society and Its Enemies* (1945; London: Routledge, 2002), chaps. 10, 25.

6 I wish to gratefully acknowledge discussions with the philosopher Timothy Macklem of King's College London, School of Law, on these points, though he is bound to disagree with my statements here.

7 Hannah Arendt, *The Human Condition,* 2nd ed. (Chicago: University of Chicago Press, 1998).

8 David Hume, *A Treatise of Human Nature,* 1896 ed., ed. Lewis Amherst Selby-Bigge (1739; Oxford: Clarendon Press, 1956), 481.

9 Hannah Arendt, *The Origins of Totalitarianism* (1948; New York: Schocken, 2004), 381.

10 Karl Marx, *The Economic and Philosophic Manuscripts of 1844* (New York: Dover, 2012).

11 Michel de Montaigne, "Of Cruelty," in *The Complete Works,* trans. Donald M. Frame (1948; New York: Everyman's Library, 2003), 372–386.

12 "Guide to the Private Sponsorship of Refugees Program," Government of Canada, http://www.cic.gc.ca/english/resources/publications/ref -sponsor/. See also presentation by professor Audrey Macklin, University of Toronto Law School, at the Harvard Canada Seminar, Spring 2016.

13 World Values Survey, http://www.worldvaluessurvey.org/WVSDocu mentationWV6.jsp.

14 Murat Iyigun and Dani Rodrik, "On the Efficacy of Reforms," in *Institutions, Development, and Economic Growth,* ed. Theo S. Eicher and Cecilia Garcia-Peñalosa (Cambridge, MA: MIT Press, 2006); Daron

Acemoglu and James A. Robinson, *Why Nations Fail: The Origins of Power, Prosperity, and Poverty* (New York: Crown, 2012).

15 Andrew Higgins and Milan Schreuer, "Attackers in Paris 'Did Not Give Anybody a Chance,'" November 14, 2015, http://www.nytimes.com/2015/11 /15/world/europe/paris-terror-attacks-a-display-of-absolute-barbarity.html.

Acknowledgments

In addition to the scholars and writers whose works are cited in the notes, and to the extraordinary individuals who opened up to me and the rest of the team from the Carnegie Council for Ethics in International Affairs during our journey, I owe special thanks to Joel Rosenthal, president of the Carnegie Council, and to the trustees of the council, for steadfast support; to Noburo Moriyama of the Uehiro Foundation in Tokyo, for the foundation's commitment to the project and for his kindness during our stay in Japan; and to Devin Stewart, program officer at the Carnegie Council, for accompanying me on our journeys and for companionship and insight throughout.

For help and advice during our visit to Argentina and Uruguay, I thank Carnegie fellows Emiliano Buis and Nahuel Maisley. In Brazil, assistance was provided by Fernanda Duarte, David Ritchie, Valeria Silva, Evan Berry, and Gabriel De Almeida. Our visit to Queens, New York, was made possible by Kavitha Rajagopalan, and our understanding of New York's immigration experience was deepened by the insights of Professor Nancy Foner of Hunter College.

In Los Angeles, we were welcomed by Lyn Boyd Judson of the University of Southern California, and preparatory research was conducted by Hebah Farrag. On our site visits we were accompanied by Professor Deen Chatterjee, a Carnegie fellow.

Our trip to Bosnia was made possible by the hard work and local contacts of Nadia Skaljic, Esmic Ganic, Mladen Joksic, and Leila Efendic. We were accompanied for part of the journey by Professor David Rodin and Sir Adam Roberts. I thank Sir Adam for his helpful comments on the manuscript.

In Tokyo and Fukushima, we relied on the assistance of Katsuhiko Mori, Hatsue Shinohara, Madoka Futamara, Malka Older, Honami Izuka, and Jean-Marc Coicaud.

In Myanmar, our translator and local point of contact was Judy Tin May Thein Ko.

During our visit to South Africa, we relied on the expertise and local contacts of Sandy Africa, Gerhard Wolmarans, Barbara Borst, and Janet Cherry.

I would like to thank Brandon Ward, my assistant at the Shorenstein Center, Harvard Kennedy School, for research, scheduling, and production assistance during this project. Stefan Roch at Central European University in Budapest provided additional editorial assistance. Ian Malcolm and the team at Harvard University Press have proven to be appreciative, critical, and helpful partners in bringing the book to life. Thanks also to Angela Piliouras of Westchester Publishing Services for her excellent work guiding my book through production.

The following friends and colleagues have read all or some of the book as it has taken shape: Janice Stein, Gary Bass, Sam Moyn, Nancy Foner, Margaret Marshall, Lindiwe Maziboko, Richard Samuels,

Arthur Applbaum, Thant Myint U, and Mark Lilla. John Tasioulas organized a workshop on the manuscript at the law school at King's College London. Ashwini Vasanthakumar, Timothy Macklem, Eva Pils, Guglielmo Verdirame, Lorenzo Zucca, Massimo Renzo, Leif Wenar, and Octavio Motta Ferraz attended the workshop and provided valuable comments. To all these readers of the manuscript I express my sincere appreciation. The many defects that remain are my responsibility alone.

Zsuzsanna Zsohar, my wife, read every word, accompanied me on some of the journeys, and, as always, proved to be my best critic.

Index